ÁSIA
in the san francisco
bay area

A Cultural Travel Guide

Asia
Society

Foreword by **Vishakha N. Desai,** President
Introduction by **Nguyen Qui Duc**

with contributions by:

Dr. Andy Anderson, Neelanjana Banerjee, Vera Chan, Jeff Cranmer,
Sarah Drew, Nicholas Driver, Marlene Goldman, Joyce Nishioka,
Barbara Jane Reyes, Thy Tran, Patricia Unterman,
Pamela Yatsko, Dr. Farid Younos

With generous support from Wells Fargo

AVALON
TRAVEL

ASIA IN THE SAN FRANCISCO BAY AREA:
A CULTURAL TRAVEL GUIDE
Avalon Travel Publishing
1400 65th Street, Suite 250
Emeryville, CA 94608, USA
www.travelmatters.com

Editor: Matt Orendorff
Copy Editors: Matt Kaye, Patrick Collins, Kay Elliott
Illustrator and Cover Designer: Justin Marler
Production Coordinators: Jacob Goolkasian and Tabitha Lahr
Book Design and Composition: PDBD
Cartographer: Suzanne Service
Proofreader and Indexer: Patrick Collins

ISBN: 1-56691-743-3
ISSN: 1548-5285

First Edition
August 2004

Avalon Travel Publishing
An Imprint of
AVALON Avalon Publishing Group, Inc.
publishing group incorporated

contents

Neighborhoods

Activities and services

Maps

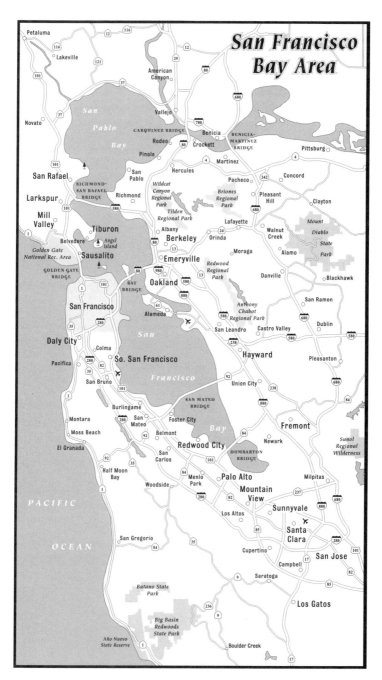

San Francisco Bay Area

FOREWORD

FOR NEARLY HALF A CENTURY, THE ASIA SOCIETY
has educated Americans about Asia in numerous ways and in many cities
across America and in Asia. From presenting major exhibitions of historical and contemporary Asian art, to showcasing performing artists and
filmmakers, to convening conferences of government and business leaders,
to changing the way Asia is taught our K-12 education system, the Asia
Society reaches a wide variety of audiences.

While headquartered in New York City since 1956, the Asia Society
opened its Northern California Regional Center in 1998. Since that time,
we have played an increasingly active role in encouraging US-Asia dia-
logue through our programs in the region. With the publication of this
exciting new book, *Asia in the San Francisco Bay Area: A Cultural Travel
Guide*, we are delighted to reach out to more people here, both residents and
tourists alike, with a resource that truly highlights the long and deep relationship San Francisco and the surrounding area has had with Asia and
Asian cultures.

Let our experts take you to the diverse communities of Asian
Americans from Little Kabul in Fremont to the historical alleyways
of Chinatown. Sample authentic fare, stop for tea, visit one of the greatest
collections of Asian art, discover a garden for reflection, shop for cutting
edge fashion inspired by centuries old tradition. Through these pages,
you will embark on interesting Asian adventures right in your own back-
yard. Encouraging you to explore and experience Asian cultures, and to
celebrate them, is what it is all about. We know you'll enjoy it and learn
something new along the way. And we invite you to come to the

Asia Society's many wonderful programs and visit our award-winning websites—AsiaSociety.org, AskAsia.org, AsiaSource.org—to make the rewards of this stimulating and fun journey to Asia last and grow, without ever having to leave the San Francisco Bay Area.

Vishakha N. Desai
President, Asia Society

INTRODUCTION

by Nguyen Qui Duc

Iт's a тypical day in San Francisco. Typical enough that unless you stop to think about it, you forget how connected to Asia you are.

Before leaving the house for work, I have a quick conversation with my new landlord. Born in Taiwan, she came to the United States and had been running a business in Virginia for some time, but has recently moved to San Francisco, to be close to a daughter who splits her time between the West Coast and Hong Kong. We talk of the expensive real estate prices in the Bay Area and I remember the building I live in was previously owned by a Japanese couple. Later in the day, I will be reminded that Asian Americans make up the fastest growing ethnic group in America, and their median household income is over $53,000, higher than any other group. Their buying power is estimated at $250 billion. As I leave, a Mercedes pulls into my parking spot: it belongs to a Vietnamese woman who owns the nail shop across the street. On the way to work, I drive past a Catholic high school. Among the students crowding the crosswalk are many Asians.

Settled into my chair at my office, I check my email: Kearny Street Workshop, the oldest Asian American art organization in the country, is having another series of readings and performances. The Pilipina American poet Barbara Jane Reyes (a contributor to this book) has invited me to another reading. I also have an email from the curator of the San Jose Museum of Art: we trade information about a Taiwanese artist and a program of performance involving the Vietnamese American poets Tran Truong and Le Pham Le, both residents of the Bay Area. The public radio show *West Coast Live* (out of San Francisco's KALW) is hosting Sri

Lankan-Anglo-American poet Pireeni Sundaralingam. My phone rings: it's Dang Pham, the executive director of the San Francisco City's Human Rights Commission. Born in Viet Nam, he has been a community activist for many years in California and was selected as a White House fellow some years back. He has called to discuss inviting former President Clinton to a gala celebrating 30 years of Vietnamese achievements in America.

I meet with some colleagues to plan our upcoming celebration of Asian American Heritage Month. KQED Public Television and Radio has selected its community heroes for the occasion. Among them is a Vietnamese psychiatrist, a Japanese American woman who runs a childrens education service, two Chinese advocates for garment workers, Dr. Chui Tsang, the Chinese-American who's the president of San Jose City College, and Dr. Samuel So, a Hong Kong native who founded the Asian Liver Cancer Center at Stanford University. We consider inviting a Vietnamese dancer who heads up the modern dance program at a college in the East Bay.

When I return to my desk, there's a message from the owner of a gallery in downtown San Francisco. This weekend, I will bring a painter friend from Shanghai to meet with her, and we will also go over some catalogues of artists in Bangkok, Tokyo, and Ha Noi. I met the gallery owner just a couple of weeks before when she hosted a reception for the Asia Society, and the Indian American writer Pico Iyer. She's been to Asia only a couple of times, but knows a great deal about Asian artists and wishes to bring more of them to San Francisco.

The day goes on with many more conversations, emails, meetings, many of which relate to the rich cultural, social, and economic life of Asian Americans. It is a privilege and a pleasure that my job involves me so much in the activities of the Asian American community, but for many Bay Area residents, exposure to Asian culture and activities is commonplace.

Driving home from work, I will drive by the Asian Art Museum at the Civic Center: Designed by the architect who designed the Musee d'Orsay in Paris, the museum now hosts one of the largest collections of Asian art in the world—and continues to mount exhibitions of some of the most prominent and exciting contemporary artists from Asia as well as local Asian American artists.

Two blocks up from the museum, I drive past some of my favorite Vietnamese restaurants. In the past 15 years, Southeast Asian businesses have revitalized the Tenderloin area, and this year, a portion of it has officially been named Little Saigon. The area attracts thousands of people each year for the annual Tet Lunar New Year festival, and I stop by at least once a week for a bowl of *pho*, the Vietnamese beef noodle soup that many of my friends consider the new champion of American comfort food.

Just before I get home, I drive through Japantown. Established in 1968, Japantown stretches for just three square blocks, but is home to numerous shops selling everything from Asian antiques and bonsai plants to books and lamps. The travel agency there always manages to find me the cheapest fares to Tokyo and Ha Noi. As I drive by the Kabuki theater, I stop to say hello to Chi-Hui Yang, for several years the director of the San Francisco International Asian American Film Festival. For 22 years, the festival has been bringing to the public a diverse film program that's unsurpassed in the country. This year, I will manage to see some 15 movies, from an historical epic from China to animated shorts from Japan, from a comedy from Thailand to a brutal and heartbreaking documentary about lost youths in Singapore. There are also superb films by Asian American filmmakers dealing with topics ranging from war to pornography to infidelity.

Before heading out to the night's cinematic offer, I take a moment to decide whether to have dinner at a Thai restaurant or Japanese sushi bar, both downstairs from my flat. I opt for sushi – and spend an hour talking to the sushi chef about family obligations. Asian traditions are never far from our minds even as we live and work in America. Tomorrow night, there's a party in San Jose: a group of Vietnamese Americans are taking their former professor in Viet Nam to dinner, and to thank him, we are offering him and his wife a trip to Hawaii.

In the 30 years since I left my native Viet Nam, I have never stopped yearning for Asia. I travel there often enough, and have lived in many parts of the United States and abroad. But I always come back to San Francisco – for its picturesque streets, its pleasant climate, the fabulous food and vibrant culture. It is also where Asia begins.

Asia in the San Francisco Bay Area is a long-overdue introduction to this gateway—visiting and getting to know some of the places and activities described by the accomplished contributors to this book will enrich any visitor's experience in Northern California. The history of Asians in San Francisco is long, with difficult episodes along the way. But Asians have been exceling in all aspects of San Francisco life, from business to politics, from the arts to education. Asian culture is undeniably one of the best features of the area, and *Asia in the San Francisco Area* is surely one of the best ways to embark on a nourishing journey that will reveal what America looks like in the 21st century.

EDITOR'S NOTE

Every effort has been made to ensure that *Asia in the San Francisco Bay Area: A Cultural Travel Guide* is as accurate and up-to-date as possible. But such information can change rapidly—stores close, new restaurants open. Still, we feel the material here has a fresh and timeless quality all its own. The world of Asia in the San Francisco Bay Area is always changing, and that's part of the fun of exploring the cities. We hope that our selections help lead you to new places, and inspire you to make discoveries of your own.

Our writers' voices are as unique and diverse as the subjects they cover, providing a real variety of tastes from the banquet that is Asian culture in the Bay Area. You may find authors of different sections talking about the same, or related, topics and events—the richness of the material at hand warrants complementary perspectives. In the same vein, we should note that our chapter listings are clearly selective, but we have taken great pains to supply a rich and representative sampling for each category—amounting to hundreds of listings throughout the book. We chose not to include prices in these listings—our concern for accuracy precluded providing them, with the Bay Area being the ever-changing place that it is.

Finally, you'll find terms throughout the body that are unique to Asian cultures in the Bay Area. Like *Desi*—a friendly term that people from South Asia (Bangladesh, Bhutan, India, Maldives, Nepal, and Pakistan) use to refer to each other. Or *pinay*, a friendly term referring to Pilipinos, used contextually in the book. We've also italicized other terms that may be new to our readers.

CHINATOWN

SAN FRANCISCO WAS LITTLE MORE THAN A VILLAGE when the first Chinese people arrived, '49ers from across the Pacific Ocean in pursuit of gold to take home to southern China. Over the next few decades, they arrived by the thousands—laborers, merchants, and revolutionaries—and together established a thriving quarter that would become the capital of Chinese America. They called it *Dabu,* or, First City.

In all, more than 200,000 Chinese people, mostly from the Pearl River Delta region in southern China, arrived in San Francisco between 1850 and 1880. Most of the earliest immigrants didn't linger in the city; instead, they headed off to the mines where they hoped to make their fortunes. The city was both a port of entry and a commercial center, where Chinese merchants, acting as middlemen, supplied contract workers to labor-hungry American companies. These early Chinese immigrants—mostly poor but eager young men—planted the first grapes in Napa Valley, toiled the mines, and helped build the railroads.

By 1870, there were more Chinese people in San Francisco than in any other city outside of Asia. The more than 12,000 Chinese people accounted for 8 percent of San Francisco's population, and "Little China" grew from two blocks along Sacramento Street in the 1850s to some 12 blocks in the

1880s, stretching across the hillside in the heart of the city, where it still stands today.

To their fellow San Franciscans they were "celestials," known for the quality of the shoes they made, their hand-rolled cigars, and their laundries. But as the economy went sour in the 1870s, the mood began to change, and the Chinese, known for their willingness to work hard for lower wages, were cast in an unfavorable light. Chinese people were assaulted and murdered, and Chinatowns burned across California. Soon local politicians, responding to pressure from the working class, were referring to Chinatown as "a den of human vermin," and debating the "Chinese question"—namely, how to get rid of them. Laws were passed to make life miserable for the community, a sidewalk ordinance prohibited people from carrying poles on the street (Chinese vendors being the only people who

© JUSTIN MARLER

Chinatown entrance gate

did so) while the cubic air ordinance targeted the quarter's overcrowded apartments. The Workingmen's Party of California was formed with a single platform: the Chinese must go. Restrictive immigration laws first targeted Asian women and then, with the 1882 Exclusion Act, Chinese laborers. New arrivals dwindled to a mere 10 in 1887, and the city's Chinese population was halved in the span of a decade.

Yet the city's Chinese held their ground, and the hostility—which extended well beyond San Francisco's city limits—solidified Chinatown's role as a haven for America's Chinese community. As the anti-Chinese hysteria grew and jobs in the mines and railroads dried up, some of the recent arrivals headed home to Guangdong Province, while others headed to Chinatown, where they felt secure and were able to find work. Chinatown became a city within a city, a self-reliant community where its residents could live, work, and eat without ever stepping into the city beyond. But the community wasn't entirely isolated. Part of a larger trans-Pacific community, San Francisco's Chinese never let their homeland entirely out of sight: there was always the possibility of heading back—indeed, many planned to do so after making their fortune, while others went home to visit wives or get married. Men wore their hair in *queues* as a sign of loyalty to the Manchu dynasty and, later, supported the republican revolution on the mainland. For its part, China rallied to their cause by boycotting American goods in 1905 to protest the harsh treatment of Chinese Americans, then lent a helping hand after the 1906 earthquake and fire.

The earthquake marked the start of a new era for Chinatown. The district was rebuilt with Chinese architectural flourishes, and thousands of savvy residents—aware that birth and immigration records had gone up in smoke along with City Hall—declared themselves to be citizens. These instant Americans could arrange to have their children in China join them in San Francisco, a process that also saw many "paper sons" arrive from the mainland, helping give rise to a second generation of Chinese Americans during the exclusion years.

As the restrictive immigration laws were eased after World War II, and then loosened further in the 1960s, Chinatown's population exploded, bringing new Chinese immigrants from beyond the Pearl River Delta as well as from Southeast Asia. At last allowed to live anywhere in the city, many, particularly the professionals and those with monetary resources, opted to live outside of the cramped confines of the neighborhood by moving to the Richmond district, the Outer Sunset, and to suburbs scattered all around the Bay Area. Today, San Francisco's 160,000 Chinese Americans make up one-fifth of the city's population, but only 8 percent live in old Chinatown. Yet Chinatown remains a bustling neighborhood: it's the densest neighborhood in the country outside of Manhattan, home to new immigrants from China and Southeast Asia as well as many elderly Chinese people who've spent much of their lives in the neighborhood. A tourist mecca, Chinatown is the cultural capital for the Bay Area's Chinese Americans.

SIGHTS

Spread across some 30 blocks between Nob Hill and the Financial District, Chinatown stretches from Kearny Street west to Powell Street, and from Bush Street north to Broadway. It can be seen easily in an hour's walk, but the neighborhood rewards those who explore beyond Grant Avenue, the main thoroughfare. One can poke around back alleys filled with the clatter of mahjongg tiles, or wander through the jostling markets of Stockton Street, where roasted pigs are wheeled on carts through rush hour traffic. The quarter's noodle shops, bakeries, and dim sum restaurants make for happy hunting for chow-hounds, while shoppers willing to dig beneath the veneer of tourist bric-a-brac will find traditional Chinese instruments, antique opium lamps, gourmet teas, herbal remedies, and fast-fashions direct from Hong Kong.

A good place to start is on the corner of California Street and Grant Avenue, where a Chinese American merchant named Look Tin Eli helped remake Chinatown's image after the 1906 earthquake. In the process he helped the Chinese community retain its coveted real estate in the heart of the city. The fire that followed the earthquake devastated San Francisco, leaving two-thirds of the population homeless and leveling every building downtown save Old Saint Mary's Cathedral (also found at this intersection). City leaders, who had long plotted to move Chinatown to the city's outskirts, saw their chance. But Look and a group of likeminded merchants had no intention of giving up their turf, and set about building a new Chinese city of "fairy palaces."

Look raised $3 million from Hong Kong and hired a team of non-Chinese San Franciscan architects. The resulting Sing Fat and Sing Chong buildings ushered in an architectural style of pagodalike towers, faux-Chinese roofs, and vibrant colors. It was neither American nor truly

Chinese, but something new: a Chinese-American style that would help to transform the district's seedy image. Pre-1906 Chinatown was a ramshackle neighborhood of Italianate buildings accented with red lanterns, seamy back alleys dotted with opium dens, and brothels. Following the earthquake, the quarter was reborn as a maze of expressive Edwardian buildings featuring red, gold, and green accents for luck, honor, and progress, and eaves that curved to ward off evil spirits.

Although dwarfed today by the glass and concrete towers of San Francisco's Financial District, the Sing Fat and Sing Chong buildings remain a gateway to the city's oldest street, Grant Avenue. A long line of festive lampposts, capped with coiling, golden dragons and tiny bells that stir in the city's windy nights, leads into the heart of the quarter, where undulating rows of mismatched low-rise buildings are layered in chinoiserie and topped with fluttering Taiwanese and, increasingly, Chinese flags. Moving north along Grant—which many Chinatown residents still call by its pre-1906 name, Dupont—souvenir shops stuffed with Alcatraz T-shirts and Giants caps give way to antique stores showcasing intricately carved ivory, and jewelry shops specializing in gold, amber, and jade. While the **Eastern Bakery** (720 Grant Ave., 415/392-4497), with its classic shopfront, elegantly aged neon sign, and renowned moon cakes, is the quarter's oldest pastry shop, **The Golden Gate Bakery** (1029 Grant Ave., 415/781-2627) on the northern end of the street boasts the longest lines. The 30-year-old store's silky egg custards have a devoted following, and during the annual Mid-Autumn Festival customers snap up their rich moon cakes. Nearby, the family owned **Wok Shop** (718 Grant Ave., 415/989-3797, 888/780-7171, www.wokshop.com) has a wealth of Asian cooking tools and offers advice on how to use them, while **Ten Ren** (949 Grant Ave., 415/362-0656, www.tenren.com) sells gourmet Chinese teas as well as quick fixes to go.

As the street continues northward, Grant's cacophony of chirping mechanical crickets yields to Canto-pop, stores hawking inexpensive clothing, and, beyond Pacific Avenue, Chinatown's strip of poultry shops, where live roosters and pheasants stalk stacked cages. Head a block west to Stockton and the quarter's markets begin in earnest. Here, shoppers elbow their way through open-air shops teeming with Wisconsin ginseng, dried scallops, bitter melons, spiky durian fresh from Thailand, and prized birds' nests going for more than $1,000 a pound. Some of the city's freshest—and cheapest—fish flop in buckets on what are easily San Francisco's most crowded sidewalks, alongside tubs of glistening green turtles, frogs, and Dungeness crabs, a local delicacy. This is where the locals hunt for bargain lunches, and Stockton's restaurants—their windows bursting with racks of golden-glazed roast ducks, trays of pigs' intestines, and chicken feet—don't disappoint, often offering heaping $3 plates of rice-and-whatever.

For a respite from the bustle, head toward North Beach, the traditionally Italian neighborhood still haunted by the ghosts of Jack Kerouac and the Beat generation, to the edge of Chinatown and the **Imperial Tea Court** (1411 Powell St., 415/788-6080, www.imperialtea.com). Passing through the wooden shopfront is like stepping into another world: birdcages and lanterns hang from the ceiling of this gourmet tea shop, and delicate ceramic tea sets adorn the shelves and tabletops as ethereal music eases away the street sounds. Co-founders Grace and Roy Fong pride themselves on offering tea of the highest quality: sample a monkey-picked tieguanyin, a richly aromatic dark-roasted oolong, or any of a number of high-grade teas, prepared using the elaborate *gongfu* method, or in the more informal *gaiwan* style. Also at the northern end of Chinatown, **Eastwind Books & Arts** (a block south at 1435 Stockton St., 415/772-5899) has an extensive selection of Chinese-language books as well as English-language texts on topics including traditional Chinese medicine, martial arts, and philosophy. A small section of the store features work by Pilipino, Japanese, Korean, and Vietnamese American writers.

On the southern side of Stockton's markets, half-a-block uphill, lies the excellent **Chinese Historical Society of America** (965 Clay St., 415/391-1188, www.chsa.org). The museum and learning center is located in the old YWCA building, built in 1932 and designed by renowned local architect Julia Morgan, whose work includes the Hearst Castle as well as several other buildings in Chinatown. A blend of Western and Asian styles, Morgan's work is celebrated for elevating the Chinatown streetscape from the splashier, stereotypically "Oriental" structures built in the years immediately after the earthquake. Here, a captivating permanent exhibit explores the Chinese American experience from the gold rush to the present, while other rotating shows highlight Chinese American artists and different aspects of the community's history. The society's archives and its journal, *Chinese America: History and Perspectives,* are good resources for those researching the story of Chinese people in America.

Back on Stockton, the longtime center of power in Chinatown can be found at 843 Stockton Street. Established in 1865 to mediate disputes between merchants, the **Chinese Consolidated Benevolent Society** soon became the protector of community interests in the face of an increasingly hostile city. For decades the Chinese Six Companies, as the Society is more commonly known, was the unofficial government of Chinatown and the voice of Chinese America. The group's influence began to wane in the 1960s, however, with the rise of social service agencies, advocacy groups, and, later, Nixon's opening of relations with the People's Republic of China (the pro-Taiwan group was an ardent anti-Communist watchdog). When the influx of immigrants in the 1960s brought new residents from beyond Cantonese-speaking Guangdong, new regional associations (catering to Taiwanese, Shanghainese, and other groups) formed to meet their needs, further diluting the organization's influence. Today, the leaders of the Six Companies are sometimes seen as out of touch, and local critics have dismissed them as *fan toong*—rice buckets—good for little more than traveling the banquet circuit.

Around the corner, the **Donaldina Cameron House** (920 Sacramento St.) is home to one of the many Christian groups that have played an important role in the Chinese community over the years. Established by the

Presbyterian Church as the Occidental Mission Home for Girls in 1874, the organization is now named for a missionary who devoted her life to liberating women and girls from the city's "yellow slave trade." Cameron is said to have rescued more than 2,000 women and girls who were smuggled into the city and sold as prostitutes or domestics in the late 19th century. The home offered them a place to stay as well as classes in language and practical skills. The organization continues to serve the Chinatown community with a range of social services.

Sacramento Street, between Stockton and Kearny, was the site of the city's earliest Chinese businesses, and in those early years it was known as *Tangren Jie*, the street of Chinese people. Among the businesses still here today is **The Clarion Music Center** (816 Sacramento St., 415/391-1317), which specializes in traditional Chinese instruments, including *erhu*, a two-string fiddle played solo or as a lead in Chinese operas and ensembles; *dizi*, a flute; and assorted gongs, cymbals, and drums for use in lion and dragon dances. Across the street, note the tiny mirrors attached to the facade of 831 Sacramento Street. As the building sits at the end of an alley, the mirrors ward off evil spirits, which are believed to only travel in straight lines.

Clarion stands at the mouth of Waverly Place—a name devotees of Bay Area native Amy Tan's *Joy Luck Club* will surely recognize—one of many lively alleyways that link the quarter's main streets. Early Chinatown residents, confined to a tiny patch of San Francisco, carved these alleys between the main streets to maximize space for shops and homes. Waverly's colorful streetscape has earned it the nickname the "street of the painted balconies." The oldest Chinese temple in the country resides on the top floor of 125 Waverly, honoring a 10th-century woman from Fukien revered as the guardian of seafarers and sojourners. A group of merchants built the **Tin How Temple** in 1852 to express their gratitude for a safe journey across the Pacific. Inside, an image of Tin How rests on an altar on the far wall, below a swath of red-and-gold lanterns tipped with dragons. Joss sticks in a wooden cup offer the chance to check one's fortune: Shake the cup until a stick pops out and ask a docent to interpret the corresponding fortune. A few doors to the south, a long, wooden stairway leads to the austere **Norras Temple,** where an altar holds three Buddha statues under a small chandelier. It's customary to leave a small donation when visiting any of Chinatown's temples.

The towering green building nearby is the local headquarters of the Hop Sing Tong, for years one of the most powerful *tongs* on the West Coast. *Tongs* had their roots in China, where during turbulent times armed groups were formed for self-protection. In San Francisco these fraternal groups took the form of merchant and workers' guilds, some of which operated protection rackets and opium dens and dabbled in prostitution and gambling. Competing interests between *tongs* made the Chinatown of the late 1800s and early 1900s a tense neighborhood, and these alleys were at times bloody battlegrounds as wars between rivals exploded in violence. According to Herbert Asbury's 1933 novel *The Barbary Coast,* one of Chinatown's most infamous kingpins, Fong Ching, lived steps away from the Hop Sing headquarters on the corner of Waverly and Washington in the 1890s. Little Pete, as he was also known, masterminded various criminal enterprises in addition to fixing the occasional horse race. Descending from his apartment for a haircut and a shave one evening in 1897, Pete sent his bodyguard off to get a newspaper with the day's racing results; moments later he was gunned down in the barber's chair, a hit that sparked a war that lasted for months. These days the opium dens are gone, and the *tongs* are crafting a new image as commercial groups.

Spofford Alley, a narrow strip between Washington and Clay Streets just to the west, sings with the clatter of mahjongg tiles, as old neighborhood friends gather to wile away the afternoon at the association halls dotting the street. These associations, bound by clan or region, have been vital community networks since the first Chinese immigrants arrived on these shores. Association members would meet a new arrival at the boat, help them find a job and a place to stay, tide them over through lean times, and ship their bones home after they died. Gatherings at one such meeting hall on Spofford targeted a somewhat grander goal: the end of the Manchu Empire. Sun Yat-sen and his fellow revolutionaries met at the Chee Kung Tong's building at 36 Spofford, just a few years before Sun would become the president of the new Chinese Republic. At the end of the alley is one business that hasn't changed much since those days, **The Great China Herb Co.** (857 Washington St., 415/441-6320). Inside this dimly lit shop bathed in the reassuring scent of ginseng and Chinese herbs, traditional pharmacists have been carefully measuring out prescriptions of seeds, roots, and bits of dried seahorse and deer's antlers—or whatever else the on-site doctor might prescribe—with handheld scales, and tallying bills on an old mahogany abacus, since 1922.

Across Washington, Ross Alley was once known as Gau Leuie Sung Hong, or Old Spanish Alley, for the Latinos who once patronized the street's gambling dens. The alley is also known as the "Street of the Gamblers" after a famous photograph by Arnold Genthe, whose images provide some of the most vivid glimpses into life in pre-earthquake Chinatown. According to a late 19th century map, there were more than a dozen gaming rooms along this narrow strip. "Look-see" boys from the *tongs* kept an eye out for police and, should any be spotted, the alley's rows of sliding iron doors would quickly clang shut. The fenced off passageway between No. 20 and No. 20$^1/_2$ Ross hints at the extent of how the labyrinthine backstreets and tiny lanes composed old Chinatown. Near the end of Ross Alley, the **Golden Gate Fortune Cookie Company** (56 Ross Alley) offers free samples and has bags of cookies for sale. The only mom-and-pop business of its kind left in San Francisco, the company churns out some 10,000 cookies a day. It's worth a peek inside to see the fabulous old cookie machine, which looks like a contraption out of a vintage Rube Goldberg cartoon. Fortune cookies, incidentally, were first introduced at the Japanese Tea Garden in Golden Gate Park.

Back on the city grid, Washington Street rumbles downhill past the not-to-be-missed **Chinese Telephone Exchange,** a colorful, multitiered pagoda that's easily the most eye-catching of the early Chinatown edifices. Built in 1909, China-5, as it was known, required its operators to be fluent in five dialects of Cantonese, and, as callers would ask to be routed by name and not number, they had to memorize every person, business, and address in Chinatown. The exchange fielded ten thousand calls a day—a number that would skyrocket to 40,000 an hour during a *tong* war, when the Chinese community would rush to call acquaintances in other cities to warn them of the impending violence. The only telephone exchange of its kind in the United States, it closed down with the advent of the rotary phone in the late 1940s. A century earlier, this site, which now houses a bank, was home to Sam Brannan's *California Star*, the state's first newspaper, which announced the California gold rush to the world.

Beyond the next intersection, **Portsmouth Square** is the birthplace of San Francisco, where U.S. Navy captain John Montgomery raised the American flag for the first time on July 9, 1846. The city was then just a tiny Mexican enclave called Yerba Buena. Today, early morning tai-chi gives way to furious afternoon gambling sessions over cards and Chinese chess by the grey-haired denizens of the district. On Saturday nights in summer and fall the square buzzes with the **Chinatown Night Market Fair,** which features martial arts demonstrations, lion dances, and performances of traditional music and Cantonese opera, plus scores of stalls where local merchants hawk their wares. Connected to the plaza via the pedestrian bridge, the **Chinese Cultural Center** (750 Kearny St., 415/986-1822, www.c-c-c.org) inhabits the third floor of the Holiday Inn Select Downtown. In addition to changing shows in the gallery, the center has a small bookshop and offers classes in Chinese opera, kung fu, language, and traditional painting. Guides from the center offer Chinatown walking tours, highlighting the history and culture of the neighborhood.

FESTIVALS

By far the biggest and most important holiday in Chinatown is the **Chinese New Year,** which is based on a lunar calendar, starting with the new moon and ending on the full moon 15 days later. The 15th and final day is the Lantern Festival, which coincides with San Francisco's Chinese New Year parade, the oldest and largest of its kind outside of Asia. The event began in the 1860s when a group of recent immigrants from southern China decided to celebrate the Lunar New Year with an American twist, a parade. They marched down Grant Avenue and Kearny Street carrying lanterns and colorful flags to the sound of drums and firecrackers, used to frighten off spirits. These days, the televised procession of elaborate floats, marching bands, and stilt walkers draws hundreds of thousands of spectators as it winds its way from 2nd and Market Streets through Chinatown to Kearny and Columbus, where it concludes with the appearance of the 200-foot-long Golden Dragon and the crackle of thousands of firecrackers. The parade is a culmination of two weeks of celebrations, street fairs, and events, which include a carnival, a flower festival, and the Miss Chinatown USA Pageant, where hopeful Chinese American beauty queens from around the country have been battling it out since 1959. Another lunar festival sees the residents take to the streets in the fall with the **Mid-Autumn Festival,** also known as the Moon Festival, a thousand-year-old tradition held on the 15th day of the 8th lunar month. The two-day celebration, which sees a heavy intake of those extra-rich moon cakes, features a parade along Grant Avenue as well as Chinese opera performances, martial arts demonstrations, and various games for the little ones.

SPECIAL CHINATOWN AREA HOTELS

Spanning 11 floors on top of a commercial building in the heart of San Francisco, the **Mandarin Oriental San Francisco** (222 Sansome St., 415/276-9888, http://mandarin-oriental.com/sanfrancisco) offers 158

OTHER CHINATOWN LODGINGS

Allison Hotel: 417 Stockton St., 800/628-6456 or 415/986-8737, www.allisonhotel.com

Amsterdam Hotel: 749 Taylor St., 800/637-3444 or 415/673-3277, www.amsterdamhotel.com

Baldwin Hotel: 321 Grant Ave., 800/622-5394 or 415/781-2220, www.baldwinhotel.com

Campton Place: 340 Stockton St., 415/781-5555

The Golden Gate Hotel: 775 Bush St., 800/835-1118 or 415/392-3702, www.goldengatehotel.com

Grand Hyatt Hotel: 345 Stockton St., 415/398-1234, www.hyatt.com

Grant Hotel: 753 Bush St., 800/522-0979 or 415/421-7540, www.granthotel.citysearch.com

Hotel Boheme: 444 Columbus Ave., 415/433-9111

Hotel Triton: 342 Grant Ave., 800/556-6085, www.hoteltriton.com

Orchard Hotel: 665 Bush St., 415/362-8879

Petite Auberge: 863 Bush St., 415/928-6000, www.jdvhospitality.com /hotels

Ritz-Carlton San Francisco: 600 Stockton St., 415/296-7465, www.ritzcarlton.com

upscale rooms and suites with panoramic views of the city. The hotel hosts an Asian afternoon tea service in the Mandarin Lounge. The amenities do not come cheap. Rooms start at about $470.

Located close to Union Square, the deluxe, Japanese-owned **Hotel Nikko San Francisco** (222 Mason St., 800/645-5687 or 415/394-1111, www.hotelnikkosf.com) is filled with Japanese touches, including the

Japanese decor of the entry and lobby. Rooms are well equipped for leisure and business travelers, with high speed Internet access, a stereo, CD player, and a fax machine. Shiatsu massage is available through the health club. Sushi and sake bar ANZU is on the premises as well.

Sophistication and luxury are the keywords to the appeal of **Pan Pacific San Francisco** (500 Post St., 800/533-6465 or 415/771-8600, www.panpacific.com). All 329 guest rooms and suites feature elegant touches, such as soft lighting, warm colors, and marble bathrooms. In addition the hotel's Atrium Court offers piano entertainment most nights, and upscale dining at the Pacific Rim-style Pacific Restaurant. Adjacent to the restaurant, the bar offers snacks and cocktails.

East meets West at the **SW Hotel** (615 Broadway, 888/595-9188 or 415/362-2999, www.swhotelsf.com), which borders both the Chinatown and North Beach districts. The SW stands for Sam Wong, the hotel's owner since 1958 who bought what was then the Columbo Hotel. In the lobby are displayed many pieces of Wong's art collection, including works by the Chinese Picasso, Cheung Dai Ching. Rooms have a European flavor.

The Asian touches in the small, reasonably priced **Alisa Hotel** (447 Bush St., 415/956-3232) give it an artsy feel. Guest rooms feature hand-crafted Pan Asian beds and furniture, as well as Asian artwork. The hotel boasts Feng Shui decor. There is also a gallery downstairs that features works by local artists.

Sitting just outside the Chinatown gate, the **Grant Plaza Hotel** (465 Grant Ave., 800/472-6899 or 415/434-3883, www.grantplaza.com) is a comfortable, very affordable option for its location. During the 1940s and 1950s the hotel was renowned as the home of the Grand View Tea Garden, one of the city's hippest nightclubs at the time. Today, the nightclub is a floor of guest rooms, and features colorful stained-glass windows.

What used to be a Hollywood star hangout in the 1950s has transformed over the years into San Francisco's hippest hotel for touring rock bands. The boutique **Phoenix Hotel** (601 Eddy St., 415/776-1380, www.thephoenixhotel.com) features the Bambuddha Lounge, serving Southeast Asian cuisine and cocktails with names like the Lotus and Lucky Bamboo.

SAN FRANCISCO'S

JAPANTOWN

GLANCE AT A PHOTO OF SAN FRANCISCO'S POST Street taken in the 1940s—with rows of Japanese-run theaters, groceries, and cafes operating out of old Victorian homes—and it's hard not to feel that today's Japantown lacks the vibrancy it held before World War II, when its entire community was whisked away to internment centers. But as the oldest Japanese American enclave in the mainland United States, and one of three historic *nihonmachi* left in the country, San Francisco's Japantown remains the heart of the Bay Area's Japanese American community, the third largest in the country after Honolulu and Los Angeles. Indeed, one need only hear the pounding of the drums by the world-class San Francisco Taiko Dojo during the annual Cherry Blossom festival or sample a freshly made *manju* from **Benkyo-Do** on Buchanan Street to know that the city's Japantown is alive and well.

The first Japanese people began arriving in San Francisco in the 1870s, mostly male students who had been encouraged by the Meiji government to travel abroad in order to absorb Western technology and bring it back to Japan. These "schoolboys" cooked and cleaned in exchange for room and board while they learned English. They socialized through the Japanese Gospel Society, the first Japanese organization in the United

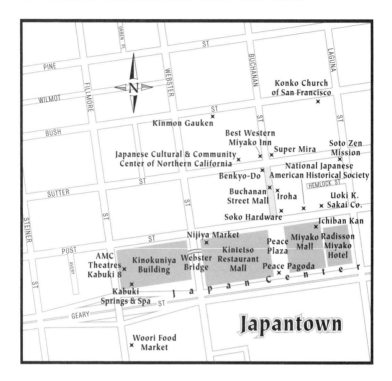

States, which originally met at the Chinese Mission on Washington Street in Chinatown, and later at Japanese Christian churches, the Young Men's Buddhist Association, as well as through *kenjin-kai,* associations that linked immigrants from the same region in Japan.

By the 1890s a new wave had already begun to arrive: Thousands of contract laborers, fleeing heavy land taxes and a military draft back home, came to work in agriculture and in mines and canneries along the coast. In 1900 nearly 2,000 *issei,* or first generation immigrants, called San Francisco home, making it the largest settlement in the mainland United States, and dozens of businesses—pool halls, hotels, and general stores— sprouted on Dupont Street (now Grant Street) in Chinatown, and in the two alleys behind the Old Mint in the South of Market area.

After the devastating earthquake and fire of 1906 left roughly two

Japantown

thirds of the city's residents homeless, many Japanese people left the Bay Area. This led to the creation of Japantowns all around California, in particular in Los Angeles, where the population of ethnic Japanese would soon eclipse that of San Francisco. Those who stayed established a new *nihonmachi* in the Western Addition, where the Japanese community would flourish for the next 30 years and still survives today.

From the start, however, the *issei,* much like the early Chinese arrivals, faced mistrust, hostility, and rampant racism. San Francisco saw the country's first large-scale anti-Japanese rallies in 1900, led by no less than the city's mayor, supported by labor groups, and egged on by the persistently hostile local press—"The Japanese Invasion, the Problem of the Hour," read a San Francisco Chronicle headline around that time. A 1906 school segregation case garnered national attention when Japanese and Korean children, some of whom were U.S. citizens, were ordered to attend the Chinese Oriental School. The Japanese government pressured President

Theodore Roosevelt to intervene. As part of the bargain, however, Japan shook on the Gentlemen's Agreement of 1907, which barred new Japanese immigrant laborers from entering the United States. Yet this seeming victory for the anti-Japanese lobby would sow the seeds of permanence for the Japanese American community. Under the deal, Japanese men could send for their wives, and many had their relatives arrange marriages through matchmakers. Between 1908 and 1924, more than 20,000 of these "picture brides" arrived to join their pioneering husbands, stepping ashore at Angel Island. What was once a bachelor society began to grow roots, and San Francisco's Japantown swelled to more than 5,000 residents.

It was only a matter of hours after the bombs fell on Pearl Harbor on December 7, 1941, that authorities had cordoned off Japantown and began arresting community leaders. Westbrook Pegler, a nationally syndicated columnist, summed up the sentiment of the time: "The Japanese in California should be under armed guard to the last man and woman right now—and to hell with habeas corpus." Soon, the orders would come for the evacuation of the community, leaving most residents to hastily sell their property, or simply abandon it. More than 120,000 ethnic Japanese from the West Coast were interned in camps throughout the Western interior, 8,000 from San Francisco.

Upon their return at the end of the war, the community members barely had a chance to make a fresh start before their neighborhood was branded as a blighted area and slated for redevelopment, one of several large-scale urban renewal projects undertaken in the country at the time. By 1960 roughly half of Japantown was seized and razed—including the area where the **Japan Center** stands today—displacing 1,500 ethnic Japanese residents and forcing the closure of more than 60 Japanese American businesses. The neighborhood would never be the same.

Today only a tiny percentage of the Bay Area's more than 100,000 Japanese Americans live in Japantown. Down from 32 blocks at its peak in the late 1930s, the neighborhood occupies a handful of blocks in San

Francisco's Western Addition, just south of the Pacific Heights neighborhood and east of Fillmore Street. Although strikingly quiet compared with
Chinatown or the Richmond district's Clement Street, and lacking in historic sights, the central commercial strip along Post Street really comes
alive on the weekend. Visiting Bay Area Japanese Americans, expats from
Japan, hungry San Franciscans, and curious tourists are drawn by the vintage kimono boutiques, sushi bars, excellent Japanese-language bookstores, and especially the Japan Center mall. And while it is no longer the
thriving community of pre-war San Francisco, the neighborhood remains a
hub for the region's Japanese Americans, a place to come and eat, shop at
Japanese markets, and celebrate festivals.

SIGHTS

Arriving in today's Japantown, the 100-foot-tall **Peace Pagoda** is the first
thing to catch one's eye. A gift from the people of Japan in 1968, the pagoda
is a focal point for the neighborhood, standing at the center of Peace Plaza
(off Buchanan Street) between Post and Geary. Occupying the three blocks
on either side of the Peace Plaza, the Japan Center stretches from the
Miyako Hotel to the east and the Kabuki multiplex on the west. Designed
by Minoru Yamasaki, the second-generation Japanese American architect
who designed New York's World Trade Center, the center opened as the
Japanese Cultural and Trade Center in 1968 and was a showcase for the
products of Japan, Inc. The construction represented a departure from the
mom-and-pop businesses of the 1950s Japantown, whose owners had
mostly moved on or retired during the long construction period. Within a
few years, the large corporate showrooms gave way to small businesses,
run by Japanese nationals, and selling Japanese goods to shoppers from
outside the neighborhood. Today, the center's three main buildings house a
variety of Japanese restaurants, stores selling everything from antiques to
anime, a traditional communal bathhouse, as well as the headquarters of a
handful of cultural institutions. What makes a wander through the center's

THE JAPANESE TEA GARDEN

Created for the 1894 Midwinter International Exposition, the Japanese Tea Garden is one of the most serene spots in San Francisco. Located on the eastern side of Golden Gate Park, the garden features elegantly gnarled trees, intricate landscapes in miniature, and exquisite artifacts from Japan. It's best enjoyed early in the morning, when the verdant grounds open themselves up to quiet reflection. Makoto Hagiwara, a successful local Japanese landscape designer, came up with the idea for the garden, which was built as part of the Japanese Village exhibit for the Midwinter Fair. For most of the next 30 years he lived there while planning, supervising and funding the garden's expansion from one acre to five. After his death in 1925, his family tended the space until their eviction and internment in 1942.

Japanese gardens evolved out of the grounds surrounding imperial palaces and Shinto shrines. Today, they are considered high art and come in a variety of styles. The Japanese Tea Garden is a stroll-garden. Popularized in the Edo Period (1603–1867), these gardens comprise a series of tableaux that unfold as one walks through the landscape, a journey of sorts meant to encourage a greater understanding of nature. The **Tea Garden,** with its rustic bridges and steppingstones across tranquil pools of water, invites one to linger. A series of paths meander past understated maples, cherry trees that burst white and pink in spring, and an English boxwood clipped into the shape of Mount Fuji, Hagiwara's home region in Japan. There are more than a few rarities here, a pair of Japanese umbrella pines and a collection of dwarf trees among them.

shops so interesting for those new to all things Japanese are the details that lend insight into a living culture: The crepe shops, the photo-sticker booths, and the countless other tidbits are a world away from the trendy boutiques of Union Street and the tourist traps of Fisherman's Wharf.

Entering the center to the west of the Peace Plaza, the Kintetsu Restaurant Mall has a dozen restaurants and coffee shops, a handful of boutiques, and various shops selling the latest in Japanese pop culture. Just

The **Sunken Garden,** located on the site of the old Hagiwara home, is designed to conjure up a faraway landscape. Not too far off, a flagstone path leads down Maple Lane to the **Zen Garden,** which is a modern version of a dry landscape—*kare sansu*—and symbolizes a mountain scene. Zen gardens have a religious and mythological meaning, an aid to monks in their quest for enlightenment, and were introduced to temple grounds in Japan when Zen Buddhism was brought to the country from China in the 12th century. This particular space was designed by noted landscape architect Nagao Sakurai, who was formerly in charge of the grounds at the Imperial Palace in Tokyo.

Stone lanterns are a fixture of stroll-gardens. Among the dozen or so found here, the 9,000-pound **Lantern of Peace** was a gift from Japan in 1953 commemorating the United States–Japan peace treaty signed in San Francisco two years earlier. The bronze Buddha, cast at Tajima, Japan in 1790, was another gift, bequeathed by the S. & G. Gump Company in 1949.

Although the garden has evolved substantially since Hagiwara's time, several of its original elements remain, including the steeply arching Drum Bridge and the old wooden teahouse, where kimono-clad waitresses serve green and jasmine tea along with a plate of fortune cookies. It was Makoto Hagiwara—and not some baker from Beijing with a penchant for whimsical prognostications, as one might expect—who gave the world the fortune cookie, introducing it here in 1914. The Japanese Tea Garden, located on Hagiwara Tea Garden Drive in Golden Gate Park, is open 8:30 A.M.–5 P.M. daily, staying open an extra hour in the evenings from March to October.

inside the entrance is **Sakura Sakura,** a textiles boutique where shop owner Mariko Sawada, a designer who hails from a family of obi weavers in Kyoto, adds modern flair to traditional obi design, transforming the kimono sashes into scroll-like wall-hangings. Sakura Sakura also features hand-painted and hand-dyed *noren* tapestries, *shibori* silk scarves from Kyoto, as well as elegant silk evening jackets designed by Sawada herself.

FOOD

However, as the name indicates, this slice of the Japan Center is all about the food, and it doesn't disappoint. Steps away are a clutch of casual restaurants, including the often packed **Mifune** (415/922-0337), an inexpensive noodle specialist serving ramen, *udon*, and *soba*, where slurping is de rigueur. Another popular spot with long lines at lunchtime on weekends is **Isobune** (415/563-1030), a lunch-on-the-go spot where sushi floats lazily past a lunch counter, adrift in little boats. Grab a plate as it goes by; the colored rim indicates the price of the item. Around the corner, **May's Coffee Shop** buzzes with regulars sampling from an eclectic menu of pancakes, hamburgers, *udon*, and *tai-yaki*, warm, fish-shaped pastries filled with sweet beans or chocolate.

SHOPPING

The strip of shops across from May's will satisfy any Japanese pop culture jones. **Japan Video** (415/563-5220) specializes in anime DVDs, offering rentals and sales, while a few shops down, **Mikado Music Japan** has the latest in J-Pop and **Mikado Kids Corner** caters to fans of Japan's ambassador of all things cute: Hello Kitty. A few shops away, **Tokyo Motor Trendz** (415/922-6388) offers an astonishing array of cell phone accessories. With a few dollars, a little creativity, and some patience for the up to half-hour wait you can have flashing lights and a shiny new faceplate added to your phone.

Nearby, a couple of cultural institutions have set up shop, including the **Ikenobo Ikebana Society of America** (415/567-1011). The nonprofit organization was founded in 1970 by Sen'ei Ikenobo, 45th headmaster of the outpost's namesake society—Japan's original such school—to promote goodwill through the art of flower arranging, which dates back to 15th century Japan. *Ikebana* supplies are available through the headquarters, as well as tips for those interested in seeking out lessons and exhibitions. There's not much to see here on most days, but on weekends deft-fingered veterans of the art sometimes set up shop in front of the society's office.

Practitioners of another Japanese art can be found down the hall along the Webster Bridge in the **San Francisco Taiko Dojo Showroom** (415/928-2456, www.taikodojo.org). Grand Master Seiichi Tanaka introduced *taiko* to the United States with the founding of Taiko Dojo in 1968, and his academy is regarded as the leading school of the Japanese-style of drumming in the West. Held sacred for centuries, the drum was first used to drive evil spirits away from crops. By imitating the sound of thunder, drumming would summon the spirits of rain; at harvest time, the *taiko* was played again in thanks for a successful growing season. The Taiko Dojo, which has played with the likes of Max Roach, Art Blakey, and Tito Puente, plays around the country as well as at local festivals, including the International Taiko Festival in Berkeley, held annually in November, and at various fairs and events in Japantown.

Across the way, narrow **Shige Kimonos** (415/346-5567) is one of the Japan Center's original shops. It features a range of kimonos, from the elaborate *uchikakes* worn at weddings to casual cotton after-bath *yukatas,* as well as vintage silk kimonos dating back to the early 20th century. For something a little less refined, grab a bite at the eclectic **On the Bridge** (415/922-7765), which serves casual, *yoshoku*-style food—essentially Western staples with a Japanese twist. The no-frills diner draws a younger crowd eager to sample off a menu that reads like a recount of an Iron Chef showdown, with dishes like chicken-and-sansai rice gratin, spaghetti, *kimchi,* and beef dry curry pilaf.

Webster Bridge, somewhat grandly billed as an ode to Florence's Ponte Vecchio, connects Kintetsu Mall with the Kinokuniya Building, which, as the name suggests, has a branch of the well known **Kinokuniya** bookstore (415/567-7625). By far San Francisco's best Japanese-language bookstore, it also features a good selection of English-language Asian-interest books as well as Japanese-language newspapers. This is perhaps the liveliest part of the Japan Center on weekends, as fashionable teenagers and twentysomethings cruise Kinokuniya's extensive magazine racks, snap pictures at the sticker-stamp photo booths, and snack on the inventive offerings at **Sophie's Crepes.** Some other nearby shops are **Café Tan Tan** (415/346-6260), a Japanese riff on a European-style teahouse; Kinokuniya's excellent stationery spin-off; and a cluster of bars and restaurants, including the tiny and elegant **Maki** (415/921-5215). One of the city's best Japanese restaurants, Maki specializes in several dishes less commonly offered on this side of the Pacific, such as *wappa meshi,* rice steamed in wooden baskets with fish, vegetables or meat.

Anchoring the western corner of the building, the **AMC Theatres Kabuki 8** takes a break from its usual blockbuster fare each March to co-host the San Francisco International Asian American Film Festival. Around the corner, **Kabuki Springs & Spa,** with a separate entrance outside the mall at 1750 Geary Blvd (415/922-6000, www.kabukisprings.com), offers the chance to indulge in a Japanese-style communal bathhouse, with a sauna, a steam room, and hot and cold pools, along with a variety of other services, including acupuncture and shiatsu massage.

Doubling back, on the eastern side of Peace Plaza, the Miyako Mall holds just a handful of shops and restaurants. **Genji** (415/931-1616, www.genjiantiques.com) specializes in traditional Japanese antiques, with ceramics, furniture, dolls from the Edo and Meiji periods, and vintage kimonos from the Taisho, Showa, and Hensei periods, in addition to modern furnishings crafted from around Asia. Upstairs, **Ichiban Kan,** stuffed with shoehorns, pens, assorted housewares, and prawn chips—all at rock-bottom prices—resembles the *hyakuen* stores of Japan (100-yen shops akin to the 99-cent stores common in the United States). Nearby is **Seoul Garden** (415/563-7664), which offers a wide-selection of Korean food, including barbecue. Exiting the Japan Center, there's more Korean food to be had across Post Street, where a small Korean enclave has taken hold on the corner of Laguna and Post. Another clutch of Korean businesses, including the small but well stocked **Woori Food Market** (1528 Fillmore St., 415/673-9888), has sprung up on Fillmore, just south of the movie theater. At 1656 Post Street, the family-run **Uoki K. Sakai Co.** grocery store (415/921-0514) is one of the three oldest businesses in Japantown. In 1942 the Sakai family sold off their perishable goods, rolled the company truck into the store, and boarded it up. After the war, they returned to find their belongings still there—a rare occurrence among Japantown's relocated residents. A few shops downhill, visit the **National Japanese American Historical Society** (1684 Post St., 415/921-5007, www.njahs.org), where excellent rotating exhibits illuminate the Japanese American experience and celebrate the work of Asian American artists. The group also publishes *Nikkei Heritage,* a quarterly glimpse into the Japanese American community's history.

Next door is the former location of one of the more legendary establishments that opened in and around Japantown during the World War II era, a time that saw the area's African American community blossom as migrants from the south came to work in the city's defense industry. Jimbo's Waffle Shop opened in an old Victorian in 1950, and the backroom soon became Bop City, one of the many jazz clubs that emerged on and around Fillmore Street. Bop City was the site of after-hours jam sessions that saw John Coltrane, Billie Holiday, Miles Davis, and many of the other jazz greats of the age grace the club's tiny stage. As with many small, family-run Japanese businesses in the area, redevelopment took its toll on the haunts of the Fillmore jazz scene; Jimbo's closed in 1965 when construction began on the **Buchanan Street Mall.**

The Buchanan pedestrian mall, between Post and Sutter streets, was built as a part of the redevelopment projects of the 1960s. The one-block strip of restaurants and shopfronts are set in a series of two-story buildings built to resemble a traditional Japanese village. The central walkway, intended to evoke a mountain stream, features two origami fountains made by local artist Ruth Asawa. The usually vacant police kiosk was added in the 1980s, the brainchild of then-mayor Dianne Feinstein, who had seen similar outposts on a trip to Asia. (A second, also little used kiosk, can be found in Chinatown.)

Anchoring the mall, **Soko Hardware** (1698 Post St., 415/931-5510) has been a neighborhood fixture since 1925. Owner Mas Ashizawa, who took over the business from his parents in 1948, led the community in the 1950s when the city first tried to redevelop Japantown. Along with an unending supply of nails, duct tape, kitchen scales, and other hardware store staples, the shop also stocks lucky cats, mini-carp streamers, and *Arita* porcelain wares, as well as seeds for growing Japanese plants.

At **Benkyo-Do** (1747 Buchanan St., 415/922-1244), the Okamura family has been waking up before dawn since 1906 to make *manju*, the sweet-bean-filled confection. Bobby and Ricky Okamura make more than 1,500 *manju* daily, but the shop, as the last major manufacturer in San Francisco and one of only two left in the Bay Area—the other, Shuei-Do Manju Shop, is in San Jose—is busiest around New Year's. This is when their *mochi*, a type of rice cake that's been an integral part of the holiday for centuries, is in high demand. *Mochi* was originally made as an offering at shrines; the offering would then be cut up and given to people for good health and fortune; later, it came to be enjoyed during festive occasions. *Kagami Kai*, a local *mochitsuki*, or *mochi*-pounding group, is often on hand at various annual festivals throughout the neighborhood, pounding rice to a *taiko* beat.

CULTURAL ORGANIZATIONS

Crossing Sutter Street, the **Japanese Cultural & Community Center of Northern California** (1840 Sutter St., 415/567-5505, www.jcccnc.org) is a touchstone for the preservation and development of the area's Japanese American community. The center was founded in 1973 in response to the turmoil the community endured in the 1940s and again in the 1960s. Although there's not much for the casual visitor here, residents may want to

JAPANTOWN HOTELS

Best Western Miyako Inn (1800 Sutter St., San Francisco, 888/466-9990 or 415/921-4000, www.bestwestern.com/miyakoinn): Completely renovated in 2002, this Best Western is a small, affordable option right in the heart of Japantown. On the premises is Cafe Mums, a fusion restaurant known for its Japanese noodle dishes, *shabu shabu*, and seafood.

Radisson Miyako Hotel San Francisco (1625 Post St., San Francisco, 800/333-3333 or 415/922-3200, www.miyakohotel.com): Rooms at this moderately priced Radisson Miyako are comforting, with natural lighting, hand-painted *fusuma* screens, and deep Japanese tubs. Western-style rooms offer Western beds and Oriental touches. There are also two traditional Japanese suites with raised sleeping platforms and *tatami* mats and *tokonomas*, or ornamental alcoves. In-room *shiatsu* massages can be arranged.

look into their wide-ranging roster of classes, which include *ikebana, washi-ningyo* (paper-doll making), *minyo* and *hauta* (Japanese singing), *odori* (classical dance), *shibori*, (textile art) and *kendo* (traditional fencing). Downstairs, the **Japanese American History Archives** (415/776-0661) has an extensive collection of books, periodicals, maps, and photographs documenting the Japanese American experience.

Located behind the community center, the **Kinmon Gakuen** ("Golden Gate Institute") at 2031 Bush Street was founded as a Japanese language school in 1911. 31 years later Japanese American families would report here for evacuation to internment camps. They received tags and numbers and were loaded onto buses headed for the Tanforan horse track, 13 miles south of San Francisco in San Bruno. Eight thousand Bay Area residents were held behind barbed wire here for six months, some sleeping in whitewashed horse stalls, before being shipped off to detention centers in remote areas, where they would wait out the rest of the war. Today, the Kinmon Gakuen building houses the Nihonmachi Little Friends, a bilingual preschool.

If you continue east for a few blocks, a handful of Japanese temples and churches lend a sense of just how far pre-war Japantown extended. The **Konko Church of San Francisco** (1909 Bush St.), was founded in 1930 in a Victorian a couple of blocks away, while the **San Francisco Buddhist Church,** on the corner of Pine and Octavia, is the oldest in the United States. The **Jodo Shinshu Buddhist Temple's** stout rooftop *stupa* contains holy relics of the Buddha, a gift from the King of Siam in 1935. Every summer, on a weekend in mid-July, the temple holds its annual **Obon** festival. According to a Buddhist *sutra,* Mokuren, a disciple of the Buddha, was able to alleviate his mother's suffering in the land of the dead by making a retreat and giving offerings to his fellow monks. Seeing his mother liberated, Mokuren danced for joy. *Obon* commemorates the spirits of ancestors with folk dances and traditional music.

FESTIVALS

Several other annual festivals bring Japantown to life each year. The **Nihonmachi Street Fair** (415/771-9861, www.nihonmachistreetfair.org) was dreamt up in the early 1970s by a group of youth activists—the first event was held on Malcolm X's birthday—who longed for a celebration that would bring out the soul of the local community. Today it's held annually over an August weekend in the heart of the neighborhood and features live bands, including the San Francisco Taiko Dojo, and food from around the Asia-Pacific.

The **Cherry Blossom Festival** (415/563-2313, www.nccbf.org) is the highlight of spring in Japantown. Taking place over two weekends in April, the festival began in 1968 as a means of drawing people to the newly redeveloped Japantown. The streets of Japantown are closed off for the festivities, which include tea ceremonies, origami and ikebana demonstrations, food stalls, and traditional dance performances, as well as the United States/Japan Taiko Festival. The event culminates in a parade, which begins at the Civic Center, winds its way down Polk Street, and then follows Post Street into Japantown. The *taru mikoshi*, a shrine constructed out of sake barrels, marks the end of the parade; it's carried by 100 young men who run down the street, spreading good wishes—and sake—to parade-goers.

ASIA IN

THE RICHMOND
AND OUTER SUNSET

Most visitors to San Francisco who have an interest in Asian American culture make a beeline for Japantown and Chinatown, the city's oldest Asian neighborhoods. As a result, many overlook the Richmond and the Sunset, districts that in the span of just a few decades have developed into two of the most diverse, dynamic—and distinctly Asian—locales in a city where more than 30 percent of the residents trace their roots to Asia.

Among the last stretches of San Francisco to attract settlers, the Richmond and Sunset districts were once a vast expanse of sand dunes collectively known as the "Outside Lands" and the "Great Sand Waste." The area was given over to squatters, resorts, racetracks, and cemeteries, including a Chinese burial ground on the bluffs at Land's End. Settlement did not begin in earnest until after the 1870s creation of Golden Gate Park, a three-mile-long swath of green stretching from Haight-Ashbury to the Pacific, which separates the Richmond from the Sunset.

The Richmond developed first, and in the first half of the 20th century its early arrivals included Eastern European Jews, Irish, and a group of Orthodox Christians, exiles from Russia who had fled their homeland to Shanghai, only to leave again with the Japanese invasion of China in the

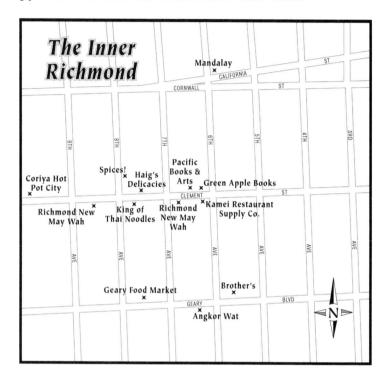

1930s. When in 1947 the city at last lifted the restrictive housing covenant that prohibited San Francisco's Chinese American community from living outside of Chinatown, the Richmond and the Sunset began to attract Asian residents, as Chinese families left the cramped confines of the old quarter for the windswept, wide avenues of the city's westernmost neighborhoods.

The growth of San Francisco's Asian populations accelerated in the 1960s, after immigration laws shifted to a policy based on labor skills and family reunification, and has continued at a steady clip ever since. With this influx, Chinatown nearly burst at the seams, and white-collar families, including new arrivals from Taiwan and Hong Kong, headed to the predominantly residential Richmond and Sunset districts in droves, where they could afford to buy a home. Chinatown, in turn, became increasingly a blue-collar neighborhood of newly arrived immigrant families and elderly who had lived there all their lives. Today, more than 40 percent of Richmond and Sunset residents are of Asian descent, and the area surrounding the Richmond's Clement Street is now often called the "New Chinatown."

With neat rows of single-family homes and three- and four-story apartment buildings stretching out to Ocean Beach, both neighborhoods have an almost suburban feel. Any given block might house families from Taiwan, Hong Kong, Korea, Japan, and the Philippines, as well as from Ireland and Russia; in one section of the Outer Richmond, a Chinese Buddhist temple, a Russian Orthodox church, and a Burmese Baptist church are all within a stone's throw of one another. Although Chinese Americans are by far the largest Asian group in the area—as well as in the city as a whole—the neighborhood's diversity still shines through. Along the two districts' main commercial strips—Clement and Geary streets in the Inner and Outer Richmond and Irving in the Outer Sunset— Vietnamese noodle shops, Chinese herbalists, sushi restaurants, and specialty food stores mingle on pleasant non-touristy streets.

THE INNER RICHMOND

For many San Franciscans, a trip to the Richmond is a chance to sample the delicacies found in the district's Asian bakeries, sweets shops, and restaurants. People who wish to explore the area need only hop the 1-California bus in Chinatown and follow the stream of residents—fresh from their afternoon mah jongg sessions or the markets of Stockton Street—who exit at the 6th Avenue stop and head toward lower Clement Street, the heart of the "New Chinatown."

Visitors may find the nickname deceiving, however. In the span of only a few blocks, Clement's restaurants offer a passport to the foods of nearly the entire region: There are zesty bowls of Vietnamese noodles, Taiwanese hot pots, authentic Thai, hands-on Korean barbecue, Chinese bakeries with steaming pork buns, as well as Burmese, Cambodian,

Indonesian, Japanese, and Indian cuisine. The tourists and tchotchkes of Chinatown have been replaced with these culinary gems (many of which have yet to catch on with Zagat savants), as well as with discount housewares stores and overflowing pan-Asian groceries. Most of the buzz is centered on Clement—and to a lesser extent on California, Geary, and Balboa—from 2nd to 12th Avenues, where afternoons find the district humming with the rituals of everyday neighborhood life: Older residents swapping Chinese-language newspapers over afternoon coffee and school kids gossiping on cell phones while slurping colorful cups of bubble tea through long straws.

The district got its name from an early resident who lived at the end of this strip in the late 19th century, George T. Marsh. Marsh, who was raised in Japan, sold Japanese art from a downtown store and had a hand in the creation of the Japanese Tea Garden for the 1894 Midwinter Exposition, held in Golden Gate Park. A native of Richmond, Australia, Marsh named his large red Victorian after his birthplace, now a suburb of Melbourne, and the district that grew up around him gradually took on its name. Today the area is anchored by the **Richmond New May Wah**, a supermarket with so much to offer the district's food shoppers that it actually has two branches within a block of one another. The larger of the two (709 Clement St., 415/221-9826), is one of the city's best Asian groceries. A pleasant upgrade from the crowded markets of Stockton Street, its long, neat aisles are packed with an extensive selection of sauces, curry mixes, and noodles from Thailand, Vietnam, China, and elsewhere around the region. Next door, the meat, produce, and fish sections overload the senses and include everything from slimy geoducks to Japanese eggplants, all at excellent prices.

Nearby, **Haig's Delicacies** (642 Clement St., 415/752-6283), a Middle Eastern specialty food store, has goods from Indonesia and India, including pappadams, chutneys, spices, and a wide range of teas, and **Kamei Restaurant Supply Co.** (507 Clement St., 415/666-9288), has everything one needs to cook up the bounty offered by these stores. Also found here is the unassuming **King of Thai Noodles** (639 Clement St., 415/752-5198), a bare bones eatery whose no-frills décor and authentic noodles are a portal to a Bangkok back *soi*. This spot has inspired a chain of popular Thai restaurants around the city since its opening in the early 1990s.

One of Clement Street's landmarks is **Green Apple Books** (506 Clement St., 415/387-2272), a dog-eared neighborhood bookstore that's regarded as one of the city's best. Upstairs, Green Apple has an extensive collection of English-language books on Eastern philosophy and religion, and good, if not expansive, offerings on Asian history and Asian American studies. There are also plenty of books on Asian cooking, as well as guides to learning languages from around the Pacific Rim. For Chinese-language books, magazines, and newspapers, head next door to the small **Pacific Books and Arts** (524 Clement St., 415/751-2238).

One block south, a cluster of Korean businesses has gained a foothold amid the clamor of multi-lane Geary Boulevard, a noisy expressway lined with auto showrooms that was expanded in the 1960s to serve the growing Richmond at the expense of part of old Japantown. A little more than a century earlier, this old rabbit hunter's trail became the district's first transit line, transporting passengers from downtown to the resorts and racetracks that hugged the city's western shore. Although San Francisco's Korean American community is too small to support a K-town to rival those of Los Angeles and New York—at roughly 8,000 it's just one percent of the city's total population—Korean food and drink is well-represented by several Geary standouts. **Brother's** (4128 Geary Blvd., 415/387-7991) is one of San Francisco's most popular spots for beef *kalbi*, which is served in a nondescript setting with grills right at the tables. The ultra-sleek **RoHan Lounge** (3809 Geary Blvd., 415/221-5095) is a hipster's shrine to *soju*, the traditional Korean liquor distilled from rice, barley, and potato. And **My Tofu House** (4627 Geary Blvd., 415/750-1818), is a big hit with Korean families hungry for *soondubu chigae*, a spicy tofu stew. For groceries,

Geary Food Market (4324 Geary Blvd., 415/668-7474) has everything one needs to prepare a Korean feast, including a selection of spicy *kimchi* and more than a dozen types of *ban chan*—the quintessential side dishes eaten at every meal in Korean households—ready to go.

It's not just about Korean cuisine, though: Nearby, Joanna and Keith Dan opened the city's first Cambodian restaurant, **Angkor Wat** (4217 Geary Blvd., 415/221-7887), in 1983, and further east, the blend of Indian, Malay, and Chinese flavors of the **Straits Café** (3300 Geary Blvd., 415/668-1783), offers a chance to taste the food of Singapore, the Southeast Asian culinary crossroads whose food is rarely showcased in restaurants in the United States.

THE OUTER RICHMOND

To the west in the perpetually foggy Outer Richmond, the golden onion-shaped domes and triple bar crosses of the Russian Orthodox Holy Virgin Cathedral rise above another concentration of Asian businesses, stretching from 22nd to 26th Avenues along Clement and Geary. Here, Eastern European and Russian businesses mix with restaurants spanning the spectrum of Asian foods. Although this cluster of commercial activity lacks the buzz of lower Clement Street—indeed, with its wide avenues and salty breezes it feels like a sleepy beach town in the off-season—the area boasts several of the city's best Asian restaurants, including **Ton Kiang** (5821 Geary Blvd., 415/387-8273), renowned for its dim sum; **Khan Toke Thai House** (5937 Geary Blvd., 415/668-6654), a decidedly shoes-off affair; and **PPQ Vietnamese Cuisine** (2332 Clement St., 415/386-8266), with its excellent *pho* and succulent roasted crab.

Another neighborhood highlight is the independent **4-Star Theatre** (2200 Clement St. at 23rd Ave., 415/666-3488, www.hkinsf.com), which shows first-run Hong Kong films shortly after their release in Asia, as well as films from around the region. Native San Franciscan Frank Lee has owned the theater since 1992, and now that Chinatown's theaters have closed, his movie house is the only one keeping Asian flicks alive in the city on a regular basis. Each August, the 4-Star holds its Asian Film Festival; with features from across Asia, it's an event that spans several weeks, making it one of California's longest film festivals. The theater also runs a summer series screening classic kung fu films.

A circuitous car ride away, **China Beach** hugs a narrow sliver of coast below the mansions of Sea Cliff, off El Camino Del Mar near 28th Avenue. Chinese fishermen would anchor their boats in the sheltered cove and camp along the beach here in the late 19th century, a time when roughly half the Bay Area's fishing crews were Chinese. They are credited with helping develop the state's fishing industry, as a stone marker here attests. The small memorial omits any mention of the discriminatory legislation and harassment that had all but chased the Chinese out of the industry by the early 1900s, however. Perhaps fittingly, the area was until 1983 called Phelan Beach, for the former mayor who pushed for the relocation of Chinatown to the outskirts of the city following the 1906 earthquake.

THE OUTER SUNSET

Located on the opposite side of Golden Gate Park, the Sunset District was still so undeveloped by the 1930s that a Hollywood director used the area to shoot desert scenes. Although the squatters, gunpowder factories, and dairy farms of the Inner Sunset had begun to give way to homes by the 1900s, the last stretches of the Outer Sunset weren't settled until the remaining dunes were at last paved over in the 1930s and 1940s. Traditionally a predominantly Irish neighborhood, Asian families began to move here in the 1960s, an influx that gained momentum in the 1980s and 1990s as new residents from Taiwan, Hong Kong, and China settled here for the affordable housing and good neighborhood schools.

Asians now make up the majority of district residents, and Irving Street, between 19th and 25th Avenues, has blossomed into the Sunset's answer to Clement Street. While the strip lacks Clement's leisurely pace and sheer diversity, this busy commercial stretch, crowned by Chinese-language billboards, features several excellent, low-key Taiwanese, Vietnamese, and Thai restaurants, and a cluster of exhaustively stocked pan-Asian supermarkets. In the largest of these, **Sunset Super** (2425 Irving St., 415/566-6504), signs hanging above the aisles direct shoppers to sections devoted to "rice sticks" and "bean thread," and a seafood counter features everything from live frogs and turtles to fresh crab and several varieties of enormous clams bursting from their shells in large tanks. A few blocks east, **Wonderful Foods Co.** (2110 Irving St., 415/731-6889), specializes in savory and sweet delights, with rows of bins stacked with colorful snacks, such as sour watermelon, honey kumquat, hot olives, wasabi peas, and a drink counter featuring dozens of flavors of tapioca bubble tea, the trendy East Asian staple of San Francisco's Asian neighborhoods. Tea purists can head to Ten Ren's Sunset branch, **Tea Oasis** (2035 Irving St., 415/566-6066), where a small selection of gourmet teas awaits.

FESTIVALS

Every September, hundreds of paddlers race colorful dragon boats in the two-day **Northern California International Dragon Boat Championships** (www.cdba.org) at San Francisco's Lake Merced, just south of the Sunset District. It's quite a spectacle: Twenty paddlers, kept in time by a drummer perched on the bow, power through 500-meter sprints in elaborately painted 50-foot-long canoes decked out with dragon heads and tails at either end. Roughly 100 teams participate in the races, including a contingent from Bay Area high schools. Dragon boat races trace their roots to the legend of Qu Yuan, an exiled poet and statesman from the former state of Chu. Qu Yuan drowned himself in the Milou River in 278 B.C., distraught over the invasion of his homeland by ambitious Qin armies, who would later bring all of China under their rule. Villagers rushed to their boats to save him, but they were too late and were left to pound the water with their paddles to scare off fish while they tried to retrieve his body. It's a festive occasion, though, and at Lake Merced dragon boat teams compete against a backdrop of food stalls, dragon dances, and martial arts demonstrations. Shuttles run from various locations downtown, including Chinatown, to the races, which are held on the north side of Lake Merced, at Skyline Boulevard and Harding Road, near the San Francisco Zoo.

PILIPINO
COMMUNITY

T HE SOUTH OF MARKET DISTRICT, COMMONLY
KNOWN AS SoMa, is the area of San Francisco bordered by Townsend
Street to the southeast, 13th Street to the southwest, Mission Street to the
northwest, and 2nd Street to the northeast. Wealthy families settled here
and built mansions during the Gold Rush era. The 1906 Earthquake and
Fire completely destroyed the district, which was then rebuilt as a low-rent
neighborhood full of warehouses, as well as a transportation hub for the
city. It became a destination for poor immigrants, including Pilipino
laborers, in the early 20th century. In the last few decades, rapid development has dramatically changed the area: Construction of the 87-acre Yerba
Buena Gardens in the early '80s, the recent (and late) dot com boom, the
building of SBC Park in nearby China Basin, and continuing gentrification
have all affected the Pilipino community in the SoMa neighborhood. *SoMa
Pilipinas: Studies 2000*, by MC Canlas, and The Wildflowers Institute
(www.wildflowers.org) have both studied the impact of this encroaching
development on the Pilipino community, examining the traditional Pilipino
cultural values and history that have made SoMa the center of Pilipino
American life in the Bay Area.

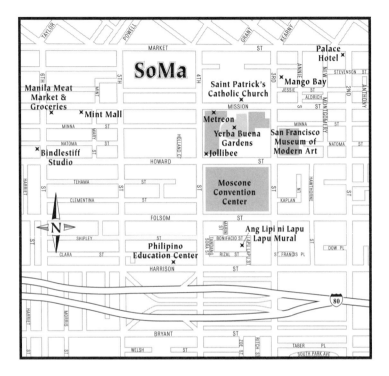

Recent demographic trends show an increase in the Pilipino population in SoMa, but an overall drop in San Francisco as a whole. The increase is primarily due to newly arrived Pilipino immigrants (the majority of whom are renters), who settle in the SoMa area as they establish themselves in a new country. The decrease in the Pilipino population throughout San Francisco, however, comes from the departure of more established community members to suburban areas in the East Bay, and even the Central Valley, where real estate is more affordable. But SoMa remains a community center and gathering place for Pilipinos in San Francisco, as well as those who have moved to the suburbs, because the neighborhood is still home to a number of highly visible institutions of Pilipino and Asian culture, and provides the social services that advocate for SoMa's Pilipino population.

PISTAHAN

Pilipino American students and families come from all over Northern California for the annual **Pistahan**, the weekend-long **Pilipino American Arts Exposition** (FAAE), which was inaugurated in 1994. Pistahan is held in the summer at the Yerba Buena Gardens Esplanade, the grassy area sandwiched between The Sony Metreon and The San Francisco Museum of Modern Art (SF MOMA), between 3rd and 4th Streets on Mission. FAAE's mission is to put on an event that is both educational and entertaining, drawing participation and attendance from the larger Bay Area Pilipino American community. Popular at Pistahan are the local food vendors and merchants, who sell everything from cheap sunglasses to tribal-print Pinoy t-shirts and sweatshirts, original Pilipino music CDs, Pilipino and Pilipino American literature, and even condominium units in Cebu City. Also popular are the musical performers, who come from as far away as Manila, and Pilipino American celebrities, most recently Paolo Montalban, who starred as the Prince in ABC's 1997 Disney movie *Cinderella*, and who was named one of *People Magazine's* "50 Most Beautiful People" of 1998 (both groundbreaking accomplishments for a Pilipino American in the entertainment industry).

Also part of Pistahan are film screenings at the Sony Metreon, and the Panama Arts Legacy Awards for literature, music, dance, film, and journalism, held in the Marriott hotel. Visual artists display their works on the far, quiet end of the Gardens, appropriately close to the SF MOMA. Of course, there's the annual parade featuring floats of Pilipino American organizations from all over Northern California—folk dancing troupes, martial arts schools, youth and church groups. San Francisco's political figures can also be counted on to make appearances. And what Pilipino parade would be complete without the Pilipina beauty queens? The parade starts at Spear and Market Streets, proceeds down Market to 6th Street and on to Yerba Buena Gardens. The entire weekend is a wonderful spectacle, showy and meaningful at the same time. Make no mistake about its mass

CHRISTMAS IN SoMa

Sponsored by Bayanihan Community Center, the annual *Parol Making Workshops and Festival* began in 2003. A *parol* is a handmade, five-pointed, star shaped lantern, representing the Star of Bethlehem, hung outside homes during Christmas season. Its three-dimensional frame is traditionally made of bamboo, but the ones being made at St. Patrick's Church and the Asian Art Museum are covered with colored paper and cellophane. Inside the three-dimensional frame are Christmas lights, the kind used to decorate Christmas trees.

These workshops are offered from October until December, and families have come from as far as Vallejo to participate; parents voice how pleased they are to have this kind of intensive creative time with their children. *Parol*-making is an exercise in community building, cooperation, and creativity. It is also in preparation for the mid-December, first annual *Parol* **Stroll and Festival,** which begins at Bayanihan Community Center, proceeds down Mission Street, and ends at Yerba Buena Center for the Arts at 3rd and Mission, where the Taste of Christmas, a showcase of Pilipino holiday specialties from Bay Area Pilipino restaurants, begins.

and commercial appeal; the well-attended Pistahan (attendance numbers in the thousands) is generously supported by public and corporate donors, as well as major media sponsors such as Radio Disney and the Philippine media giant ABS-CBN. Without this high level of corporate support the festival certainly wouldn't exist.

LANDMARKS

Local landmarks serve as history lessons, preserving the presence and visibility of Pilipinos in an area that simultaneously supports and discourages them. Pilipino American (or Pinoy/Pinay) history, culture, and literature are rarely taught in American primary and secondary schools, despite the growing numbers of Pilipinos in the Bay Area's cities and suburbs. What does exist of Philippine Studies in local colleges and universities is sparse, and, like much of the curriculum, is now threatened by state budget cuts. This absence of material in the classroom has caused Pinays to take their lessons to the streets.

At the corner of Market Street at New Montgomery, there is a plaque on the corner of the posh **Palace Hotel**: "Doctor Jose P. Rizal, Philippine National Hero and Martyr, stayed at the Palace Hotel from May 4 to 6, 1888 in the course of his only visit to the United States." The plaque was installed on December 30, 1996 in commemoration of the first centennial of his assassination, and explains that Rizal is known as the author of two novels, *Noli Mi Tangere* and *El Filibusterismo,* scathing critiques of Spanish patriarchy and the corruption of the church. For these contributions to the Philippine Revolution, the first successful uprising in Asia against a Western colonial power (Spain), he was executed by firing squad. The plaque is a potent reminder of the struggle for Philippine independence, which turned from a battle with Spain to the United States, which assumed colonial power in the Philippines at the end of the Spanish-American War. Commodore George Dewey's victory over the Spanish in Manila Bay on May 1, 1898, is marked by the monument at the center of upscale Union Square, and was dedicated by Rough Rider-turned-President Theodore Roosevelt on May 14, 1903.

The naming of streets can be seen as merely a symbolic, even benign attempt at cultural and political activism. But the naming and dedication of four streets in the SoMa neighborhood in 1979 asserted a community's presence, and also served as San Francisco's official acknowledgment of that presence. Just down 4th Street from Market, past the massive edifices of the Sony Metreon and Moscone West Convention Center, in the middle of the block created by 3rd and 4th Streets and Harrison and Folsom Streets, **Mabini Street** leads to **Bonifacio, Tandang Sora, Rizal,** and **Lapu Lapu** Streets, which make a small square. At the corner of Bonifacio and Lapu Lapu, the mural funded by the Office of Community Development, *Ang Lipi* *ni Lapu Lapu* (the descendents of Lapu Lapu), painted by Johanna Poethig, with the help of Vic Clemente and Presco Tabios, in 1984, covers the wall of 50 Rizal Street—The San Lorenzo Ruiz Center. Named after a Pilipino saint, the center houses primarily low-income Pilipino seniors. Originally called the Dimasalang House, the center was named after the fraternity of Pilipino workers formed in the 1920's—the Caballero de Dimasalang— and was built in 1978.

It's a fitting location for the mural, which depicts the legendary female warrior, Princess Urduja, and a Philippine eagle, from whose left wing sprouts the Philippine Islands. Most significantly, the *bayani* (heroes) of the Philippine Revolution are also depicted: Dr. Jose Rizal, known as the Philippines' National Hero; Apolinario Mabini, the intellectual and revolutionary; Katipunan leader Andres Bonifacio, holding his bolo knife in the air and uttering a war cry; and Katipunera Melchiora Aquino, more commonly known as Tandang Sora, tending to those wounded in battle. In the center of these figures stands Senator Benigno Aquino, whose August 21, 1983, assassination fanned the fires of the 1986 People Power Revolution, in which the dictator Ferdinand Marcos was overthrown. Numerous other Pinay political and cultural heroes populate the remainder of the mural, which seeks to condense the entire history of the Philippines on a single wall.

ART

As the home of Pinay culture and community, the SoMa area is also a center for the arts. But like other small entities in the neighborhood, arts organizations were pushed out of their spaces by the recent dot com boom, and development continues to jeopardize the existence of those that hung on. Despite the marginalization of noncommercial arts organizations, local Asian American and Pinay groups have found that survival and success is still possible (as is the case with FAAE), when partnering with large, well-established organizations. One such arts center, **Bindlestiff Studio** (415/974-1167) is an "epicenter of Pilipino American Performing Arts," where young Pinays perform in a blackbox theatre. Bindlestiff shows include home grown stand-up and sketch comedy, spoken word, independent film, and book launchings for Pinay authors. At press time, the Plaza Hotel at 185 6th Street, the company's space since its foundation in 1988, had been demolished. However, Bindlestiff, which relies mostly on the community for its funding, continues to perform at a temporary site just across the street in Natoma Alley, and is raising money for a new and improved theatre at the original 6th Street location.

One of the most successful (and loudest) events staged at Bindlestiff Studio is the brainchild of brothers Ogie and Jesse Gonzales. The annual **piNoisepop**, a festival of Asian Americans in the independent music scene, is now in its eighth year (piNoisepop 8 was presented in cooperation with the Zellerbach Family Fund and Intersection for the Arts). Well-organized chaos, it's a wild, loud (ear plugs are recommended), grungy weekend of garage and pop punk, hip hop, jazz, reggae, funk, film, video, and animation shorts. Fans will find CDs, stickers, and t-shirts for their favorite groups. Bands and performers come from all over the country to participate in piNoisepop's wall-to-wall packed house—nothing like it really exists anywhere else in the country. In fact, piNoisepop shows have been so successful that the Gonzales brothers have taken to infiltrating the larger underground music scene with the **Roadkill Tour**, booking piNoisepop bands in local clubs, including Gilman Street, Cafe Eclectica, and the Stork Club in the East Bay, and Bottom of the Hill, Voodoo Lounge, and Brainwash Cafe in SF.

Farther south of Market, the **Kearny Street Workshop**, located at **SomArts Cultural Center** (934 Brannan St., 415/503-0520), is the oldest Asian American Arts organization in the country. Founded in 1972, KSW was originally located in the International Hotel at 854 Kearny Street, but was evicted in 1977 with the rest of the building's tenants. Subsequent development and the dot-com boom has forced KSW out of various spaces over the years, and they remind us on their website that they are lucky to be

ST. PATRICK'S

Indisputably, the center of many Pilipino communities is the Catholic church. SoMa is no exception. Located across the street from the Yerba Buena Gardens Esplanade, St. Patrick's Catholic Church at 756 Mission Street (between 3rd and 4th Sts.) was founded in 1851. Its original mission was to minister to San Francisco's growing Irish population during the Gold Rush era. The church was rebuilt after the 1906 Earthquake and Fire, and underwent a seismic retrofit in 1996. In 1968, it was designated San Francisco Historic Landmark No. 4. Today, St. Patrick's entire pastoral staff and 90 percent of its parish are Pilipino. Its Young Adult Choir Organization is also predominantly Pilipino. Tagalog mass is conducted every first Sunday of the month. Other uniquely Pilipino services and organizations include Charismatic Mass and Healing, Mother Ignacio de Espiritu Santo, Santo Niño de Cebu, and San Lorenzo Ruiz. Far from insular, St. Patrick's is also a member of the Yerba Buena Alliance, and has a voice in the development of the neighborhood.

housed at SomArts, whose facilities include rehearsal and exhibition space, a theatre, design studios, and administrative offices. Today, KSW's mission is to "produce and present art that enriches and empowers Asian Pacific American (APA) communities." They have a long and illustrious history of nurturing young Asian American artists, many Pinays included, in many disciplines, through gallery showings, workshops in creative writing, drawing, and painting, and stand-up comedy. The small KSW press has produced such publications as the anthology *Without Names: A Collection of Poems* by 15 Bay Area Pilipino American Writers, and Jaime Jacinto's *Heaven is Just Another Country*, a 1998 nominee for the Pushcart Prize and a 1998 finalist for the Bay Area Book Reviewers' Association (BABRA) Award.

KSW-Next was created in 1998 as a growing space for the next generation of artists, those between 18 and 35, living and/or working in the San

Francisco Bay Area. Their annual multidisciplinary arts festival **APAture,** which is in its fifth year, takes place in the fall. APAture is an entire weekend of panel discussions on the state of APAs (Asian Pacific Americans) in the arts, presenting performances ranging from poetry readings, to spoken word, single-act plays, and music in various genres. Many of the local piNoisepop bands participate, as loud and rowdy as ever. Also featured at APAture are zine, chapbook, and comics tables, film and video screenings, and visual and conceptual art displays. APAture is an important and respected venue for artists who struggle to find places to exhibit their work.

MINT MALL

In 2000, the Mint Mall Organizing Committee was formed when three Pilipino businesses and art groups, including the theatre group Teatro ng Tanan, were served eviction notices. Other businesses in the space were also informed of their imminent evictions in order to make room for office space. But tenants and community members fought hard to stay in **The Mint Mall** (953 Mission St., between 5th and 6th Sts.), and today the establishment is still standing and filled with Pilipino businesses and organizations.

Likha Folk Ensemble (www.likha.org) formed in 1992, collects and preserves "indigenous Philippine art forms, as expressed in music, literature, dance, arts, crafts and costumes." They perform dance with live musical accompaniment internationally, and offer dance workshops throughout the Bay Area. Check out their online store to purchase their DVD *Dekada*, or a CD of their Rondalla (stringed instrument ensemble) and percussionists.

The **Pilipino American Development Foundation** was founded in 1997 "to develop initiatives and resources to strengthen the social, physical and economic well-being of Pilipino Americans in the San Francisco Bay Area with special attention to those segments of the population that are underserved." The associated **Bayanihan Community Center,** a centralized

LAKAS SAMBAYAN/
PEOPLE POWER 1986

Close to SoMa, in Daly City, one can find the Office of Community Development–funded mural *Lakas Sambayan/People Power 1986,* painted by Johanna Poethig, Vic Clemente, and Presco Tabios. This mural is not easily accessible if you don't have a car, but it is well located for its visibility, at the intersection of Highway 101 and I-280. Like Poethig's earlier *Ang Lipi ni Lapu Lapu,* this second Pilipino mural is both a history lesson and a reminder not to be complacent in our suburban comfort. The mural depicts the continuation of Philippine revolution in a contemporary context, making it relevant for those of us who have no memories of revolution.

At the center of this mural is a stone monument, the head of former dictator Ferdinand Marcos, which was carved and cemented into the mountains of Benguet Province as a display of power almost as showy as his wife's thousands of pairs of shoes, which is shown in the mural spilling out from under Marcos's collar. Also scattered around his wife's shoes, American dollars, a human skeleton with bound wrists and ankles, and children scavenging on Smoky Mountain, Manila's massive garbage dump that the city's impoverished have made their home. Forcing itself out from inside Marcos's stone

meeting place whose programs consist of Pilipino business assistance, advocacy for families and individuals seeking affordable housing (especially in SoMa), and guided "ethno-tourism" walking tours of the area. Check out their website at www.bayanihancc.org or call 415/348-8042 for information on their programs and services.

The **Manilatown Heritage Foundation** (415/777-1130) was established in 1994 to advocate for the building of a new International Hotel on the site of the original at the corner of Kearny and Jackson Streets, just outside Chinatown. The area was once a bustling and vibrant Manilatown, and one of MHF's projects is the Manilatown Center, to be located on the ground floor of the new International Hotel. Currently being rebuilt after nearly 30 years, the International Hotel will contain 104 units of section 8 head is a brown fist, brandishing a fiery torch, much like Athena's birth through the head of Zeus.

To the left on the mural you can see a bronze *agong*, a large percussive instrument from predominantly Muslim Mindanao, the southernmost Philippine Island. You can also see Generala Gabriela Silang, who led the northernmost province of Ilocos in a rebellion against Spain in 1762-1763. Behind her on the mural is a jungle of bamboo, in which guerrilla soldiers hide. Above her lies a festive Christmas *parol*, a lantern representing the Star of Bethlehem. To the right of Marcos's shattered stone head is the assassinated Senator Benigno Aquino, fallen in the arms of his wife Corazon Aquino, who became Philippine president after the People Power Revolution of 1986. They are embraced by the torch's flame, which folds into a golden dove taking flight. Behind them can be seen religious figures kneeling and praying with their crucifixes and Santo Niño statues. Masses of protestors take to the streets: young men and women, in blue jeans and *tsinelas* (rubber flip-flops) overturn an army tank, next to a sunrise over the beleaguered city of Manila.

senior housing and supportive tenant services. The Center will provide performing and visual arts space, and a permanent collection of historical photos, artwork, and artifacts of the original hotel and Manilatown. To find out more about Manilatown, pick up *Rappin With Ten Thousand Carabaos in the Dark*, a good, nonacademic read by Al Robles. A community institution himself, Robles has transcribed the stories of the Manongs (Pilipino elders) into poems. Many of these elders have since passed away. For the kids, check out the wild and colorful *Lakas and the Manilatown Fish*, by Tony Robles (translated into Tagalog by Eloisa de Jesus and Magdalena de Guzman).

You can find these books and many more on the street level of the Mint Mall, at **Arkipelago Philippine Arts + Books + Crafts** (415/777-010), the best place in the Bay Area to stock up on Pilipino and Pilipino American literature. Arkipelago carries books published in the Philippines that are difficult to find anywhere else in the United States. In an effort to support this Pilipino American–owned business, some Asian American and Philippine Studies professors from San Francisco State University, City College of San Francisco, and University of San Francisco (USF) send their students to Arkipelago on scavenger hunts and to buy their textbooks. USF Professor Joaquin Gonzalez, of the Yuchengco Philippine Studies Program, takes his Pilipino Culture and Society students here on a SoMa walking tour. Arkipelago also features a small selection of Pilipino and Pilipino American CDs, literature, and music produced by Arkipelago Books Publishing, along with all manner of Philippine cultural artifacts.

RESTAURANTS AND MARKETS

Located at street level in the New Mint Mall, the **New Pilipinas Restaurant** serves food *turo-turo* style, meaning that everything—the *sinegang* (tamarind soup), *sinangag* (garlic fried rice), eggplant tortas, and menudo—is on display behind the glass case. Diners simply point to what looks good, and it's served in Styrofoam bowls and plates. Also on display are individually wrapped desserts, which are usually very sticky, and loaded with coconut milk. New Pilipinas is a no frills experience; patrons bus their own tables and share the many bottles of banana ketchup, *patis* (a salty, fermented fish sauce) and *toyo* (soy sauce) set out for everyone's use. Perhaps even more important than the wonderful homemade food offered in New Pilipinas is the company of the other diners. On any given day, Al Robles and other community leaders might be found sharing stories over a plate of fried fish and garlic rice—a wonderful way to learn about the history of the Pinay community in San Francisco.

For those who love Pilipino food and want to try preparing it themselves, a shopping trip to **Manila Meat Market and Groceries** (also known as **Shar-Vi's**), at 987 Mission Street, is a great place to start.

Pastries (*pan de sal, pan de leche, bibingka*), many varieties of *pancit* noodles, banana ketchup, and mango and *calamansi* juice, are just some of the essentials on sale.

Inside the International Food Mall on 3rd Street, between Market and Mission, is **Mango Bay** (415/369-9888), which was opened in 2002 by San Francisco resident Barry Picazo, who had always wondered why Philippine cuisine seemed so inaccessible to San Franciscans. One look at the artful presentation of *dinuguan* (pork stew, made with a small amount of pig blood) in this turo-turo-style restaurant could convince anyone to try this most traditional of Pilipino dishes. Still, for those who haven't yet "acquired" the taste for dinuguan, Mr. Picazo has chosen the "safer" and more aesthetically pleasing paella, and Arroz a la Cubana (complete with fried saba banana), in its place. Since Mango Bay has opened, he's learned to adapt other traditional Pilipino recipes to suit the palates of those unaccustomed to some of the rare ingredients. Traditional *kare kare* (peanut stew) is made with ox tails and tripe, but at Mango Bay it's made with mussels, shrimp, and scallops, which are not only more palatable than tripe, but healthier as well. Mr. Picazo has also become quite good at teaching non-Pilipinos traditional ways of eating Pilipino cuisine. For example, essential to tasty *kare kare* is adding just the right amount of *bagoong* (very salty fermented shrimp paste); too much can be overpowering and even unpleasant. Mango Bay is open Monday to Saturday from 7 A.M. TO 5 P.M., and is also available for event catering. There are plans to open a second Mango Bay in the future, also in the SoMa area, for sit-down (rather than turo-turo) dining.

From enterprising local businesses to global fast food, the SoMa neighborhood covers the full spectrum. **Jollibee** (200 4th St., 415/546-1246), the Philippines' number one fast-food chain, is perhaps most well known for its fried chicken, oddly named "Chickenjoy," and for the Philippine spaghetti—don't ask, just try it. The banana-langka (jackfruit) and mango turnovers are served warm and gooey on the inside, crunchy on the outside, and taste best washed down with a coco-loco pearl cooler (green because of the *pandan* in it). Jollibee may be an example of a Western phenomenon, but it is a uniquely Pilipino experience.

THE BAY AREA'S

DESI
COMMUNITIES

Before the technology bubble burst, BART platforms up and down the Silicon Valley corridor were full of young Indian professionals. Men and women toting computer bags lined up in droves, powering the IT revolution of the late 1990s. The bottom may have dropped out of the tech boom, but the *Desi* (Hindi word meaning anyone from the homeland, which has come to signify anyone from South Asia) influence in the San Francisco Bay Area has roots deeper, older, and stronger than any economic trend. From San Francisco hipster-*Desi* nightclubs to historical Sikh *Gurdwaras* to numerous tea and snack cafés, the Bay Area is a true mecca for the fusion of South Asian and American cultures.

Indians were the fastest growing Asian American population over the last decade, and that growth is highly evident in the Bay Area, which has the largest number of Indians outside of the New York metropolitan area—some 158,000 people—along with thousands of South Asians from Pakistan, Bangladesh, Sri Lanka, and Nepal.

While the major population growth happened over the last 30 years, the Bay Area was one of the first areas to host Indian immigration in the United States, a rich history that goes back to the 1800s, when Sikhs began arriving as laborers. The new immigrants, settling mostly into the suburbs of the East and South Bay, initiated the cultural depth that infuses those areas today. Unlike other ethnic enclaves crowded into one corner or neighborhood of a city, the *Desi* community in the Bay Area is spread throughout the many cities, suburbs, hills, and valleys of Northern California.

Home to scores of high-tech entrepreneurs, such as Hotmail creator Sabeer Bhatia, the Bay Area is also home to world-renowned artists like Indian classical musician Ali Akhbar Khan, who runs a school across the Golden Gate Bridge in Marin County. Novelist Chitra Divakaruni, who lived for many years in the Bay Area, has brought the nuanced lives of Bay Area Indians to light in her novels *Mistress of Spices* and *Sister of My Heart.* Her book of poems, *Leaving Yuba City,* fictionalizes the lives of women in the heavily Sikh populated town some 150 miles north of San Francisco.

While the epicenter for all things Indian has become the East Bay city of Fremont, day trips exploring the random yet delightful treats of San Francisco, the historical and agricultural side of Yuba City, the shopping extravaganzas of Berkeley's University Avenue, or Sunnyvale's Gandhinagar, are all enriching ways to indulge in the Bay Area's *Desi* offerings.

FREMONT

About 40 miles southeast of San Francisco in the East Bay, and BART accessible, Fremont is exemplary of the New California where the once-dubbed "minority" is becoming the majority. Not your typical suburb, Fremont is home to huge populations of *Desis,* Chinese Americans, and the largest Afghan population outside of Afghanistan. Driving through the wide boulevards and past the strip malls, you might think Fremont was like any other suburb. But take a closer look: You might see a group of Chinese and Indian grandmothers out on a power walk, or perhaps a group of Afghan men in traditional dress playing volleyball in the park. On a Saturday afternoon, you'll probably smell barbecues and hear people working on their cars—but you'll be smelling tandoori chicken from the grill and hearing Bollywood's latest hits blaring out of garages.

Fremont, like typical suburbs, is heavily spread out—meaning that the best way to travel there, and around the city, is by car. From San Francisco, the drive should take about 40 minutes, barring traffic. A good first stop might be the **Fremont Hindu Temple and Cultural Center** (3676 Delaware Dr., 510/490-9597). Founded in the late 1970s by early Indian immigrants to the area, it was one of the first Hindu temples in the Bay Area. The burgeoning community bought a church nestled deep in a Fremont neighborhood and converted it into a place of worship and community center, which it continues to be to this day. Call ahead to check for *pujas* (worship services) or community events.

At the intersection of Fremont Boulevard (one of the city's main arteries) and Washington, you'll find a shopping center that exemplifies the diversity of this little city and houses two great *Desi* stores. **Bharat Bazaar** (510/623-0390), a large *Desi* grocery store, opened in 1974, carries a huge selection of spices, snacks, and ready-made mixes for all sorts of South Asian dishes. A Bay Area institution, Bharat Bazaar also features a huge selection of Indian/Asian produce—from bitter melons and cinquas to jackfruits and turmeric root. They also offer a large selection of henna shampoos and, of course, an entire corner dedicated to Bollywood DVDs and CDs. A few doors down you'll find **Lovely Sweets** (41031 Fremont Blvd., 510/657-1412), a classic Indian snack and sweet shop whose glass cases are filled to the brim with sticky delights like foil-wrapped coconut *barfi, sohan papri* (made from boiled milk skin), *kaju kattli* (cashew bars), and crispy, fried *jalebis*. These *Desi* treats are intensely sweet and best enjoyed with a cup of tea.

Catch the latest Bollywood movie at **Naz 8 Cinemas** (39160 Paseo Padre Parkway, 510/797-2000), "the nation's first multicultural entertainment megaplex." Now in its second location—in the Princeton Gateway Plaza Shopping Center in central Fremont—the theater boasts some 3,000 seats and even more parking spaces. A perfectly Bay Area invention, the vibrantly postered lobby is no different from the local chain theater—until

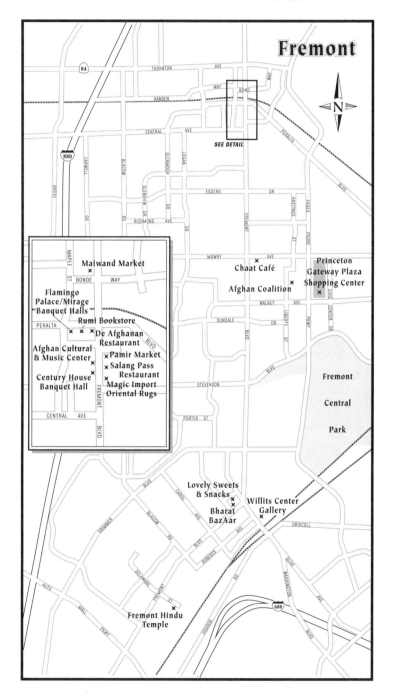

you read the concession stand menu, which offers a lamb and *naan* plate alongside the standard popcorn. Owner Shiraz Jivani bought a run-down, one-screen theater in Fremont back in 1992 in order to show South Asian films—now, as other multiplexes are struggling, the Naz 8 is hoping to open new locations across the country. If you don't speak the language of the film, be sure and double-check whether the movie you are going to see is subtitled or not—the Naz runs different versions at different times.

Fremont's hub, at the intersection of Fremont Boulevard and Mowry Avenue, is home to **Chaat Café** (3954 Mowry Ave., 510/796-3408), a hangout for young *Desi* residents. Serving a wide range of snack type foods like *samosas* and *naan* wraps, you'll find a line heading out the door on most weekend nights. *Chaat*—a broad term for snacks and appetizers—has become a popular way to eat *Desi* food in the Bay Area, with "cafes" popping up all over the place.

Fremont is home to the annual **Festival of India** held in mid-August to celebrate India's independence from the British. A huge event that show-cases the size and influence of the Bay Area's *Desi* community and boasts legendary Bollywood actors as parade marshals, this two-day festival sees upwards of 70,000 *Desis* out eating, socializing, and enjoying the festival activities. Go to www.fiaonline.org for festival dates and information.

SAN FRANCISCO

Though San Francisco's South Asian population is small compared to other parts of the Bay Area, the city has some of the most interesting attractions and eateries—beginning right in downtown San Francisco. The bronze statue of Gandhi at the Embarcadero Ferry Building, portraying the famous spiritual leader in stride on one of the many *padyatras* (long marches) he took throughout his native country, was a gift from the Indian Council for Cultural Relations (ICCR), headed by the Vice President of India in 1988.

San Francisco's gritty Tenderloin neighborhood has recently become home to numerous cheap, tasty, and quick *Desi* eateries. From the original

YUBA CITY'S SIKH COMMUNITY

Though this agricultural town of 79,000 has the distinction of being known as the prune capital of California, Yuba City is gaining more recognition for its large community of Sikhs and a growing population of other South Asian immigrants. Since the early 20th century, newcomers from the Punjab province of India have settled down to work in and operate rice, plum, and peach farms, and processing facilities.

Exclusion laws in effect from the 1900s to mid-1940s prohibited many South Asians from entering the country, but some were able to immigrate by way of Canada and Mexico. There are stories of those who took five years to reach California—walking up from Panama to California via Mexico. When immigration laws were relaxed after World War II, Sikhs arrived in Yuba City in droves, gradually changing the entire demographics of the area. Today 9 percent of the city's population are Sikh, and other South Asians have moved to the area as well. The Sikh community calls Yuba City *Chhotta Punjab.* "Sat Sri Akal" is the preferred form of greeting. You can speak Punjabi at the local gas station, in the doctor's office, or at the farms.

The Sikh culture pervades daily life in this region of the Upper Sacramento Valley. When Sikhs first moved to Yuba City they became

---

Shalimar (532 Jones, 415/928-0333), to **Naan 'n' Curry** (478 O'Farrell, 415/775-1349), to the new vegetarian **Haveli** (35 6th St., 415/546-1238), which serves up one meal per day cafeteria–style. These places offer great food and tons of character.

Further west near Japantown, the front room of the **Maharani** (Empress) restaurant (1122 Post St. at Polk, 415/775-1988) might look like a normal Indian restaurant, but first impressions can be misleading. To really impress a date, diners choose the Fantasy Room, where they are seated on cushions secluded behind beaded curtains, while images from the *Kama Sutra* decorate the walls. The place isn't all ambiance though—the set, seven-course Fantasy Room meals for two can include a salad sprinkled with pomegranate seeds, heady lamb stew, and luscious meats.

involved in the local business of agriculture, and to this day many of the local peach and other farms are run by South Asians. While times are changing and the Sikh families are diversifying their trade, you may still be able to meet them—and purchase their wonderfully fresh produce—at local **Yuba City Farmer's Markets.** The main one is in the middle of town on Center Street and runs from April 29 to mid-October. For information call 530/671-3346.

For a more solemn experience of the Sikh culture, you may visit the *Gurdwara* at 2468 Tierra Buena Road. At this Sikh temple, large murals visually document Sikh religious history and the history of Sikhs in Yuba City. Also on-site is a library containing various books on Sikhism, and you might even get a free meal if you're there during lunchtime—be sure to check in with the kitchen. Also in town are Islamic mosques (the newest one is located at 2626 Tierra Buena Road) and Hindu temples. Please dress appropriately and wear head coverings at all places of worship.

Yuba City is located about 125 miles northeast of San Francisco, in Sutter County. To get there from San Francisco, take I-80 East, drive for approximately 60 miles, then take Highway 113 to Highway 99.

Mango ice cream sprinkled with chocolate and vanilla sauces makes a wonderful dessert. Call ahead for reservations or special occasions.

Like the Naz 8 Cinema in Fremont, **Kennedy's Irish Pub and Curry House** (1040 Columbus Ave., 415/441-8855) is another uniquely Bay Area cultural mixture. Featuring over 200 kinds of beer and wine, pool tables galore, darts, and of course delicious Indian snacks at low prices—the mix of dingy dive and gaudy Indian restaurant makes Kennedy's a favorite for happy hour or reveling concert-goers heading to a show at Bimbos across the street. In San Francisco's Mission District the blending of cultures continues. Dalvinder Multani opened **Zante's Pizza** (3489 Mission at Cortland, 415/821-3949) some 20 years ago. Upon first arriving in the United States he made pizza in Brooklyn, then moved to San Francisco where he bought a pizza restaurant named, for whatever reason, after a Greek island—he kept the name and the pizza, but added Indian toppings and dishes. Pizzas topped with *saag,* curried vegetables, tandoori chicken, or even lamb are on the menu at Zante's. For dessert, **Bombay Ice Creamery** (522 Valencia Street, 415/431-1103), near the intersection of 16th, features *Desi* ice cream flavors ranging from cardamom to *chai* to saffron-pistachio.

The **Gadar Memorial House** (5 Wood St., 415/668-0662) is a must for those interested in Indian history. The Hindustan Gadar Party, founded in 1913 to join the struggle for India's independence, started its operation from 436 Hill Street in San Francisco. The original building was known as *Yugantar Ashram* and it was from here that the freedom fighters of the Hindustan *Gadar* Party, also known as *Gadri Babas,* were active from 1913 to 1917. The modest three-story building provided an environment for thinkers, activists, and volunteers who came to live, work, organize, and run a printing press that sent their message of Indian independence around the world. In August 1914, when the Party called on overseas Indians to return to India to fight for its freedom, no fewer than 8,000 of them were said to have returned home to take part in the revolution. The party's headquarters subsequently moved to Wood Street, where they are still located. Visitors can browse the Gadar Memorial Library's collection of Hindi and English books on Indian history and other subjects. Call the Indian Consulate for more information.

SOUTH BAY

The Information Technology revolution brought a huge number of H-1B (temporary) visa holders to the Bay Area, many of them settling in the heart of Silicon Valley—Milpitas, Sunnyvale, Mountain View, and Palo Alto. The intersection of Lawrence Expressway and El Camino Real in Sunnyvale has seen a huge number of *Desi* shops and restaurants recently opened, creating what is unofficially called Gandhinagar, or Gandhi Town.

Komalavilas (1020 E. El Camino Real, 408/733-7400) is a small, traditional restaurant serving mostly young South Indian bachelors who long for some home-cooked food. Very strict in its cooking style, the restaurant uses absolutely no garlic and a bare minimum of onions—trademarks of the traditional South Indian Brahmin style of cooking. In Mountain View, **Saravana Bhavan** (600 W. El Camino Real, 650/635-0460), a South Indian chain that has made the move to America, serves delicious *masala dosais* (large crepes filled with curried vegetables), *sambar* (thin tomato soup with vegetables), and coconut chutney-dishes that are fast making South Indian food more popular than the heavier North Indian styles. Saravana Bhavan is no longer a well-kept secret in the Indian community—the place is usually crowded, but definitely worth the wait.

The **Indian Community Center** (555 Los Coches St., 408/934-1130) in Milpitas is a good resource for information on events happening in the South Bay. The Center hosts community events and classes, as well as a schedule of local events, such as concerts, plays, and dance performances.

SAN JOSE'S

VIETNAMESE
COMMUNITY

T HE FLAG OF SOUTH VIETNAM STILL FLIES HIGH IN San Jose. Its three red bands cross a wide, golden-yellow field: Vivid red for the blood spilled during centuries of rebellion, and one stripe each for the country's northern, central, and southern regions. Vietnamese landscape, language, food, and dress all adhere to these regions' contours. Despite the passing of decades, the three-striped flag remains an emotionally laden symbol for "Free Vietnam," and flutters throughout San Jose as an emblem of the Vietnamese American community's cultural pride and political persistence. The Mayor of San Jose recently signed a proclamation to officially recognize the flag of old Vietnam, an act that highlights the growing importance of Vietnamese immigrants in the city.

The first wave of Vietnamese immigrants arrived in the United States as refugees. Many left their country unwillingly, believing they would soon return. Their lives here in America were only temporary, they insisted, but as children grew and grandchildren were born and as bitter memories gave way to new identities, Vietnamese families began setting roots into American soil.

During the late 1970s and through the 1980s, increasing numbers of overseas Vietnamese, known as Viet Kieu, settled in San Jose. They were

attracted to the city's affordable housing and found abundant work in Silicon Valley's high-tech factories and nearby agricultural fields. A nascent "Little Saigon" promised to revitalize the Tenderloin District in San Francisco, and Oakland's Chinatown attracted its share of Southeast Asian immigrants. The South Bay, though, pulled a much larger number of Vietnamese people into its neighborhoods. Today, Santa Clara County has the second largest population of overseas Vietnamese in the world. San Jose itself is home to more Vietnamese Americans than any other city in the nation—nearly 79,000 according to the 2000 census. Many have settled in the eastern districts of San Jose, near where the wide lanes of I-280, I-680, I-880, and the infamous Highway 101 gather into a loose knot just beyond the southern tip of the San Francisco Bay.

San Jose was the first civilian settlement in Alta California and then

© MATT ORENDORFF

fresh produce at a local market

later became the state's first capitol. With its burgeoning, diverse population and continued economic growth, it may soon reclaim its place as the
region's central city. The U.S. Census Bureau has already given the city top
billing over its more famous northerly neighbors, calling this the San Jose-
San Francisco-Oakland area. It's only a matter of time, some say, before
"San Jose Bay Area" will be the correct name for Northern California's
sprawling metropolis.

SIGHTS

A drive along the stretch of Tully Road east of the Capitol Expressway
reveals the heart of the Vietnamese commercial district. Here, the businesses are concentrated into convenient strip malls and shopping centers,
each a nexus of Vietnamese American needs. Young women visit custom
dress shops to be measured for the latest *ao dai* fashions. Couples pore over
samples of bilingual wedding invitations before selecting reception treats
from both Chinese and European-style bakeries. Turning the pages of
Calitoday or *Thoi Bao,* men linger over the day's news from Vietnam, while

FRESNO'S HMONG COMMUNITY

In the student center of the California State University in Fresno, a hanging quilt tells the story of the Hmong people. Stitch by tiny stitch, it recounts their long trek from southern China to the highlands of Southeast Asia, from the refugee camps of Thailand to their new homes in the United States. While they faced persecution and prejudice for hundreds of years as an ethnic minority in Asia, the Hmong people suffered even greater casualties when they were recruited as CIA mercenaries during the Vietnam War. After 1975, they fled the harsh reprisal of the Laotian and Vietnamese governments to find a refuge in the United States. Over 50,000 Hmong now make their home in California's Central Valley, and almost half of them live in or around Fresno.

Every year during the last week of December, Hmong from around the world converge at the Fresno Fairgrounds for the lively **International Hmong New Year Festival.** It has grown into the largest Hmong event in the United States, attracting more than 150,000 people for seven full days of song, dance, art, food, and games. Modern life blends with centuries-old traditions: Contestants for the Miss Hmong International beauty pageant change from elaborate tribal wear to sequined gowns, and teenagers switch between tossing *pov pob* balls to dialing their cell phones. Open to the public, the festival is an excellent way to learn more about the Hmong people and their rich culture.

beneath posters advertising gala concerts, music lovers flip though CDs released by their favorite singers on each side of the Pacific. Eyeglasses and cell phones, rice cookers and soy bean grinders, plastic flip-flops and designer handbag knock-offs—it's all here.

Lion Plaza (1818 Tully Rd., at King Rd.) and the **Grand Century Mall** (1111 Story Rd., at McLaughlin Ave.) are two well-known sites for finding and buying all things Vietnamese. Near these malls are smaller business strips, such as Sun Plaza on South King Road, or Caribbees Center and Senter Road Plaza on Senter Road. Their formal names become

The Hmong identify themselves by clan and tribe, the latter depending on their specific dialect, geographic origin, and dress. Here in the United States, though, these distinctions have less meaning day to day. Although various countries have given them many different names, the Hmong now designate themselves into two major groups: the White Hmong and the Green (or Blue) Hmong. **The Hmong Cultural Heritage Center** preserves the art, music, and dance of the diverse tribes and presents classes to the community in Hmong, English, computer literacy, and health. The Center also offers workshops to the public on specific aspects of Hmong tradition, such as marriage ceremonies and funeral rituals.

The University of California, Irvine maintains an extensive collection of Hmong textile art. Hmong women have refined the art of *paj ntaub*, or flower cloth, for over 2,000 years. Ceremonial clothing and baby carriers, for example, are elaborately decorated, involving a complex and colorful blend of weaving, dyeing, wax resist, pleating, appliqué, and embroidery that helps define each tribe. Their abstract patterns are named evocatively after forms in nature: Rooster combs, elephant foot, bird wings, snails with seeds, and tiger's face all find elaborate expression on fabric. More recently, while detained in refugee camps, Hmong women were encouraged to record their memories. They turned to cloth and thread to tell their stories. Their narrative quilts, known as storycloths, depict the Hmong community's exodus in extraordinary detail and has developed into a new, unique art form.

less important as these strips begin to blur together into one nearly continuous corridor of Vietnamese businesses. When developers created Lion Plaza at the nondescript intersection of Tully and King in the 1980s, it was billed as the largest Asian mall in Northern California. Bigger, flashier shopping centers have since been built, but Vietnamese families still crowd Lion Plaza. Cars line Tully Road waiting for parking spaces to open during busy weekends and holidays. To herald the new lunar year, children and adults light long, loud strings of firecrackers, sending drifts of paper down to blanket the courtyard like red snow.

Further north, Grand Century Mall sits far back from Story Road. Its high columns and fancy fountain create an imposing façade, but enter its doors and you'll find the same eclectic mix of shops and stands that define other Vietnamese shopping centers. Up front, kumquat trees and orchid plants spill out onto the sidewalk from Phuong Nam Plants. Inside the store are miniature bamboo stands, money plants, garden fountains, and lucky red blossoms of all types. Shoppers will also find an abundant stock of pots, from large ceramic urns to little gold containers in the shape of Chinese ingots. Stop by Imperial Tea for a lesson in traditional tea service, or browse in Y Nhu Tailoring to select fabric for a flowing Vietnamese dress.

It's easy to forget, once you enter the gates of **Chua Duc Vien,** (2420 McLaughlin Ave, 408/993-9158, www.geocities.com/NapaValley/9004 /ducvien.htm) that you're not far from the busy intersection of Tully and McLaughlin. Known also as the Perfect Virtue Buddhist Temple, the beautiful grounds provide a peaceful setting for Vietnamese families to pray and study. The late Thich Dam Luu and the Vietnamese Buddhists she inspired, from small children to elders, raised money to build the temple by collecting and recycling cans, paper, and cardboard for years. (*Thich* is Vietnamese for "Venerable," the title of respect for monks and nuns.)

Chua Duc Vien is the only Vietnamese Buddhist temple in Northern California, and one of the few in the nation, run by nuns. During the weekends and especially on holidays, Vietnamese Buddhists fill the temple grounds. They quietly pray, burn incense, walk in the gardens, and pose for family photos on the Grand Hall's front steps. Along with their daily recitations, chanting, bowing, and studying, the nuns also lecture on Pure Land Buddhism, sell gifts, and teach Vietnamese language classes. The temple welcomes visitors, and on Sundays, the nuns serve vegetarian food and special sweets such as sesame-covered *banh cam* (fried cakes filled with sweetened mung bean paste) to the public. On the south side of the Grand Hall lies a tiny divination chapel with just enough room for two or three to kneel and ask the gods for guidance. Gently shaking wooden containers filled with flat, numbered sticks, they wait for the release of a fortune. The number on the stick corresponds to printed poems stacked neatly along one wall. Revealing the Taoist influence on Buddhism, these thought-provoking verses offer supplicants divine counsel for problems at hand.

Less than one-tenth of the population in Vietnam practices Catholicism, but over a third of Vietnamese Americans are Catholic. Having left the north during the division of Vietnam in 1954, Catholics again fled their homes after the fall of Saigon, fearful of persecution by the Communist government. Over 10,000 of them resettled in Santa Clara County. Deep rifts once divided the Vietnamese Catholics as they struggled to establish a personal parish in San Jose. During this period, the community maintained strong ties to several churches where Vietnamese priests conducted masses daily in their native language. In 1999, the bishop declared **St. Patrick's Proto-Cathedral Parish** (389 E. Santa Clara St., 408/294-8120) a personal parish for Vietnamese Catholics. In 2002, in a final move for reconciliation, the Chapel of Vietnamese Martyrs became a part of **St. Maria Goretti Church** (2980 Senter Rd., 408/363-2300).

FOOD

The food courts of American-style malls are perfect for Vietnam's street food fare. Virtually all Vietnamese shopping centers include both tiny stalls and full-scale restaurants serving a wide selection of foods: noodle soups, *banh mi* sandwiches, fluffy steamed *banh bao* buns, crispy rice crêpes and silky steamed rice rolls, bubble teas, and technicolor *che* desserts. Look for the *nuoc mia* vendors, easily identified by the tall stalks of sugar cane gathered on their counters. They'll press sugar cane juice to order and then mix it with a fruit or flavoring of your choice. Follow your nose to find the Belgian waffle stands, made distinctly Vietnamese with a startling swirl of green *la dua*, the essence of a fragrant tropical plant.

VIETNAMESE CUISINE

Blending influences from India, China, Thailand, and France, Vietnamese cuisine boasts complex layers of flavors. Enjoying Vietnamese food is a hands-on experience—from wrapping shrimp in lettuce leaves to dipping beef in a simmering broth, from flavoring your soup to mixing your own sauce. Many dishes require diners to cook, mix, assemble, garnish, or season right at the table. Vietnamese cooks grant guests their personal preferences and consider them an important part of the creative process. Even a simple bowl of soup may call for a squeeze of lime, a sprinkle of bean sprouts, perhaps a dollop of chile or hoisin sauce, and then a few fragrant leaves of basil—each added to individual taste.

Except for formal wedding banquets, Vietnamese meals are generally not served in distinct courses. In family-style restaurants, dishes are brought to the table as soon as the kitchen finishes them. If you resist any attempts to slow the pace of their arrival, don't be surprised when your host or the server begins delicately stacking and overlapping platter upon platter to create more space on the table.

Vietnam's gastronomic specialties number into the hundreds. Fortunately for the devoted diner, certain favorites reappear frequently on Vietnamese restaurant menus. For a taste of the country's traditional cuisine, look for the following dishes.

Banh hoi: The name refers to delicate rice noodles that have been pressed and cut into flat "cakes." Topped with a variety of grilled meats or seafood, *banh hoi* are wrapped in lettuce leaves with fresh herbs and vegetables.

Banh mi: Vietnamese sandwich filled with meats such as grilled chicken, roast pork, or pâté, served on a French-style baguette roll with cucumber, carrots, cilantro, and chile.

Banh uot: Steamed rice sheets rolled around savory fillings such as pork or mushrooms.

Banh xeo: Sometimes translated as sizzling or happy crêpe. Made from rice flour and tinted gold with turmeric, the crisp crêpe is folded over a filling of pork, shrimp, and mung bean sprouts. Diners tear off small pieces to wrap in lettuce with fresh vegetables and herbs.

Bo bay mon (bo mon): A celebratory meal consisting of seven courses of beef, including a carpaccio flavored with lime juice, thin slices grilled in *la lot* leaves, and a rice and ground beef soup.

Bo nhung giam: Thinly sliced beef cooked at the table in a broth spiked with onions, vinegar, and black pepper.

Bun: Referring to the thin, vermicelli-like rice noodles, *bun* can be either a soup (as in *bun rieu,* a crab and tomato soup) or a noodle salad (such as *bun thit nuong,* or rice noodles and fresh greens topped with grilled pork).

Ca kho: Catfish steaks braised in a rich, mahogany-hued sauce with a distinctive sweet-salty flavor. Shrimp, pork, chicken, and tofu can also be cooked in this style.

Cafe sua da: Chicory coffee that is brought to the table in individual metal drip filters, stirred into sweetened condensed milk, and then poured over ice. *Café sua nong* is the version served hot, while *café den* is black and strong.

Canh chua: A sour and spicy soup with tamarind-based broth and a vibrant mix of pineapple, tomato, taro stem, and bean sprouts. Traditionally eaten with a dollop of rice or paired with *kho* dishes.

Cha gio: Crisp, fried spring rolls, also called imperial rolls, filled with ground pork and shrimp. A tofu-based vegetarian version is also popular.

Chao tom: Shrimp ground to a smooth paste and grilled on skewers of fresh sugar cane.

Che: Sweet, brightly colored snacks often offered as dessert, *che* is a cross between a drink and a pudding. Though the specific combinations vary, common ingredients include tapioca, banana, coconut milk, dried longan, agar agar strips, seaweed, taro, red beans, and mung beans.

Goi: A refreshing salad of thinly cut vegetables and meat garnished with fresh herbs and peanuts. Highlighted ingredients might include shrimp, squid, jackfruit, jellyfish, pomelo segments, banana blossoms, or lotus stems.

Goi cuon: Fresh "salad rolls" usually served as appetizers. Thin, translucent rice paper, once softened, becomes the perfect wrapping for sliced pork, shrimp, and fresh herbs and vegetables. The dipping sauce may be based on either fish sauce or ground peanuts.

Hu tieu: With a crystal clear broth sprinkled with crisp-fried shallots, this delicately flavored rice noodle soup is a specialty in the south. Diners can choose various combinations of shrimp, crab, fish balls, fish cakes, and thin slices of pork.

Lau: The Vietnamese interpretation of hot pot. Thin slices of meat or fish, fresh greens, and rice noodles are cooked convivially at the table in a simmering broth.

(continued on next page)

VIETNAMESE CUISINE

(continued from previous page)

Mi bo kho: A rich stew of beef, carrots, and potatoes served over rice noodles. *Banh mi bo kho* is served with thick slices of French baguette.

Mi vit: This Chinese-style soup pairs toothsome egg noodles with five-spice roasted duck.

Nuoc mam: Fish sauce is the salt of the Vietnamese kitchen. This pungent, amber-colored liquid is pressed from fermented anchovies and appears as a seasoning, a table condiment, and a base for numerous dipping sauces.

Pho: Considered by many to be the national dish of Vietnam. At its most basic, this soup combines rice noodles, paper-thin slices of rare beef, and a fragrant broth infused with star anise, ginger, and cinnamon. Add-ins include long-cooked brisket, tripe, beef balls, and tendon. A version made with chicken, *pho ga,* may also appear on the menu.

Sinh to: Smoothies made from fresh fruit. Avocados (*sinh to bo*) make an especially luscious shake.

Across the street from the Grand Century Mall is a landmark as venerable as it is quirky: **Lee's Sandwiches,** (four San Jose locations: 990 Story Rd., 408/295-3402; 2525 South King Rd., 408/274-1596; 3276 S. White Rd., 408/274-8166; 640 N. 9th St., 408/298-6389), home of the towering French baguettes. In 1981, Chieu Le and his younger brother, Huong "Henry" Le bought a single lunch truck. With a little bit of English and a lot of hard work, they quickly grew their business to 500 trucks. Within three years the family opened the first Lee's Sandwiches of San Jose. *Banh mi,* a popular street food throughout Vietnam, pairs crisp French bread with distinctively Asian fillings. Cheiu's son, Minh Le, a business student at San Jose State University, had dreamed of a modern sandwich store that would showcase Vietnamese flavors and American efficiency. His family successfully carried out his vision of Lee's Sandwiches. There are now over 16 locations in California, and more are opening every year as the stores adapt, franchise, and begin redefining the meaning of fast food in the United States. The Le family continues to play a vital role in the San Jose community, respected for their civic leadership as well as their business savvy.

Another growing Vietnamese chain, **Pho Hoa** (1834 Tully Rd., 408/238-1481), also had its humble beginnings in the South Bay. From one tiny soup joint a multinational franchise has grown. Specializing in that most comforting of Vietnamese meals, a steaming bowl of beef and rice noodle soup, Pho Hoa restaurants from San Jose to Singapore boast bright interiors and menus with photographs and friendly English translations. Though some locals still hunt down their favorite bowl of pho in independent, family-run restaurants, the Pho Hoa chain is bringing Vietnam's beloved national dish to many outside the Vietnamese community.

In addition to the sheer number of mom-and-pop noodle shops, rice plate joints, and sandwich stores scattered throughout the Bay Area, a new generation of restaurateurs hopes to transform Vietnamese cuisine in the United States. **Citronelle** (826 S. Winchester Blvd., 408/244-2528) and **Dragonfly** (2847 S. White Rd., 408/532-8989) in San Jose, as well as **Tamarine** (546 University Ave., 650/325-8500) in Palo Alto, have roots in first generation Vietnamese restaurants, family businesses that served classic dishes to a mostly Vietnamese clientele. These new establishments, however, are rising to the challenge of developing contemporary Vietnamese cuisine. While exploring new culinary ground, they also remain closely linked to the community: The owners display the work of modern Vietnamese artists, and their special events benefit local nonprofit organizations.

ARTS AND CULTURAL ORGANIZATIONS

In the early 1990s, a group of young Vietnamese American writers and artists came together in the basement of a furniture store. A few bottles of wine later, Ink and Blood was born. Challenging and inspiring each other, the group's creative sessions led to art performances and publications. They also sowed the seeds for important contributions to Vietnamese institutions throughout the Bay Area. Members of Ink and Blood went on to play influential roles in academia, the arts, and journalism. Isabelle Thuy Pelaud, now a professor at the pioneering Vietnamese American Studies Center at San Francisco State University, organizes programs for the public that showcase the top Vietnamese American writers, poets, and dancers in the nation. Nguyen Qui Duc hosts KQED Public Radio's "Pacific Time," while Andrew Lam is a correspondent and editor for Pacific News Service. As publisher of *Viet Mercury*, the Vietnamese language weekly of the *San Jose Mercury News*, De Tran provides international news and in-depth features for the Vietnamese émigré community. Poet Truong Quoc Tran directs the Kearny Street Workshop in San Francisco, an organization dedicated to presenting the art of Asian Americans.

Based in San Jose, the **Association for Viet Arts** (www.vietarts.org) has focused on Vietnamese American visual, performing, and literary artists since 1992. Past programs include a fusion of traditional and contemporary Vietnamese music with the Phu-Sa Ensemble at Montgomery Theatre, le thi diem thuy's multimedia performance of "Red Fiery Summer," Club of Noodles' improv drama and comedy, and "Salt and Pepper," an exhibition of Vietnamese American artists at the San Jose Institute of Contemporary Art.

Transforming personal experience into universal meaning is particularly challenging for Vietnamese American artists, as the war still looms darkly in the public's consciousness. One of the artists in the "Salt and Pepper" exhibit, Trung Quoc Tran, represents the individual's search for an aesthetic beyond ethnic identity. His large, abstract canvases explore the natural course of decomposition and transformation, a process with cultural as well as physical meaning. Understanding this delicate balance, **Pacific Bridge** (510/654-3212) promotes the work of contemporary Southeast Asian artists in a more complex context. It sponsors an artist-in-residence program that has brought influential Vietnamese painters to the United States and represents numerous professional Vietnamese American artists in the Bay Area. Their work, such as Kai Hoang's somber colorfield paintings and Thai Bui's organically urban sculptures of found objects, can be viewed at Pacific Bridge's online gallery, Asian Art Now (www.asianartnow.com).

Though young in the history of the city, San Jose's Vietnamese community is itself diverse. A younger generation has come of age entirely in the United States, and as commercial and cultural institutions establish themselves in the wider flow of the Bay Area, the community will transform itself again and again. Artists like Thai Bui, commissioned to create public art for the City of Palo Alto, and civic leaders like Madison Nguyen, the first Vietnamese American to be elected to public office in Northern California, are helping to lead the way. San Jose and the surrounding South Bay will continue to be home to a vibrant, successful Vietnamese community.

FESTIVALS

Vietnamese people find numerous occasions to celebrate during the year, from death anniversaries to Buddha's birthday, but the most important Vietnamese holiday by far is **Tet Nguyen Dan**, or "the Feast of the First Day." Commonly called Tet, it combines Thanksgiving's focus on food and family, Christmas' gift giving, and New Year's Eve's parties and personal renewal. The holiday marks the beginning of the lunar year, which falls on the new moon between late January and mid-February. Throughout the city, festive banners declare "Chuc Mung Nam Moi" (Wishing you a happy New Year) or "Cung Chuc Tan Xuan" (Wishing you a new spring). Two different weekend festivals bracket the traditional week of celebration.

SAN JOSE HOTELS

Hotel De Anza (233 W. Santa Clara St., 408/286-1000), built in 1930 in a Moorish style, has been declared a national landmark. The 101-room hotel was renovated and reopened in 1990, with attractions including a hand-painted ceiling and a central location. The Hedley Club jazz bar is popular with guests.

Other San Jose lodgings include **Moorpark Hotel** (4241 Moorpark Ave., 408/864-0300), **Fairmont San Jose** (172 S. Market St., 408/998-1900), and **Radisson Plaza Hotel—Mineta San Jose Airport** (1471 N. 4th St., 800/333-3333 or 408/452-0200, www.radisson.com).

The **Tet Festival** at the Santa Clara County Fairgrounds (344 Tully Road, 408/295-9210) and the **Vietnamese Spring Festival and Parade** in downtown San Jose (Market St. and Park Ave., www.vsfsanjose.com) together provide four full days of activities and cultural events. Companies and diverse community groups across the city build elaborate floats to take part in the parade. Miss Saigon and her court preside over the festivities, while artists, performers, and food vendors all contribute to the revelry.

Another holiday with a special appeal for Vietnamese children is **Tet Trung Thu.** Known as the Mid-Autumn Festival, it falls on the 15th day of the 8th lunar month (between mid-September and early October). Tet Trung Thu celebrates the harvest moon, when the full moon shines its brightest and clearest. With the heavy work of the harvest finally done, parents once took this time to reconnect with their children. Today, the holiday still retains the song and dance, the colorful lanterns, and the rich moon cakes of this ancient festival, but the Vietnamese community also now commits to teaching children about the history and art of their homeland. Numerous schools and cultural organizations organize smaller scale celebrations. During certain years, a community-wide Mid-Autumn Festival may be held in Guadalupe River Park in downtown San Jose.

Every year, as April 30th approaches, thousands of Vietnamese people gather in public spaces to commemorate the fall of Saigon in 1975. **Black April Remembrance Day** inspires a wide range of expression in the community. It is a distinctly *Viet Kieu* memorial, with quiet candlelight vigils for victims of the war, rowdy demonstrations against Hanoi's policies, and modern art performances exploring the meaning of refuge and resettlement.

LITTLE
KABUL

B EFORE THE SOVIET INVASION OF AFGHANISTAN IN 1979, most Americans were unfamiliar with both the country of Afghanistan and the cultural practices of its citizens. During the invasion and subsequent war, which lasted for 10 years, the United States absorbed almost 50,000 Afghans as refugees—20,000 of whom settled in the San Francisco Bay Area, particularly in the city of Fremont.

Afghans, like other immigrant groups, brought with them their lifestyle and culture, adding to the diversity of the Bay Area. Now, 25 years later, Afghan Americans have established a successful community. Respected for their hard work and achievements in business, social, and educational circles, They have established a successful presence throughout the Bay Area. Afghans are justifiably proud of their success in this country as business professionals, doctors, lawyers, police officers, social workers, beauticians, car technicians, hotel and motel owners, taxi service workers, and high school and university students.

Recently, due to American political involvement in Afghanistan and the ousting of the Taliban, Afghans surfaced noticeably in the nationwide media after September 11, 2001. Afghan laymen and scholars were interviewed on a variety of topics, and the country and its citizens have since taken center-stage in world politics—particularly in American foreign policy. With this newfound exposure, Americans began to understand that many Afghans are living in the United States—specifically in the Bay Area, and they began to learn more about Afghan culture and traditions. Local independent news station KRON featured "Little Kabul" on its *Bay Area Backroads* program, and a delegation from Fremont was invited to make a presentation on the community at The Wayne County Museum in Goldsboro, North Carolina.

Taken from the name of Afghanistan's capital, Little Kabul is located in the heart of Fremont between Parish Avenue and Bonde Way on Fremont Boulevard. Spend any time in this two block cluster of primarily Afghan businesses and you will often hear both national languages of Afghanistan, Dari or Pashto, being spoken, as well as experiencing the true sights, sounds, and smells of Kabul City.

In 1995, the small **De Afghanan** restaurant (510/745-9599) opened at 37405 Fremont Boulevard and established the distinctive character of what has come to be known as Fremont's Little Kabul. Offering a small (just two) but very traditional Afghan menu of *Chapli Kabob* and *Boulani,* the restaurant takes its name from a small district in the heart of Kabul City. *Chapli Kabob* is similar to an American burger but larger, much flatter, and full of spices and leeks. *Boulani,* a sort of appetizer in Afghan cuisine, is bread stuffed with leeks and spices, and is usually consumed with either yogurt or *chatni gashneez,* a mild dip made of chili peppers, garlic, coriander, and cilantro. Serving authentic, domestic Afghan food, De Afghanan offers diners an atmosphere typical of restaurants in Kabul City.

Another distinguished restaurant in the Little Kabul area, the **Salang Pass Restaurant** (37462 Fremont Blvd., 510/795-9200) offers fine Afghan cuisine to patrons seated on the floor at tables surrounded by large mattresses covered with Afghan rugs and luxurious pillows. Not located in the Little Kabul area, but definitely worth the trip two miles west to Newark, the **Afghan Village** restaurant (5698 Thornton Ave., 510/790-0557) is the

Abu Bakr Sidique Mosque

place for ice cream lovers to try the tasty Afghan variety. Owner Omar
Amerie's business card reads, "We cater *halal* food," meaning that all the
meat at Afghan Village is slaughtered according to Islamic law. Ninety-
nine percent of Afghans are Muslims and their religion has a strong impact
not only on their daily life, but also on their dietary routines. Afghans normally do not consume alcohol or pork, as it is not allowed in their dietary
laws. *Halal* (permissible) meat is an intrinsic part of the daily dietary life of
a Muslim, similar to the concept of kosher food for Jews.

CUISINE

Afghanistan was part of the Silk Route in ancient history, and due to its
strategic location in the heart of Asia, at the crossroads between China,
Persia (modern-day Iran), and India, it has also been called the "Highway
of Conquest." These trade route connections have had a great impact not
only on Afghan culture, but also on the cuisine, which is different than the

food from other parts of Asia (adopting a little bit of flavor from each culture that passed through). Today, each adopted food enjoys a distinctive Afghan touch. The basic *kabob* (skewered grilled meat), inherited from the Greeks and Alexander the Great (356 B.C.–323 B.C.), has developed into more than eight varieties marinated in a mix of onions, salt, pepper, cinnamon, and turmeric.

Afghan cuisine is neither hot and spicy like Indian dishes nor as mild as Iranian food. Unique in its ingredients and flavors, the main staples are bread, called *naan,* and two types of rice (*chalaw* and *pallow*), which constitute the base for a wide variety of dishes. *Chalaw,* or plain white rice, is served with different gravies called *quorma,* made from various vegetables and meat—usually lamb, beef, chicken, or goat, and sometimes fish. All gravies constitute side dishes for *chalaw.* Among *chalaw* menus, the most famous is *sabzi chalaw,* containing spinach cooked with cubed lamb or beef, chili pepper, and green onion in a stew flavored with onion, cumin, and coriander. *Sabzi chalaw* is popular in Afghanistan as a special dish prepared on the first day of spring and the New Year, March 21st. *Sabzi* (spinach) signifies spring (its growing season), happiness, and good luck because of its vivid green color. The most popular type of *pallow* in Afghanistan, *kabili pallow,* originated in northern Afghanistan. Basmati rice is cooked with a sauce of meat (either lamb or chicken) turning it brown, covered with fried carrots, raisins, roasted almonds, and pistachios, then seasoned with onion, caramelized sugar, *char masala,* (four Indian spices crushed together), saffron, and cumin. Pasta made its way into the Afghan diet by way of China. *Aashak,* similar to Italian ravioli, is stuffed with leeks, onions, and spices, topped with ground-beef sauce, mint, yogurt, and a sprinkle of dry coriander for extra flavor—a favorite among travelers. Afghans love desserts after a meal. The most popular is *firnee,* a pudding dessert made from cream, cornstarch, and sugar, and seasoned with cardamom, rose water, and pistachios.

Nowadays, Afghan bread is as ubiquitous in America as the French baguette. The standard recipe contains plain flour, yeast to make it rise, and salt as needed, but *naan* can also be found in white, whole-wheat, and seasoned varieties. An important staple in the Afghan diet, *naan* is prepared in loaves almost three feet long, and while it has enough flavor to be eaten plain, it is most often served as an accompaniment to a meal. *Naan* baked with sesame seeds and black seeds is called *naan-e-khasa* (special), and *naan-e-roghani*, which is made with flour and clarified butter, is usually consumed either with breakfast or afternoon tea. Both the **Pamir Market** (37436 Fremont Blvd., 510/790-7015) and **Maiwand Market** (37235 Fremont Blvd., 510/796-3215) in Little Kabul bake this delicious bread every morning.

Groceries/Shopping

The Afghan grocery stores in Little Kabul are stocked to meet almost all of their customers' daily needs—similar to a supermarket but on a smaller scale. The first grocery store to open in Little Kabul, **Pamir,** (37436 Fremont Blvd., 510/790-7015), was named after the famous Pamir mountain range in Afghanistan. Besides cooking supplies, ingredients, and spices, Pamir offers a bakery, butchery, and a selection of Afghan books and music. **Maiwand Market** (37235 Fremont Blvd., 510/796-3215), named for a victory over the British during the second Anglo-Afghan war, is a larger market that also offers a butchery. Besides groceries, books, and music, you can find Afghan candies and sweets made in California—some in the Bay Area. Traditionally, Afghans drink tea with candies after a meal—any sweet eaten with tea is called *dashlama*. The most popular types of *dashlama* are *noqul*, a sugar-coated almond, and *shirpira*, a soft sweet made of milk. Afghans, like the British, have the custom of an afternoon tea, typically drinking either a black or green tea while relaxing with some *shirpira*.

The **Rumi Bookstore** (510/744-3692) specializes in books on the history of Afghanistan plus a rich collection of music and videos on Islam and the Middle East. Named for the famous 13th-century poet, philosopher, and Sufi, Maulana Jallaludin Rumi Balkhi, the Rumi Bookstore offers poetry by its namesake as well as books for children and families, along with political and religious works.

MUSIC

Under the Taliban, artistic expression in Afghanistan was severely limited—they burned books, destroyed musical recordings, and banned music from radio and television. As a result, America has become the largest producer of Afghan music in the world, and recordings of past and current musicians are easily found in most chain music stores, as well as many Afghan grocery stores. An intrinsic part of Afghan culture, music has always united those divided by politics. Traditional Afghan instruments such as the *dutar* (a long-necked, 14-string guitar-like instrument), *rubab* (a short, wooden-bodied, stringed instrument played with a small wooden paddle), and *tanbur* (a long-necked, 18-string instrument, usually made from a gourd) are rare in America and many Afghan musicians have become acculturated to Western music. They still play traditional and folk songs, though often with modern instruments.

Homayoun Sakhi, the famous Afghan rubabist, offers rubab classes at the **Afghan Cultural and Music Center** (37415 Fremont Blvd., 510/792-4746). The rubab is the "plucked lute," known among Afghans as *Kabuli rubab*. They regard it as their national instrument. A complicated instrument, the *rubab* is built with two sound chambers and multiple sets of strings: melody, drone, and "sympathetic" strings. It is the sympathetic strings (vibrating indirectly from the plucking of the other sets) that give the instrument its unique sound. Some evenings the center hosts small recitals of traditional rubab music for enthusiasts, usually by appointment.

RELIGION

Afghans are moderate Muslims but maintain a high level of devotion in their adherence to the daily practices of Islam. Eighty percent of Afghans practice Sunni Islam and the other 20 percent practice Shi'i Islam. Many Afghans left their country during the Soviet invasion because of Communist religious oppression. On arriving in the United States, they immediately established locations for worship, leasing space for a mosque in Hayward. Today, there are 12 mosques in the Bay Area—2 belong to the Shi'i school of thought. Afghans locally supported the building of a Grand mosque in Hayward called **Abu Bakr Sidique Mosque** (29414 Mission Blvd., 510/393-5648)—named for the first Khalif of Islam. The official name of the center is **Afghan Islamic Refugee Community.** Built in 2001, the center is considered a landmark in the city of Hayward. The ceramic *Mehrab* (an ornamental, arched niche—the central feature of the mosque) and the calligraphy around the main chamber follow 15th century *Timurid* architectural styles, common to the city of Herat in Northwest Afghanistan. Besides religious services, the center provides facilities for full funeral services, residential homes, and two cemeteries.

ART

America also absorbed a good number of Afghan artists and entertainers. Renowned Afghan poet and painter Yusef Kohzad lives in the Bay Area. Mr. Nadi, a sculptor, and Mr. Rashid Binesh, a calligraphist and writer, enrich Afghan cultural offerings in the San Francisco Bay Area. **The Willits Center Gallery** (3755 Washington Blvd., www.willitscenter.com) exhibits the art work of Nadi and Kohzad.

Rug weaving is a tradition of primarily northern and western Afghanistan, where each province produces its own variety, distinguished by design and color. Prior to the Soviet invasion, Afghanistan was a major exporter of traditional rugs to the rest of the world. Rugs woven there were world famous in design, color, and texture. Many experienced weavers left

FREMONT LODGINGS

Belvoir Springs Hotel: 36990 Mission Blvd., 510/791-5711, www.belvoirsprings.com

Lord Bradley's Inn: 43344 Mission Blvd., 510/490-0520

Marriott Fremont: 46100 Landing Pkwy., 510/413-3700

the country during the war, and Afghan rugs were made in neighboring countries and exported under the trademark of that country. Now, however, many weavers have returned to Afghanistan and are again producing authentic Afghan rugs. In Fremont **Magic Import Oriental Rugs** (37468 Fremont Blvd., 510/745-7691) offers a good selection of imported rugs from Afghanistan.

AFGHAN HOLIDAYS

Afghans traditionally celebrate two religious holidays and two national holidays during the year, though which "year" can be confusing for Westerners. The Afghan calendar (*Jantari*) is based on the Islamic era which began with the emigration of the Prophet Muhammad from Mecca to Medina in 622 A.D. The calendar shows two dates for each day—for Islamic festivities, Afghans consult the Arabic lunar (*Qamari*) calendar and for administrative purposes the Persian solar calendar (*Shamsi*). The Afghan solar year begins on March 21st, Navroz. In the West, the Gregorian calendar is standard—it is solar based, so the year 2004 corresponds to the Persian solar year 1382 or Arabic lunar year 1424.

The Eid ul-Adha commemorates the Prophet Abraham's sacrifice of his son Ismail at God's command. It is during the Eid ul-Adha that Muslims make a pilgrimage to the House of God in Mecca, Saudi Arabia—the journey that all Muslims must make at least once during their lifetime. Eid ul-Fitr is the feast celebrating the end of *Ramadan* (fasting month). Muslims fast for one full lunar month every year, every day from dawn to dusk. In fasting, they are not only fulfilling God's command, but also purifying their souls and cleansing themselves from sin. Both religious holidays are celebrated according to the lunar calendar, so every year these events move 10 or 11 days backwards.

Afghans celebrate the New Year on the 21st of March. Fittingly for the first day of spring, they frequently celebrate with a picnic either at Elizabeth Lake in Fremont or the Pleasanton Fairgrounds. Traditionally, Afghans celebrate *Mila-e-Navroz* (New Year Picnic) by preparing *sabzi-challow* with yogurt and *haft-miwa* (seven fruits), alluding to the concept of seven heavens and consisting of walnuts, red and green raisins, almonds, pistachios, black raisins, and dried apricots. People spend much of the day outdoors enjoying various area festivals, praying for a productive year, visiting the tombs of their loved ones, and planting new trees.

Afghanistan obtained independence from the British Empire in 1919 after the third Anglo-Afghan war. Although never a British colony, the country was under the influence of the British Empire, namely British-India, for 80 years. On August 8th, every year, local Afghans celebrate their independence in one of the area's banquet halls with music, poetry readings, and speeches.

In the Fremont area, the Afghan community holds holiday feasts and celebrates weddings and other events at a number of locally owned banquet halls. **The Flamingo/Mirage Palace** (4100 Peralta Blvd., 510/792-9999) accommodates up to 1,000 guests and was designed for large Afghan weddings where families typically invite 400 or more guests. The associated **Mirage** banquet hall was designed with smaller parties in mind. Both offer traditional Afghan cuisine for wedding ceremonies, but can accommodate weddings and special occasions for other groups as well.

FOOD
AND DRINK

ON THE WORLD MAP OF FOOD, SAN FRANCISCO
virtually defines the Pacific Rim. Asians have been journeying across the
Pacific to San Francisco for 150 years, and today dozens of diverse communities throughout the Bay Area support vibrant, ever-renewing culinary
cultures. Thanks to countless Asian supermarkets and bakeries, tea salons
and dinner houses, butchers and produce stores, and food stalls and delicatessens, there's no more exciting place in America for lovers of Asian food
to shop, cook, and, of course, eat.

And everybody, it seems, shares in the feast. In San Francisco, the
Japanese go for Korean; the Cantonese love sushi. Indians look for Sichuan.
Chinese and Vietnamese restaurants are popping up all over the Latino
mission. There are long lines outside dim sum houses on weekends, endless
queues at favored sushi bars at midnight, and crowds milling in the
parking lots of South Indian cafes on the Peninsula. One reason that Asian
food is so good here is the emphasis on using only the best ingredients.
Small, local farms grow beautiful Asian herbs and vegetables to meet the
demand. Chinatown was offering free-range ducks and chickens before
anyone else understood how superior they were; local fish glisten and live
crabs wiggle in Chinatown markets. What cannot be produced locally

flows in through our harbors: spices, condiments, tea. As a port city, San Francisco has always been willing to embrace new ideas and ingredients, but is also home to a culinary crosscurrent: California influences Asian cooks here, and Asia has long inspired Californians.

San Francisco got its first taste of Asian cooking in the 1860s when the Chinese population began to grow. A third of these immigrants were laborers from South China who came without families to build the Central Pacific Railroad. It was in San Francisco's Chinatown that the first East-West culinary exchange took place, as Cantonese American hybrids like chop suey, chow mein doused with gravy, and egg foo yung caught on—invented by Chinese workers who had to cook with whatever they found in the New World. Until well into the 20th century, generations of San Franciscans encountered these dishes on Chinatown menus, alongside prime rib and apple pie. Meanwhile, dim sum parlors, noodle joints, family restaurants, and fancy dinner houses were proliferating. But not until the mid-1980s did Cantonese cooking take a major leap towards authenticity when Alice Wong brought a branch of her family's sophisticated **Hong Kong Flower Lounge** (renamed **Parc Hong Kong,** 5322 Geary Blvd., 415/668-8998) to the Bay Area. She ushered in a new era of smart Hong Kong style restaurants that cook with a much wider range of ingredients—especially seafood—and pick up on the latest dishes emanating directly from Hong Kong. The reversion of Hong Kong to mainland China in the '90s brought a wealthy new wave of Chinese immigrants to the Bay Area who demanded a quality of dining comparable to the one they left.

Though Canton is the region best represented in the Bay Area's Chinese restaurants, other regional cuisines have been arriving since the early '60s, culminating in the first northern Chinese restaurant in the United States, Cecilia Chiang's elegant Ghiradelli Square restaurant **The Mandarin,** which opened in 1968. Since then Sichuan, Shanghai, and Chiu Chao restaurants have joined the huge array of Chinese eateries flourishing here.

Japanese immigrants settled in the Western Addition shortly after 1900, though San Franciscans first experienced the pleasures of a Japanese tea garden when one was built in Golden Gate Park for the Exposition of 1894. The Japanese living in what was then called "Little Osaka," now known as Japantown, were evacuated to internment camps during World War II, but 10,000 returned to their old neighborhood. Now the Japan Center—a redevelopment project from the '60s—takes up most of those original blocks, and the streets are lined with restaurants, snacks shops, noodle places, and Japanese grocery stores. Mirroring geography, excellent Korean restaurants opened right across the street from the Japan Center.

Today, Japanese restaurants and sushi bars are no longer confined to Japantown; they've dispersed throughout the city, along with the resident Japanese community. Visitors to San Francisco can stay at Japanese-owned hotels downtown; and all San Franciscans frequent the restaurants.

By the late '70s and early '80s, little Vietnamese places offering sandwiches and *pho* (beef noodle soup) were popping up around the Civic Center in San Francisco. Now a large Vietnamese community in San Jose and the South Peninsula supports many excellent Vietnamese restaurants with extensive menus. As for the rest of Southeast Asia, both northern and southern Thai restaurants thrive, and Indonesian, Singaporean, Burmese, and even intricate Cambodian food have popular outposts throughout the Bay Area.

The Pilipino community in the Bay Area is the largest outside the Philippines. During the 1970s, branches of Manila restaurants began opening in San Bruno and Daly City, as did several major Pacific Island supermarkets. The '80s saw an explosion of Indian restaurants and food shops in Silicon Valley and the East Bay, following the path of Indian computer engineers who moved here as part of the high tech boom. Afghan, Pakistani, and Turkish immigrants all support culinary communities as well.

CHINESE

There are three Chinese communities in San Francisco, each with restaurants spanning China and Southeast Asia. Start your culinary tour with a crawl down the always packed Stockton Street, the great Chinatown market street, and then walk one block over to Grant Avenue for a sizzling claypot at **Bow Hon,** (850 Grant Ave., 415/362-0601) particularly the house special of fluffy, white-fish dumplings braised with black mushrooms, Napa cabbage, and Chinese barbecue pork, in a luscious, smoky, pot gravy. Shiny, lacquer-skinned Chinese barbecue ducks and chickens, and roasted pig with crackling skin, hang temptingly in many Chinese deli windows. I always head to **Yee's** (1131 Grant Ave., 415/576-1818) for either takeout or a sit down meal of Chinese roasted poultry and meats, with rice and braised lettuce—fabulous and inexpensive. The entire late shift in Chinatown slurps *congee* (Chinese rice porridge) until the wee hours at **Hing Lung** (674 Broadway, 415/398-8838) where it comes to the table boiling hot. The basic porridge, seasoned with cilantro, ginger, and scallions, is dressed up with such tidbits as sliced hard head (a fish); or bits of shrimp, fish, lettuce, and peanuts (called *Sampan* porridge); or soulful pork giblets, including velvety liver, kidney, tripe, and meatballs.

For birthdays, holidays and weekly get-togethers, the oldest Chinatown families head for **Lichee Garden,** (1416 Powell St., 415/397-2290) a handsomely appointed Cantonese cafe with wooden chairs, dark green carpeting, and wood paneled walls. Chef owner Chak-Siu is famous for his crisp-skinned whole chicken; glazed pork spareribs, pan fried noodles that boast the much prized taste of the wok; fresh crabs and lobsters; and simple fresh vegetables like pea greens and *choy sum.*

When you want cutting-edge Hong Kong-style seafood, head straight for the modern, three level **R&G Lounge,** (631 Kearny St., 415/982-7877) known for deep fried salt and pepper coated Dungeness crab; Washington State geoduck clam served two ways—the adductor as sparkling sashimi, and the body in a sublime chowder with Chinese watercress and tofu—and

THE EAST–WEST PHENOMENON

A unique culinary movement in America was founded in the Bay Area by Western restaurateurs and chefs who fell in love with Asia. The trend began in 1934 with **Trader Vic's** in the East Bay (9 Anchor Dr., Emeryville, 510/653-3400), where Vic Bergeron pioneered a menu of Chinese-, Javanese- and Polynesian-themed dishes, many cooked in a Chinese smoke oven. Many years and branches of Trader Vic's later, sinophile Barbara Tropp opened her groundbreaking China Moon Cafe, and Bruce Cost mounted his ambitious Monsoon (now both closed), highly personal restaurants that presented classic Asian dishes in a Western context. Current pan-Asian restaurants like **Betelnut** (2030 Union St., 415/929-8855) in San Francisco and **Grasshopper** (6317 College Ave., 510/595-3557) in Oakland carry on the legacy with stylish looking dishes from many Asian countries. These restaurants explore Asian ingredients and reproduce authentic dishes in each chef's own style, pairing them with Western amenities such as wine lists, cocktails, and desserts based on Western technique.

savory minced seafood in lettuce cups. Owner Kinson Wong, who makes frequent trips to Hong Kong and Shanghai for ideas, has fashioned a user-friendly menu with photos of the kitchen's specialties. Even first-timers can't go wrong, though the cognoscenti call ahead to arrange for a banquet for 8 or 10. In the Richmond District, residents enjoy juicy little pork dumplings and fortifying noodle soup with bits of pickled vegetables and pork at **Taiwan.** Dim sum abounds at **Ton Kiang** (5821 Geary Blvd., 415/387-8273) during both lunch and dinner, at take out shops like **Wing Lee** (501 Clement St., 415/831-7883), and at upscale restaurants like **Mayflower** (6255 Geary Blvd., 415/387-8338) and **Parc Hong Kong** (5322 Geary Blvd., 415/668-8998), both known for creative seafood cookery at night.

On Irving street in the Sunset, the third Chinatown, everyone stops at **New Hai Ky** (2191 Irving St., 415/731-9948) for a bowl of Preserved

CHINESE SAVORY PASTRIES AND BUBBLE TEA

One of the pleasures of a stroll in San Francisco's original Chinatown is devouring warm, flaky, savory pastries from the **Golden Gate Bakery** (1029 Grant Ave., 415/781-2627) where lines of Chinese schoolchildren and adults spill out the door waiting for the next batch to come out of the oven. The curry beef turnover filled with saucy, curry-scented ground beef, sweet corn, and carrots is addictive. The glazed crust, made with lard, melts in your mouth. And don't walk out without taking away a barely sweetened egg custard tart with that same amazing pastry.

Bubble tea is all the rage now. Strong, milky, often-perfumed black tea is poured over ice and a layer of big purple tapioca berries soaked in caramelly brown sugar. The best tapioca berries have a firm, chewy texture. All require a special large straw to drink the tea with the tapioca bubbles. Beware of aspirating on the balls until you get the hang of sucking them up through the straw and stopping them in your mouth to chew. You will find bubble tea down Grant Avenue but a favorite is made by a Double Rainbow ice cream shop on Irving Street—a bubble shake of fresh strawberries, strawberry ice cream, shaved ice and sugar syrup blended together with a layer of tapioca berries at the bottom—an East–West delicacy.

Orange Skin Duck with Egg Noodle Soup, an elegant dish of noodles and clear broth topped with a glistening barbecued duck leg garnished with a big pouf of perfect, bright green cilantro leaves. The dish could grace the centerfold of a glossy food magazine. And lovers of hearty northern Chinese food order plates of the juicy pork dumplings at **San Tung** (1031 Irving St., 415/242-0828), along with a bowl of seaweed soup. Way out on the edge of the Sunset near the beach, the **Old Mandarin Islamic Restaurant** (3132 Vicente St., 415/564-3481) warms its patrons with spicy lamb-stuffed dumplings, fried flatbreads filled with spicy minced lamb, and stir-fried slices of lamb redolent of cumin. The mid-Peninsula around Millbrae is a nexus for distinguished Hong Kong style eateries, including

Fook Yuen (195 El Camino Real, 650/692-8600) and **Hong Kong Flower Lounge** (51 Millbrae Ave, 650/692-6666), much patronized by Asian travelers who want a good meal between flights in and out of SFO. Closer to San Francisco, **Koi Palace** (365 Gellert Blvd., 650/992-9000) in Daly City reigns supreme for both dim sum and seafood.

Everyone in the Bay Area loves dim sum, or Chinese tea lunch, where diners get to choose little bamboo steamers of dumplings from trays or carts brought to the table. Henry Chan's continually innovative **Yank Sing** (101 Spear St., 415/957-9300), in the dramatic Rincon Center, and the Hong Kong-inspired **Harbor Village** (4 Embarcadero Center, 415/781-8833) in the Embarcadero make tea lunch an event. Funky little **Dol Ho** (808 Pacific Ave., 415/392-2828), bustling **Pearl City** (641 Jackson St., 415/398-8383), and **Kay Cheung** (615 Jackson St., 415/989-6838) feed hundreds of Chinatown denizens a day.

At George Chen's soignée **Shanghai 1930** (131 Steuart St., 415/896-5600), patrons nestle into posh booths to eat Shanghai delicacies with French wines. A jazz combo plays in the bar room, where people drink cocktails and nibble on *xiao long bao* (juicy little Shanghai-style pork dumplings), and, appropriate to this hip bar, drunken squab.

VIETNAMESE

The Vietnamese comprise the second largest Asian group in the Bay Area after the Chinese, so the wealth of Vietnamese restaurants should come as no surprise. The largest Vietnamese community now lives in San Jose and Vietnamese *pho* houses, sandwich places, delicatessens, and restaurants dot the lower Peninsula on both sides of the bay. (A listing of many of them can be found at www.gocee.com/viet/restaurants.htm, a website devoted to all things Vietnamese.)

Vung Tau 1 (6092 Mowry Ave., Newark, 510/793-8299), a large restaurant in what looks like a converted 1960s steak house, executes a huge menu of sparkling Vietnamese dishes, including big bowls of *pho*

VIETNAMESE SANDWICHES

One holdover from the French colonial period in Vietnam is the baguette. This soft, gently crusted loaf is used as the base for Vietnamese sandwiches, filled with five-spice chicken, roast pork, or Vietnamese meatballs. The sandwiches are garnished with shredded carrots, sprigs of cilantro, hot green chiles, and a splash of *nuoc cham*, the sweet and sour dipping sauce. The magic ingredient is a swipe of mayonnaise. These sandwiches are cheaper than fast food hamburgers, quickly made to order, and a thousand times more delicious. Join the lines at **Saigon Sandwich Shop** at 560 Larkin Street to get one of the best.

---

served with a side plate of crisp bean sprouts, lemon wedges, minty Thai basil, and sliced green chiles. You slide these raw ingredients into the bowl and smell their fragrance as it is released into the hot broth. Tissue thin rice papers are the wrappers for savory self-made spring rolls of grilled pork meatballs, fresh herbs, and tender lettuce leaves. The lettuce leaves in turn become wrappers for crisp, hot spring rolls with skinny rice noodles. Everything is dipped into *nuoc cham*, a clear sweet and sour sauce that acts like a vibrant dressing for the salady rolls. The juxtaposition of hot and savory, raw and crisp, defines Vietnamese cuisine, a natural for salad-loving Californians.

In San Francisco, older restaurants like the **Golden Turtle** (2211 Van Ness Ave., 415/441-4419), with a hand-crafted, wood-paneled interior, offer traditional Vietnamese cooking based on the freshest components. The casual **Pho Hoa Hiep II** (1833 Irving St., 415/664-0469) makes the best shrimp cakes, golden, deep-fried pillows of coarse shrimp paste studded with moist pieces of fresh shrimp. You eat them rolled into lettuce leaves with raw *daikon*, carrot and cucumber. The superb **Vietnam II** (701 Larkin St., 415/885-1274) *pho* makes a heavenly sweet and sour prawn soup from the most pristine ingredients, and a memorable dish of salted fish with chicken fried rice. And don't miss **Yummy Yummy** (3040 Taraval St., 415/759-1818) for its signature squid salad.

But San Francisco also boasts innovative and modern Vietnamese restaurants, like Charles Pham's wildly popular **Slanted Door** in the San Francisco Ferry Building, where traditional and tweaked Vietnamese dishes get chic presentations on a collection of ceramics from all over Asia, and a pastry chef creates imaginative East-West desserts. Sophisticated **Ana Mandara** (891 Beach St., 415/771-6800) in Ghirardelli Square and Charles Lam's happening **Butterfly** (1710 Mission St., 415/865-8999) and **Butterfly Lounge** use Vietnamese ingredients and techniques as a springboard for exotic, original dishes. **Le Colonial,** (20 Cosmo Pl., 415/931-3600) a stage-set inspired by the French colonial era, fits right into the old Trader Vic's digs. The Vietnamese experience in San Francisco crosses the city from the Tenderloin to the Sunset to the chic Ferry Building, and it's all exceptionally good.

THAI AND CAMBODIAN

Both northern and southern Thai restaurants delight chile aficionados throughout the Bay Area. For meaty northern Thai food try **Chiang Mai** (5020 Geary Blvd., 415/387-1299), especially the fiery minced pork served with cool cucumber slices; and pork stew with noodles. The food of the South can be explored at cornerstone Thai restaurants like **Siam Cuisine** (1181 University Ave., 510/548-3278) in Berkeley, known for its very liberal use of super hot peppers; or the classic and more modulated cooking at **Khan Toke Thai House** (5937 Geary Blvd., 415/668-6654). San Franciscans have long appreciated the cooking at **Angkor Borei** (3471 Mission St., 415/550-8417), a Cambodian restaurant that offers ravishingly complex dishes with layers of flavor. **Burma's House** (720 Post St., 415/775-1156) in San Francisco decodes its exotic menu with small color photographs of selected dishes, like their famous ginger salad, spicy, toasted, and fresh ingredients served in little piles tossed together at the table by the waiter to create a roller-coaster of flavors.

JAPANESE

A walk through the three long buildings of the Japan Center will lead to bowls of house-made *soba* and *udon* noodle soup at **Mifune** (1737 Post St., 415/922-0337), and the lyrical steamed and braised dishes at the tiny **Maki** (1825 Post St., 415/921-5215). Meats, fish, and vegetables all come on skewers at **Juban Yakiniku House** (1581 Webster St., 415/776-5822) where you cook them yourself at grills embedded in the tables. You get better and better at it as you fortify yourself with many glasses of Japanese beer.

But blissful Japanese immersion happens a few blocks away at the tiny **Kiss** (1700 Laguna St., 415/474-2866), run by one inspired chef and one waitress. A beautiful, *kaiseki*-like meal, each course made more exquisite by presentation on hand-made Japanese ceramics, is the specialty here. Consider yourself lucky to get one of the few coveted seats. San Franciscans are also willing to wait for a seat at Sachio Kojima's **Kabuto** (5121 Geary Blvd., 415/752-5652), a sushi bar, where Kojima and his son spin some wild creations and many traditional ones as well.

Sushi bars abound in San Francisco. Among the best are **Anzu Sushi Bar** (222 Mason St., 415/394-1100) in the Nikko Hotel; the intimate, homey **Hama-Ko** (108B Carl St., 415/753-0608) where you can call ahead to order an expensive but special meal of sushi and sashimi; and the upscale **Kyo-Ya** (2 New Montgomery St., 415/512-1111) sushi bar in the Palace Hotel—all have discovered sources for high quality local and imported fish and seafood.

The opening of **Ozumo** (161 Steuart St., 415/882-1333) in 2001, the dream-restaurant of a former professional baseball player in Japan, who happens to be a Caucasian American, marked a breakthrough in Japanese dining in San Francisco, combining cutting edge Japanese design with similarly up-to-the-moment food. Designed by Tokyo's Noriyoshi Muramatsu, the resplendent rooms were crafted from only the natural materials of a Japanese tea garden—stone, wood and paper. Chef Sho Kamio's menu

SAKE IN SAN FRANCISCO

Artisanal sake has taken San Francisco by storm. Many sushi bars, restaurants, and even an eccentric barbecue joint (**Memphis Minnie's,** 576 Haight St., San Francisco, 415/864-7675) have sake lists, and some places like **Betelnut** (2030 Union St., San Francisco, 415/929-8855), **Grasshopper** (6317 College Ave., Oakland, 510/595-3557), and **Ozumo** (161 Steuart St., San Francisco, 415/882-1333) serve tasting flights. At San Francisco's **True Sake** (560 Hayes St., San Francisco, 415/355-9555, www.truesake.com) the only shop in America dedicated solely to hand-brewed sake, owner Beau Timken will explain the whole process and describe each sake's distinctive quality. Artisanal sake, always served chilled, offers an astounding range of flavors. Some suggest tropical fruits like bananas, passion fruit, or pineapple; others, pears, melons, green apple, or muscat grapes. Floral overtones are woven into the mix. The most important factor of all is balance. Fine sake must perch comfortably between acidity and sweetness, fullness, and delicacy. There can be no overpowering fragrance, off flavors, or jagged edges.

Within the realm of sake there exist three levels of refinement: *Junmai, gingjo,* and *daiginjo,* which indicate the degree to which the rice grains are polished before they are mixed with pure water and fermented. In *junmai* sake the rice is polished to at least 65 percent of its original size, while in *daiginjo* it may be polished to 40 percent or less. *Junmai* sake, often the least costly of the fine sakes (but not always), is usually bigger in flavor and more versatile, and goes with a wide range of food. The more refined *gingjo* and *daiginjo* sake call for more subtle pairings.

encompasses colorful, intricate sushi rolls wrapped in pastel yellow and pink soy bean skins; layered salads that reveal secrets in each bite; and perfectly grilled and marinated black cod and kobe beef. Fine sake, wine, and cocktails accompany.

In Berkeley, David Vardy's **O Chamé** (1830 Fourth St., 510/841-8783) is a peaceful tea room with handcrafted wooden furniture and a menu of noodles, soup, bento box lunches, and seasonal Japanese dishes. Vardy was

TWO FAVORITE KOREAN DISHES

New Korea House (1620 Post St., 415/931-7834), a restaurant across the street from the Japan Center mall, specializes in two fantastic dishes. *Tofu chi gae,* a powerfully hot and sour, chile-laced red broth with big squares of soothing tofu and bits of pork, oyster and pickled vegetables, served in an earthenware casserole, tastes particularly good during a cold spell. One bite leads to another and pretty soon you'll find that your internal organs start radiating heat.

Delectable little oyster pancakes or mini-omelets, each containing one plump, juicy oyster, deliver a gentler experience. They're delicate and fresh; you dunk them in a soy-chile-scallion dipping sauce to complete the dish. Midway through the oyster pancake service, the waitress brings hot, crisp, mung bean pancakes, which taste like the best potato pancakes.

The *tofu chi ga*e and the oyster pancakes, like all dishes at New Korea House, are preceded by a table full of starters—pungent Korean pickles, soft tofu, marinated cucumbers, bean sprout salad, *daikon* and carrot slaw, spicy pressed tofu—each in a tiny pottery plate or bowl. Just make sure that you eat this hot, garlicky meal with the person you sleep with or you may get kicked out of bed.

studying *tai chi* in a monastery in Taiwan with a Taoist master when he found himself fascinated by *kaiseki* and the tea ceremony instead. As O Chamé's local founder can attest, the lure of Japan and all things Japanese has become part of San Francisco's ethos.

NORTH AND SOUTH INDIAN

Though the orderly traffic flowing down the six-lane thoroughfares of Silicon Valley seem about as far away as anyone could get from the chaos of India's clogged streets, a sizable new community of computer experts and their families have exerted their influence on the strip malls with Indian markets, snack shops, and restaurants. "Little India" runs along El Camino Real through Sunnyvale, Mountain View, and Santa Clara. **Bharat Bazaar**

ASIAN SUPERMARKETS

The scope and depth of the pan-Asian selection at the two Sunset Supers in San Francisco is unsurpassed in the Bay Area. The fresh and dried noodle departments offer every shape, every grain, and every national style of Asian noodle. The pickled vegetable section spans all of Asia, as do the refrigerated tofu shelves, and the bottled sauce aisles. The fish counter is one of the best in the city. These supermarkets are a cook's paradise.

In the East Bay's **Pacific East Mall** (take the Central Ave. exit off I-80), the all-inclusive **99 Ranch Market** (3288 Pierce St., Richmond, 510/558-2120) invites customers to pick out a fish at the fish counter and get it fried to order at the deli counter. Always worth a stop is **Daimo** (3288 Pierce St., Richmond, 510/527-3888), a casual restaurant owned by a master chef, in the same shopping center, for brisket noodle soup, salt-and-pepper fried spareribs, and shrimp-filled rice noodles.

(3680 El Camino Real, 408/247-4307), an Indian grocery and produce store overflowing with merchandise, is tucked in on the side of a gigantic K-Mart in Santa Clara.

Decidedly "small box" in concept, unlike its neighbor, Bharat's cardboard cartons of green mangos, green papayas, banana blossoms, and *tindola* (a squash that looks like a gherkin) sit outdoors under a cement overhang. Inside, shelves are bursting with packaged Indian snacks, cooking oils, ghees, sambar mixes, flours, pulses, incense, spices in cryovac, pickles, heavy stone mortars—a cornucopia of imported goods from Calcutta and Bombay. Plus, shoppers can buy freshly prepared Indian treats at two stalls inside Bharat Market. At one, a young girl stands behind a steam table of South Indian snacks, constantly replenished from a kitchen in the back. She fills a styrofoam plate with your choices—perhaps an aromatically spiced *pongal* (a thick rice and lentil "risotto" seasoned with whole black pepper and curry leaves) or crumbly, crunchy, deep fried *bajji*, a patty of ground yellow *dal* larded with whole spices. The Punjabi snack plate from a longer counter might include the delicious Punjabi winter dish *makki ki roti*, a griddled, grainy, cornmeal pancake served with a silky, *ghee*-rich puree of aromatic, long cooked mustard greens. Thin, garlicky yogurt with *boondi*, tiny balls of deep fried chickpea flour; and a dab of sharp, bright red pickle complete this luscious little meal, presented on a compartmentalized, stainless steel plate.

Saravana Bhavan (600 W. El Camino Real, 650/635-0460) in Mountain View, a branch of a popular chain from Madras, resides in a white, wood frame building that looks as if it could have been a House of Pancakes. But the pancakes are *utthapam* and *masala dosas*, the delectable South Indian favorites made with a delicately sour batter of ground rice and lentils. If you want to taste a variety of things, start with the mini-tiffin, which includes baby *idlis* (steamed dumplings) about the size of large marbles, *in sambar* (spiced vegetable and lentil soup); and a delicious *uppma*, a grainy, light, stuffing-like preparation made of semolina with toasted cashews and whole spices. Don't miss *medu vada*, a crisp, savory doughnut made of ground rice and lentils served with coconut chutney. Saravana Bhavan also makes addictive South Indian *dosas* (huge, crisp, crepe-thin pancakes stuffed with potatoes and chiles) and *utthapam* (a thicker, softer, rice batter pancake), both beloved throughout the subcontinent.

Whatever you order, do have a real South Indian coffee at the end of the meal. This milky, chicory-based coffee comes in a stainless steel glass set in a deep metal saucer. If you stir in a big spoonful of sugar, pour the super hot coffee into the saucer to cool it, and drink it from that, you will feel like a bonafide South Indian. In Berkeley you'll find **Udupi Palace** (1901 University Ave., 510/843-6600)—to my mind, the best South Indian restaurant on the West Coast—as well as excellent groceries like **Milan International,** and snack shops including **Vik's Chaat Corner** (726 Allston Way, 510/644-4412,).

San Francisco has been colonized by two popular, cheap, self-serve curry houses: **Shalimar** (532 Jones St., 415/928-0333), which whips up spicy, searingly hot Pakistani curries and superb kebabs; and **Naan 'n' Curry** (533 Jackson St., 415/693-0499), which turns out thin, buttery, tandoori baked flat breads and tamer curries. **Gaylord India Restaurant,** (415/771-8822) with a view of the Bay from its location in Ghirardelli Square, has been serving the white tablecloth crowd for decades.

PILIPINO

Pilipino cooking reflects the diverse peoples who settled in the 7,100 Pacific islands that comprise the country. Indigenous Malays, Chinese traders, Spanish colonizers, and Americans who won the islands in the Spanish-American War in 1898 have all left their mark on the food. There are also some Indian and Arab influences, especially among the Muslim population of Mindanao, a large island in the south.

You can taste the different ethnic mix at **Max's of the Philippines** (1155 El Camino, 650/872-6748), a small, very popular family restaurant in a strip mall in South San Francisco, a branch of a Manila chain with four outposts in California. My favorite Pilipino dish, Max's Crispy *pata,* is a pork knuckle that's deep fried until the outside becomes a thick layer of crunchy, pork crackling, and the inside is a mass of gelatinous and meltingly tender morsels. The *pata* is served with a dipping sauce of distilled vinegar, soy and garlic. Sublime. With it, customers drink aromatic calamansi juice, an intense lemonade made from this pleasantly sour citrus, a hybrid of a mandarin and a kumquat.

Alido's (3560 Callan Blvd., 650/869-4457), a sprawling, ranch-style building on a hill overlooking South San Francisco and the Bay beyond, specializes in dishes made with coconut milk from *Pampanga,* a region north of Manila in the Luzon Province. *Buko,* shredded fresh young coconut in its own juice with water, sugar, and ice is the drink of choice here. Don't miss halo-halo, a colorful Pilipino sundae which is made with shaved ice, creamy purple *ube* ice cream (ube is a purple sweet potato), red gelatin cubes, red *azuki,* beans, red-dyed *kaong* nuts, crisped rice, and

---

A LANDMARK INDONESIAN RESTAURANT

In 1969, the late Leonie Hool launched her charming, bamboo-paneled **Rice Table** (1617 4th St., 415/456-1808) in San Rafael, where she offered just what the name of her restaurant promises—tables full of home-cooked Javanese specialties. Her family continues to run this landmark Indonesian restaurant, preparing her signature dishes. Every meal starts with three extraordinary sambals, or dipping sauces, of graduating heat followed by waves of salads, satays, and curries. The feast ends with creamy deep fried bananas and cinnamon-scented Indonesian coffee, a last nod to Indonesia's culinary identity as the Spice Islands.

---

evaporated milk. It's juicy, cold, and refreshing.

Tito Rey of the Islands (3 St. Francis Square, 650/758-5815) in Daly City prepares a classic chicken and pork *adobo,* the meats stewed in a deft balance of soy sauce, vinegar, garlic, bay leaves, and peppercorns. *Adobo* is the national dish of the Philippines and stewing foods in vinegar is a technique unique to these islands. The vinegar preserves the meats, and makes the *adobo* tasty whether it's eaten hot or cold.

Pilipinos take *merienda,* an afternoon snack, at the **Red Ribbon Bake Shop** (6877 Mission St., 650/755-2376) in Daly City, one of a chain that stretches up the coast from San Diego. The Red Ribbon is famous for its fresh mango cake, airy chiffon layers filled and iced with whipped cream and fresh mango. The purple *ube cakeroll* is layered with *macapuno* (coconut jelly) and whipped cream. On the savory side, warm chicken *empanadas* (from Mexico, a direct result of the galleons sailing between Manila and Acapulco during the 300 years of Spanish occupation of both countries) have a sweet, flaky crust filled with mashed chicken and raisins. The *adobo* rolls, light buns of airy American bread (in Chinese *bao* form) are stuffed with sweet, salty pork *abodo.* The wild diversity of all these flavors, textures, and ingredients exemplifies the melting pot nature of Pilipino cuisine.

AFGHAN

Afghan food weaves Persian, Indian, and Middle Eastern flavors into an exquisite culinary cloth. **Helmand** (430 Broadway, 415/362-0641) in San Francisco skillfully prepares the whole repertoire of Afghan dishes—deep, hearty soups enriched with yogurt; braised lamb dishes accompanied by a light rice pilaf studded with whole spices; *koufta callow,* large soft meatballs in spicy, cinnamon-scented tomato sauce; and *dwopiaza,* grilled lamb kebabs sauced with vinegared onions and yellow split peas, presented on a square of flatbread that soaks up the juices. (These are served medium rare—inauthentically, but deliciously). The national dish of Afghanistan is *aashak:* large, tender ravioli filled with sautéed leeks, topped with a mild, buttery meat sauce and served on a bed of yogurt speckled with fresh mint. *Kaddo borawni,* or pumpkin, also sauced with garlic-scented yogurt, achieves a miraculous melting texture. The gracious, informative service, the linen, the wine list—all these amenities, not to mention the refined cooking, make the inexpensive Helmand a real bargain.

In the Little Kabul area of Fremont, the Afghan community supports restaurants, kebab shops, food stores, bakeries, and butchers, most of them along Fremont Boulevard. Here you'll find **Salang Pass** (37462 Fremont Blvd., 510/795-9200), an authentic Afghan restaurant. There are Western tables in the colorful dining room decorated with wall murals, or you can sit at low tables on a platform carpeted with intricate hand woven rugs. But the food is the thing. Two bright sauces on the table—one a cilantro chutney spiked with vinegar and garlic; the other a sweet, red, fruity chile oil—set the high tone of the cooking. Always start with *bolani,* a thin, griddled, flat bread lusciously filled with mashed potatoes and leeks seasoned with cilantro and red chiles, well worth the long wait while it is rolled out and slowly cooked to order. It's cut into triangles that you dip into a cup of rich, thick yogurt. *Borani badenjan*, long, skinny, eggplants cooked to an almost jam-like consistency, also benefits from the refreshing sauce of yogurt and dried herbs. *Mantoo* are square, open-face ravioli with curled edges, holding spicy, ground beef and topped with meat sauce, yellow split peas, and yogurt.

Everyone orders *pakawra* at Salang Pass—long, narrow, cats-tongue-shaped potato slices rubbed bright yellow with turmeric, and souffléd in the fryer so that they puff. Thin and crisp, they expel a sexy little potatoey breath when you bite into them. For a main course, have the other national dish of Afghanistan, *Quabili Pallow*, a regally mounded platter of saffron-and-tomato tinted rice with hunks of flavorful lamb on the bone hidden in the middle of the pile, the whole thing decorated with sweet, shredded carrots, raisins, and almonds.

After a meal of this heft, the only dessert that really makes sense is a refreshing *jala* or *faloodeh*. This features *kulfi* (dense ice cream made of boiled-down milk) sprinkled with pistachios, afloat in a dish of rosewater-scented syrup, thick with transparent rice noodles (*faloodeh*) and shaved ice. Afghan *faloodeh* is crowned with the frozen skin of boiled milk, which is like thick, dense, whipped cream. This dessert achieves the impossible—balancing creamy and rich with clean and juicy.

At the **Pamir Market** (37436 Fremont Blvd., 510/790-7015) next door, a couple of bakers pull long, flat, Afghan breads out of a tiled pizza oven. You can watch them tug the soft dough into shape and then dimple the top with their finger tips. Customers take the hot breads away wrapped in newspapers. Bulk spices, *halvah*, honey; buttery new crop California pistachios; green Afghan raisins that taste just like grapes and tiny, hard dried apricots for braising with meats—they're all available here. Don't miss the crunchy *jelabi*—a sweet made of dough piped out into boiling oil, then soaked in sugar syrup—prepared by a local woman.

Newark Square, a shopping center a couple of miles north, is another center of Afghan commerce. The ornate **Afghan Village** (5698 Thornton

Ave., 510/790-0557) is a large, multi-room restaurant decorated with a pot-pourri of tiffany lamps, French crystal chandeliers, bas relief wall murals in pounded copper, Indian screens, and sentimental oil paintings. It's easy to visualize the joyful marriages celebrated here, where Afghans gather in a suburb of San Francisco, eating traditional dishes transplanted to a new land.

RESTAURANTS

Chinese

House of Nanking. Atmospheric dive with all the trimmings of a tourist trap, save the food, which is excellent. 919 Kearny St., San Francisco; 415/421-1429.

Hunan Home's Restaurant. This Chinatown restaurant has long been regarded as one of the city's top Hunan restaurants. Despite the tacky décor, the flavors are excellent, whether it's the hot and sour soup or one of the restaurant's renowned platters, such as moo shu chicken or barbecued pork. 622 Jackson St., San Francisco; 415/982-2844.

Imperial Tea Court. Premium teas served in a traditional style amid soothing surroundings. 1411 Powell St., San Francisco; 415/788-6080; www.imperialtea.com.

Jai Yun. Hailing from Nanjing, a couple of hundred miles from Shanghai, Chef Ji Nei' focuses on light and delicate flavors, often steaming or brining the food. He is said to shop every day in Chinatown which means the menu changes nightly depending on his finds. Foo yung abalone, scrambling eggs with shellfish is one specialty. He's also known for his quail soup and basil-mushroom stir fry. 923 Pacific Ave., San Francisco; 415/ 981-7438.

Koi Palace. As evidenced by the 1,500 gallon live fish tank inside Koi Palace, this restaurant is known for its seafood. Customers can choose one of the fish or shellfish from the tank—Dungeness and Alaskan king crabs, Pacific clams, catfish, etc.— and chef Kam C. Leung will prepare it. The Hong Kong style eatery is often quite busy. 365 Gellert Blvd., Daly City; 650/992-9000.

R&G Lounge. Hong Kong–style restaurant renowned for its seafood. 631 Kearny St., San Francisco; 415/982-7877.

San Tung No. 2. There is often a line out the door for the bowls of hand-made noodles and steamed dumplings at San Tung. The cuisine is based on the northeastern Chinese province of Shandong. Other delicacies include jellyfish or seaweed salad and chicken marinated in wine. 1031 Irving St., San Francisco; 415/242-0828.

Spices! A colorful spot off Clement Street that buzzes with Chinese pop music and animated conversation, and serves zesty, inexpensive Sichuan food that more than lives up to the restaurant's exclamatory name. Spices I and II: 294 Eighth Ave. (near Clement Street), San Francisco; 415/752-8884; 291 Sixth Ave., San Francisco; 415/752-8885.

Ten Ren. Cups of tea to go and a wide-range of gourmet teas take home. 949 Grant Ave; 415/362-0656; www.tenren.com.

Ton Kiang. Features Hakka cuisine of southern China, including regional specialties such as salt-baked chicken, fish balls, and stuffed bean curd. There are many quality seafood items on the menu, such as smoked black cod and salt and pepper shrimp. Also known as one of the best dim sum spots in the city. 5821 Geary Blvd., San Francisco; 415/387-8273.

Yank Sing. Yank Sing, San Francisco's oldest teahouse, opened in Chinatown in the late 1950s but 30 years later moved to the city's financial district. There are more than 100 kinds of dim sum served, though not all at once—usually about 60 of those are offered daily. 49 Stevenson St., San Francisco; 415/541-4949; Other location: One Rincon Center, 101 Spear St., Financial District; 415/957-9300.

Y Ben House. Banquet hall serving some of the best dim sum in Chinatown. 835 Pacific Ave., San Francisco; 415/397-3168.

Great Eastern. 649 Jackson St., San Francisco; 415/986-2550.

Hang Ah Tea Room. 1 Pagoda Pl., San Francisco; 415/982-5686.

Little Shin Shin. 4258 Piedmont Ave., Oakland; 510/658-9799.

Ming's. 1700 Embarcadero Road, Palo Alto; 650/856-7700; www.mings.com.

Parc Hong Kong Restaurant. 5322 Geary Blvd., San Francisco; 415/668-8998.

Shangri-La Vegetarian Restaurant. 2026 Irving St., San Francisco; 415/731-2548.

Dim Sum

Canton Seafood and Dim Sum House. 655 Folsom St., San Francisco; 415/495-3064.

Gold Mountain. 644 Broadway, San Francisco; 415/296-7733.

Jade Villa. 800 Broadway, Oakland; 510/839-1688.

Lichee Garden. 1416 Powell St. (between Broadway and Vallejo), San Francisco; 415/397-2290.

Tina's Tea House. 701 Webster St., Oakland; 510/832-7661.

Japanese

Benkyo-Do. Revered manju shop that's been a neighborhood fixture since 1906. 1747 Buchanan St., San Francisco; 415/922-1244.

Ebisu. Ever popular with the local crowd, Ebisu is known for its creative special rolls. The Swamp Roll, for example, has spicy albacore tuna, yellow onion and seaweed salad, and the Arch Deluxe combines soft shell crab,

crab, isowabi, cucumber, green onion, mayo and garlic. Be prepared for long lines, especially on weekends. 1283 9th Ave., San Francisco; 415/566-1770.

Iroha. Cozy booths, intimate lighting and excellent noodles. 1728 Buchanan St., San Francisco; 415/922-0321.

Isobune. An inexpensive "sushi boat" restaurant. Kintetsu Mall, San Francisco; 415/563-1030.

Kyo-ya. Its location and exquisite surroundings in the Palace Hotel make for an expensive menu, but the quality makes up for the cost. Kyo-ya serves a variety of tempuras, grilled fish and meats, tasty teriyaki dishes, and a vast array of sushi. 2 New Montgomery St., Palace Hotel, San Francisco; 415/546-5000; www.kyo-ya-restaurant.com.

Maki Restaurant. Tucked into a small nook in Japan Center, Maki offers a modest, yet authentic menu that never disappoints. Highlights include the Wappa-meshi dishes (steamed fish, vegetables and rice), savory custard (chawan mushi), and miso soup. The small restaurant also boasts 19 different sakes. 1825 Post St., San Francisco; 415/921-5215.

Mifune. Quick and cheap noodles. 1737 Post St., Japan Center, Kintetsu Bldg., San Francisco; 415/922-0337.

On the Bridge. Diner offering yoshoku-style food—Western dishes made with Japanese flair. Webster Bridge, San Francisco; 415/922-7765.

Ozumo. Caters to an upscale business crowd, but its half sushi, half rogata grill menu appeals to any Japanese food connoisseur. Grill dishes include originals such as Hirame-hime—halibut and scallop carpaccio with grape-Grand Marnier dressing. Ozumo also offers more than 40 sake choices, nearly all are imported from Japan. 161 Steuart, San Francisco; 415/882-1333; www.ozumo.com.

Grandeho's Kamekyo. 943 Cole St., San Francisco; 415/759-5963. Other location: 2721 Hyde St., San Francisco; 415/673-6828.

Kiss. 1700 Laguna, San Francisco; 415/474-2866.

O Chame. 1830 Fourth St., Berkeley; 510/841-8783.

Sushi Bars

Blowfish Sushi to Die For. What used to be the dot.com hangout still packs the city's hipsters in with the restaurant's unique sushi concoctions and sake cocktails. Walls are lined with Japanese animation cells, while the menu is filled with maki rolls like the Super Dynamite Roll— Hamachi, bincyo, sake, scallions, chili sauce; lightly fried. 2170 Bryant St., at 20th Street, San Francisco; 415/285-3848. Other location: 335 Santana Row Suite 1010, San Jose; 408/345-3848.

Kabuto Sushi. Consistently praised by critics and locals as the best sushi spot in the city, Kabuto wows with its innovations, such as foie gras sushi, and its vast menu, whether it be sushi, sashimi, or cooked dinners. A seat at the bar allows customers to watch Chef Sachio Kojima in action. There is also a large selection of sakes. 5121 Geary Blvd., San Francisco; 415/752-5652.

Sushi Groove South. While Sushi Groove's Russian Hill location is still a popular neighborhood spot, Sushi Groove's second location has become a trendy spot. The bar is filled with young patrons sipping sake cocktails while the sushi bar serves up unusual items such as sushi pizza. A DJ is on hand most evenings. 1516 Folsom St., San Francisco; 415/503-1950. Sushi Groove North: 1916 Hyde St. at Union, San Francisco; 415/440-1905.

Tokyo Go Go. The retro '60s, brightly colored, playful décor in this sushi hang mirror the upbeat atmosphere. Tokyo Go Go is a local standout, excelling at sushi staples such as barbecued eel, tuna, and yellowtail as well as cooked entrees like miso-marinated sea bass. It's also known for its sake sangrias. 3174 16th St., San Francisco; 415/864-2288.

Anzu Sushi Bar. 222 Mason St., San Francisco; 415/394-1100.

Hamano Sushi. 1332 Castro St., San Francisco; 415/826-0825.

Minami Sushi. 1900 Clement St., San Francisco; 415/387-5913.

Moki's Sushi and Pacific Grill. 830 Cortland Ave., San Francisco; 415/970-9336.

Murasaki Sushi Bar. 211 Clement St., San Francisco; 415/668-7317.

Ryokos. 619 Taylor St., San Francisco; 415/775/1028.

Vietnamese

Ana Mandara. Though the restaurant is located in the middle of San Francisco's tourist zone, Ana Mandara is anything but a tourist-quality restaurant. Co-owned by Don Johnson and Cheech Marin, the upscale Vietnamese cuisine is robust and well presented. Starters such as Crunchy Green Papaya Salad with Prawns, Jelly Fish and Chili Vinaigrette, and entrees like Chilean Sea Bass Steamed in Banana Leaf with Shiitake Mushrooms and Miso Sauces impress with their complex flavors. 891 Beach St., San Francisco; 415/771-6800; www.anamandara.com.

Anh Hong. Tucked back in the corner of Lion Plaza, this Vietnamese restaurant specializes in *bo bay mon*, or 7-course beef. It's a favorite destination for big family get-togethers and celebratory dinners, where cooking at the table together is all part of the fun. 1818 Tully Rd. #150, San Jose; 408/270-1096.

Citronelle. A stylish restaurant serving Vietnamese cuisine with a contemporary California twist. 826 S. Winchester Blvd., San Jose; 408/244-2528.

Dragonfly Restaurant. Located in the growing Evergreen district, the chef presents contemporary Vietnamese food with a French accent and a California feel. 2847 S. White Road, San Jose; 408/532-8989.

Golden Flower. Fantastic, inexpensive *pho* shop that's always packed with hungry locals. 667 Jackson St., San Francisco; 415/433-6469.

Kien Giang. Causal restaurant specializing in seafood and home-style Vietnamese cooking. 2060 Tully Road, San Jose; 408/270-4350.

Le Colonial. The lively atmosphere, 1920s-era French colonial décor, and zesty, high-end Vietnamese fare all contribute to Le Colonial's success. Whether it's an order of Bo Bia Choy spring rolls with spicy chile dipping sauce, or Tom Rang Me (sauteed giant black tiger prawns). Save room for one of the special desserts. Guests can linger in the upstairs cocktail lounge. 20 Cosmo Place, San Francisco; 415/931-3600.

Lee's Sandwiches. A locally based, Vietnamese chain that serves *banh mi* sandwiches, *che* desserts, Asian-inspired smoothies, puff pastry treats, and other food-to-go. Four San Jose locations: 990 Story Rd., 408/295-3402; 2525 South King Rd., 408/274-1596; 3276 S. White Rd., 408/274-8166; 640 N. 9th St.; 408/298-6389.

Nha Trang. Located in the Lion Plaza complex, this cozy restaurant has an extensive menu of Vietnamese favorites. 1820 Tully Rd., San Jose; 408/274-6666.

Pho Hoa. An international chain that's figured out the formula for pho, the fragrant Vietnamese beef and rice noodle soup. 1834 Tully Rd., San Jose; 408/238-1481.

Pho Kim Long. Just down the road from the Great Mall, this restaurant specializes in Vietnamese noodle soups such as *pho; bun rieu* with tomato and crab; and *bun bo hue*, a spicy mix of beef and pork trotters. 2082 N. Capitol Ave., San Jose; 408/946-2181.

PPQ Vietnamese Cuisine. Fabulous *pho* and celebrated roasted crab. 2332 Clement St., San Francisco; 415/386-8266.

Slanted Door. Slanted Door has made quite a name for itself for its quality, authentic Vietnamese food at reasonable prices. Some favorites are the fresh spring rolls, caramelized shrimp, and lemongrass tofu. All produce is organic. Slanted Door moved to the renovated Ferry Plaza Building in early April 2004, and also plans to re-open at its original Valencia Street address in the future. 1 Ferry Building, San Francisco; 415/861-8032; www.slanteddoor.com.

Tamarine. Much lauded Vietnamese food in a sleek setting with a contemporary, California spin. Family-style service encourages sharing dishes, including shrimp in tamarind sauce, spice-infused rice in banana leaves, and their signature Ha Long Bay soup. 546 University Ave., Palo Alto; 650/325-8500.

Thanh Long. Outer Sunset Vietnamese that's long been revered for its roasted crab. 4101 Judah St., San Francisco; 415/665-1146.

Tofoo Com Chay. "If animals could speak, we'd all be vegetarians" says the sign on the wall. Meatless versions of Vietnamese favorites—banh mi sandwiches, pho and bun rieu soups, grilled satay—are popular with nearby SJSU students. 388 E. Santa Clara St., San Jose; 408/286-6335.

Vung Tau. A favorite in downtown San Jose, this bustling family restaurant serves dependable Vietnamese dishes. 535 Santa Clara St., San Jose; 408/288-9055.

Vung Tau II. Vung Tau ranks as a favorite among San Jose locals for its overwhelmingly extensive menu and tasty fare. Shrimp cupcakes with fish sauce are a popular starter, while sour soup with shrimp also rates high. Also on the menu: broken rice, fire pots, five eel dishes, frog legs, and mixed vegetables with tofu. The kitchen can adapt many of the meals for vegetarians. 535 E. Santa Clara St., San Jose; 408/288-9055. 1750 N. Milpitas Blvd., Milpitas; 408/934-9327.

Dac Phuc. 198 W. Santa Clara St.; San Jose; 408/297-5517.

Golden Harvest. 377 N. Capitol Ave., San Jose; 408/272-7254.

La Vie. 5830 Geary Blvd., San Francisco; 415/668-8080.

Le Cheval. 1007 Clay St., Oakland; 510/763-8495.

Le Soleil. 133 Clement St., San Francisco; 415/668-4848.

Minh Tri. 534 Irving St., San Francisco; 415/566-5335.

Pho Ga An Nam. 740 Story Rd., Unit 3; San Jose; 408/993-1211.

Pho Hoa-Hiep II. 1833 Irving St. (at 19th Ave.), San Francisco; 415/ 664-0469.

Tulan Restaurant. 8 Sixth St., San Francisco; 415/626-0927.

Yummy Yummy. 3040 Taraval St., San Francisco; 415/759-1818.

Pilipino

Carmen's Restaurant. Carmen's is a blend of Pilipino and American dishes, including tasty lumpia rolls filled with peas, green beans, carrots, pork, and other veggies. This restaurant attracts a local, old-time following. 998 Fourth St., San Francisco; 415/495-9265.

Jollibee. Jollibee is an international enterprise with all of its eight USA locations in California. Come here for Filipinized American or Americanized Pilipino food. Chickenjoy and Pilipino spaghetti are an adventure. Noteworthy are the mango, and the banana langka pies. San Francisco Convention Center, 200 Fourth Street (at Howard Street), San Francisco; 415/546-1246; jb-convention@jollibeeca.com.

Mango Bay. Opened in 2002 by San Francisco resident Barry Picazo, who is an artist as much as he is a chef. You won't find tripe in your kare kare at Mango Bay; you will find beautifully presented food, turo-turo style, and Pilipino breakfast all day Saturday. 53 Third St. (between Market and Mission Sts.), San Francisco; 415/369-9888, www.mangobaysf.com.

Manila Meat Market and Groceries (Shar-Vi Groceries). Also known as Shar-Vi Groceries (probably a combination of the names of the owners or their children), this market's got fresh fruit and a good selection of Philippine breads and pastries from local bakeries. 987 Mission St., San Francisco; 415/284-0656.

New Filipinas Restaurant. Very casual, cafeteria-style restaurant, or turo-turo, as Pilipinos call it. But the food is good quality. Traditional fried lumpia rolls as well as tamarind soups are specialties here. There are also a variety of well spiced dishes using coconut milk and chiles and other Southeast Asian touches. 953 Mission St., San Francisco; 415/896-2475.

Alido's. 3560 Callan Blvd., South San Francisco; 650/869-4457.

Carmila Pilipino Restaurant. 53 3rd St., San Francisco; 415/495-4440.

Clarita's Pilipino Cuisine. 905 E. Duane Ave, Sunnyvale; 408/735-1721.

Grill House. 138 6th St., San Francisco; 415/522-1183.

Islands. 3 St. Francis Square (South Gate Ave. and St. Francis Blvd.), Daly City; 650/758-5815.

Manila Eatery. 851 Cherry Ave., San Bruno; 650/588-4929.

Manila Garden Café. 370 12th St., Oakland; 510/645-1262.

Max's Restaurant—Philippines. 1155 El Camino Real, South San Francisco; 650/872-6748.

Red Ribbon Bake Shop. 6877 Mission St., Daly City; 650/755-2376.

Solita Club and Pilipino Restaurant. 120 Hazelwood Dr., South San Francisco; 650/952-8769.

Taste of Manila. 2619 Oliver Dr. Hayward; 510/783-6737.

Indian

Ajanta Distinctive Indian Cuisine. With constant kudos from locals and critics, Ajanta stands out among the East Bay's myriad of Indian eateries. The menu pulls dishes from all over the country, including Kolhapuri Gosht, a lamb dish from Maharashtra, on the West Coast of India, and Murg Mumtaz Mahal, a Moghlai dish from Delhi. 1888 Solano Ave., Berkeley; 510/526-4373; www.ajantarestaurant.com.

Chaat Café. Chaat, popular snack foods in India, makes up a large part of the menu at this busy Berkeley venue. Snack foods include basic samosas to more complex offerings such as Raj Katori—puri stuffed with lentil dumpling, potatoes, garbanzo beans, yogurt, chutneys and spices. Chaat is also known for its tandoori wraps and stuffed naans. 1902 University Avenue, Berkeley; 510/845-1431. 3954 Mowry Rd., Fremont; 510/845-1431. 5134 Stevens Creek Blvd., San Jose; 408/247-9010. 320 3rd St., San Francisco; 415/979-9946.

Gaylord India Restaurant. Fine Indian cuisine. 3rd floor, Chocolate Bldg., San Francisco; 415/771-8822; www.gaylords.com.

Indian Oven. The plain white tablecloths don't reflect the zesty North Indian food. More exotic choices include fish Tandoori with Chilean sea bass marinated in herbs and spices, chicken Madras, cooked in spicy coconut sauce with raisins, or basic sabji—vegetable curry. Sides include a variety of breads like goat cheese naan. 233 Fillmore St., San Francisco; 415/626-1628.

Naan 'n' Curry. A Bay Area chain with four restaurants, serving an inexpensive menu of spicy Indian dishes. 478 O'Farrell St. (near Jones), San Francisco; 415/775-1349. Open 11:30–midnight Sunday–Thursday, until 2 A.M. Friday and Saturday. 533 Jackson (near Kearny), San Francisco; 415/693-0499. 642 Irving (near Seventh Ave.), San Francisco; 415/664-7225. 2366 Telegraph Ave. (near Channing), Berkeley; 510/841- 6226.

Haveli. 35 Sixth St., San Francisco; 415/348-1381.

Kennedy's Irish Pub and Curry House. 1040 Columbus Ave., San Francisco; 415/441-8855.

Khana Peena. 1889 Solano Ave., Berkeley; 510/528-2519. Second location across from Cal campus: 2136 Oxford St., Berkeley; 510/849-0149.

Little Nepal. 925 Cortland St., San Francisco; 415/643-3881.

Maharani (Empress) Restaurant. 1122 Post St. at Polk, San Francisco; 415/775-1988.

Saravana Bhavan. 600 W. El Camino Real, Sunnyvale; 650/635-0460.

Shalimar. 532 Jones St. (near O'Farrell), San Francisco; 415/928-0333. Open noon–11 P.M. daily. Other locations: 1409 Polk (near Pine), San Francisco; 415/776-4642. 3325 Walnut Ave. (near Liberty), Fremont; 510/494-1919.

Udupi Palace. 5988 Newpark Mall, Newark; 510/794-8400. 1901 University Ave., Berkeley; 510/843-6600.

Vik's Chaat Corner. 726 Allston Way, Berkeley; 510/644-4412.

Zante's Pizza. 3489 Mission at Cortland, San Francisco; 415/821-3949.

Afghan

Afghan/Persian Cuisine Paradise. This has been highly rated by *San Jose Mercury News, Mountain View Voice,* and *Palo Alto Weekly.* Specializes in Afghan and Iranian cuisine. 1350 Grant Rd., Mountain View; 650/968-5949.

Bamyan Restaurant. The name of this restaurant comes from the Bamyan province where the giant statue of Buddha had been carved in 5th century A.D. The Taliban destroyed it in March of 2001. This is a classy Afghan restaurant in San Rafael, Marin County. The Marin Independent Journal, the San Francisco Chronicle, a local paper, Pacific Sun Weekly, and the Gazette have rated this restaurant highly. 227 3rd Street, San Rafael; 415/453-8809.

De Afghanan Kabob House. The specialty is the stuffed, grilled breads, which should be ordered in advance, as the crowd can get thick here. The Chapli kabob and Boulani get rave reviews. 37405 Fremont Blvd., Fremont; 510/745-9599.

Helmand. The name of the restaurant came from the Helmand province of Afghanistan. This classy restaurant belongs to the Afghanistan interim President's brothers, and has been awarded the Traveler's magazine Restaurant Award of 1994, and for the last four years has received the

Award of Distinction by *Zagat*. It offers authentic Afghan cuisine in a very serene atmosphere. 430 Broadway, San Francisco; 415/362-0641; Reservation required.

Kabul Restaurant. This specializes in different kabobs, and has been highly rated by the *San Francisco Chronicle, Daily News,* and also recommended by the *California Best Places* book. 135 El Camino Real, San Carlos; 650/594-2840.

Roya Afghan Cuisine. In Farsi/Dari, roya means vision or dream. The atmosphere is a mingling of Afghan tradition décor and American style. Roya has been highly rated by the *San Jose Mercury News* and the *San Francisco Chronicle*. 1510 N. Main St., Walnut Creek; 925/943-1289

Afghan Village. 5698 Thornton Ave., Newark; 510/790-0557.

Asmara Restaurant. 5020 Telegraph Ave., Oakland; 510/547-5100.

Kandahar Cuisine. 2118 Mount Diablo St., Concord; 925/676-2243.

Salang Pass. Little Kabul, 37462 Fremont Blvd., Fremont; 510/795-9200.

Zazoo's Restaurant. 15 Embarcadero W., Oakland; 510/986-5454.

Korean

Brother's. Roll-up-your-sleeves, no frills Korean barbecue joint that's so good it inspired a sibling a few doors down. 4128 Geary Blvd., San Francisco; 415/387-7991.

Korea House. Korea House rates above most Korean barbecue spots in San Francisco. The restaurant also excels with its varied soups and stews. There is also a healthy portion of side dishes and a wide selection of kimchee. 1640 Post St., San Francisco; 415/563-1388.

New Korea House. Filled with the smells of grilled meat and spicy kimchee being prepared, New Korea House impresses even Korean natives.

The restaurant serves its kalbi, bulgoki, and array of kimchee in a clean, friendly environment. 1620 Post St., San Francisco; 415/931-7834.

Seoul Garden. A variety of Korean food, including barbecue. Miyako Mall, San Francisco; 415/563-7664.

Brother's Korean Restaurant II. 4014 Geary Blvd., San Francisco; 415/668-2028.

Korean Palace. 2297 Stevens Creek Blvd., San Jose; 408/279-9686.

Koryo Wooden Charcoal BBQ. 4390 Telegraph Ave., Ste. J, Oakland; 510/652-6007.

Thai

Khan Toke Thai House. Khan Toke offers a relaxing atmosphere to enjoy the Thai cuisine. A host or hostess takes everyone's shoes at the door and visitors sit on cushions at low tables. Wood paneling, carved wooden tables, and a glass atrium filled with orchids add a romantic touch. The menu features standard Thai entrees such as chicken in yellow curry with sweet potatoes, all cooked to perfection. 5937 Geary Blvd., San Francisco; 415-668-6654.

King of Thai Noodles. A hole-in-the-wall that dishes up authentic staples so tasty it spawned a chain that spans the city. 639 Clement St., San Francisco; 415/752-5198.

Marnee Thai. Always one of the city's most bustling Thai restaurants, Marnee Thai can get downright chaotic. Favorites include dim sum-like prawns, string beans, tofu, and mushrooms sautéed with hot chili paste, and a variety of curries. 2225 Irving St., San Francisco; 415/665-9500. Other location: 1243 Ninth Ave., San Francisco; 415/731-9999.

Chiang Mai. 5020 Geary Blvd., San Francisco; 415/387-1299.

Koh Samui and the Monkey. 415 Brannan St., San Francisco; 415/369-0007.

Manoras Thai. 1600 Folsom St., San Francisco; 415/861-6224.

Sabuy Sabuy. 5231 College Ave., Oakland; 510/653-8587.

Siam Cuisine. 1181 University Ave., Berkeley; 510/548-3278.

Sukhothai. 1319 9th Ave., San Francisco; 415/564-7722.

Thep Phanom. 400 Waller St., San Francisco; 415/431-2526.

Other San Francisco Asian Cuisines

Angkor Wat. San Francisco's first Cambodian restaurant still turns out dependable dishes and hosts the occasional Khmer classical dance performance. 4217 Geary Blvd., San Francisco; 415/221-7887.

Coriya Hot Pot City. Don't come alone to this do-it-yourself Taiwanese hibachi spot that's something of a cross between Korean barbecue and Japanese *shabu shabu*. 852 Clement St., San Francisco; 415/387-7888.

Mandalay. Longstanding Inner Richmond Burmese restaurant serving excellent tea leaf salads, stir-fries with mango and chicken, samosas and curries plus a smattering of Mandarin dishes. 4348 California St., San Francisco; 415/386-3895.

Straits Café. Slightly more upscale than most Inner Richmond Asian eateries, Chris Yeo's Singaporean standout has had a loyal following for more than a decade. 3300 Geary Blvd., San Francisco; 415/668-1783.

Angkor Borei. 3471 Mission St., San Francisco; 415/550-8417.

Burma Super Star. 309 Clement St., San Francisco; 415/387-2147.

Jakarta. 615 Balboa St., San Francisco; 415/387-5225.

Lhasa Moon. 2420 Lombard St., San Francisco; 415/674-9898.

Rice Table. 1617 4th St., San Rafael; 415/456-1808.

Pan-Asian

Grasshopper. Asia meets California at this Rockridge hot spot. Specialties at Grasshopper include Indonesian peanut chicken; Pilipino pork adobo; or a Thai coconut mild stew with crab and mussels. 6317 College Ave. (at Alcatraz), Oakland; 510/595-3557.

Betelnut. 2030 Union St. (at Buchanan), San Francisco; 415/929-8855.

The Citrus Club. 1790 Haight St., San Francisco; 415/387-6366.

Ponzu. 401 Taylor St., San Francisco; 415/775-7979.

White Lotus. 80 N. Market St., San Jose; 408/977-0540.

Zao Noodle Bar. 3583 16th St., San Francisco; 415/864-2888. Other locations: 2406 California St., San Francisco; 415/345-8088. 822 Irving St., San Francisco; 415/682-2828. 2031 Chestnut St., San Francisco; 415/928-3088.

Grocery Stores

Geary Food Market. A small grocery with an extensive selection of Korean foods, including freshly made *ban chan*. 4324 Geary Blvd., San Francisco; 415/668-7474.

Haig's Delicacies. A Middle Eastern specialty food store stocking Indian and Indonesian spices, curries, and sauces as well as a wide range of teas. 642 Clement St., San Francisco; 415/752-6283.

Richmond New May Wah. Pan-Asian supermarket features products from around Asia, as well as fresh meat, seafood and produce. 709 Clement St., San Francisco; 415/221-9826.

Sunset Super. Expansive grocery store stocking a wide-variety of products from China, Thailand, Vietnam and beyond, in addition to fresh fruits and vegetables, fish and meat. 2425 Irving St., San Francisco; 415/566-6504.

Bharat Bazaar. 3680 El Camino Real, Santa Clara; 408/247-4307.

Maiwand Market. Little Kabul, 37235 Fremont Blvd., Fremont; 510/796-3215.

Pamir Market. Little Kabul, 37436 Fremont Blvd., Fremont; 510/790-7015.

Bakeries

Eastern Bakery. The oldest bakery in Chinatown still churns out moon cakes for sale around the country. 720 Grant Ave., San Francisco; 415/392-4497.

Golden Gate Bakery. A Chinatown favorite for its tasty egg custard tarts. 1029 Grant Ave., San Francisco; 415/781-2627.

Red Ribbon Bake Shop. A favorite stop of Pilipinos looking for an afternoon snack (*merienda*). 6877 Mission St., Daly City; 650/755-2376.

SHOPPING,
fASHION,
AND BEAUTY

SAN FRANCISCO HASN'T BEEN DESIGNATED THE most Asian American city for nothing: Census figures from 2000 showed that 240,000 Asians call the city of San Francisco home, while more than 1.2 million live in the Bay Area as a whole. Many are immigrants from large countries like China and India, while others come from smaller countries like Bhutan and Laos.

The Bay Area offers residents and visitors a diverse look at Asia in America. Here, recent immigrants rub shoulders with second-, third-, and fourth-generation Asian Americans, but they no longer do so only in traditional enclaves like Chinatown or Japantown; in fact, Eastern accents are palpable throughout the city's distinct neighborhoods, from the predominantly Latino Mission District to trendy Hayes Valley.

For those interested in clothing, there are stores galore that offer traditional as well as contemporary fashions from Asian American designers and boutique owners. Spas and beauty salons tout the newest techniques from Asia, as well as ancient treatments updated for today's men and women. And the jewelry and ceramics imported to the Bay Area from Asia are sure to please even the most discriminating connoisseur.

CLOTHING

Barong Tagalog

Pilipino men have been wearing the *barong tagalog*, or some variation of it, for more than 400 years. Though it evolved from dress worn before the Spanish arrived, the modern *barong tagalog* is certainly inspired by Western wear. During their rule from the mid-1500s to the late 1800s, the Spanish demanded that Pilipinos wear the button-down shirt un-tucked, as a mark of inferior status. The material had to be transparent so that the men could not hide weapons.

While early versions of the shirt were made from coarse cloth, by the 19th century, with increasing interaction with Europeans, the barong took on a romantic look, with finer, lighter material, decorated with embroidery. The fabric of choice was *jusi*, raw silk from the fibers of a butterfly's cocoon. As that material became scarce, fibers from a banana stalk became an alternative in producing a lightweight, earth-colored silk that was ideal for embroidery. Worn over a *camisa de chino* (collarless T-shirt), the *barong tagalog* evolved into fashionable business and formal attire. In 1975, President Ferdinand E. Marcos, who wore a *barong tagalog* in all of his official outings, named the shirt the national attire of the Philippines.

Today, young men in San Francisco can be seen sporting *barong tagalogs* with jeans or khakis for an updated ethno-chic look. **Tatak Pilipino** (284 Serramonte Center, Daly City, 650/992-7960), one of the few stores to sell *barong tagalogs* in the Bay Area, carries the shirt in *juji* and in the more affordably-priced frosted and ecru organza with finely crafted embroidery.

Women wear a more billowy variation of the *barong*. More common, however, is the *kimona*, a blouse with a straight, lacy bodice and three-quarter-length puff sleeves. At Tatak Pilipino, *kimonas* come in a variety of colors, including baby pink, mint green, and peach, many bejeweled with sequins and embroidery. The shirts can be worn with wrap-around skirts, based on the ancient *tapis*, sewn from thick woven cloth. Tatak Pilipino also sells shell necklaces, beaded belts with large gold clasps, baskets, and tchotchkes direct from the Philippines. Much of the artwork depicts Catholic icons, evidence of the strong Spanish influence on the Philippines today.

Cheongsam

The body-accentuating *cheongsam* dress worn by Chinese women since the 1930s evolved from the bannermen's robe of the Qing dynasty (1644–1911). The bannermen, who stood at the top of China's social classes, were trained in traditional Manchu arts and enjoyed economic privileges. The women wore straight, loose-fitting silk dresses called *qipao*, though on ceremonial occasions the *qipao's* rounded collars were outfitted with stiffer, more upright Mandarin collars. In the late Qing period, an upright collar replaced the rounded one altogether, and the body of the garment became narrower and longer. Some 20 years later, the modern *cheongsam* arrived in 1930s Shanghai, then the center of fashion in China. Young women paired the body-fitting *cheongsam* with Western-style coats, scarves, and shoes.

While numerous shops along Grant Street in Chinatown hawk *cheongsam* and *cheongsam*-inspired fashions (including jackets, suits and halter tops), there's one preferred dress shop for this classic Chinese dress for those in the know. Established 25 years ago by Thomas Tam, **Dragon Seed** (1325 Indiana St., 415/285-8848) has created *cheongsams* for Chinese movie stars and for contestants of the prestigious Miss Chinatown USA pageant, held each year during the Lunar New Year. He even designed an emperor's robe for former Mayor Willie Brown. He also designs *cheongsams* for travelers who are looking for a unique evening gown to take back home. Most of the dresses, though, take at least a couple of weeks to complete, so he often takes a customer's measurements and mails the finished garment to them.

Tam, who was a tailor in Hong Kong, says a good dressmaker can make any figure look good in a *cheongsam*. He shows off a photo of one plus-size customer in a flattering deep-red *cheongsam*, explaining that a well-crafted design can hide figure flaws and make a short person appear taller. Tam's elaborate one-of-a-kind dresses are made from rich silks and velvets imported from China and Hong Kong.

Kimono

Kimono in Japanese actually means "clothing," but the word has now been associated with the renowned wrap dress with long butterfly sleeves. The style first appeared during the Heian period of the late 8th century. Using a straight-line-cut tailoring technique, robes were produced that could be wrapped to fit almost any body type. During this early period of the kimono, women would typically wear 12 layers of robes, while royalty would don 16 layers.

The dress adopted a more casual style, with shorter sleeves and fewer layers, during the rise of the samurai in the Kamakura period (1133–1185). In the Tokugawa period, beginning in 1615, the dress became an indication of social status, as rulers adopted Confucianism, creating a more hierarchical society. Tailors during that time produced some of the most beautiful kimonos ever created, with ornate fabrics and extravagant designs.

But with the West's increasing influence on Japan in the late 1800s, Japanese began opting for Western-style clothing, and from the start of the Showa period (1926–1989), kimonos and the materials to make them became simpler and less expensive. Today, Japanese women save the kimono for special occasions. Men and older women usually wear kimonos in earth tones, while young women prefer lighter colors, such as cotton-candy pink, cantaloupe, or lime green.

The modern kimono ensemble not only requires the robe, but also an undergarment, an *obi* to wrap around the waist, an *obi-age* sash to hold the kimono in place, and an *obi-jime*, a decorative rope that is tied around the *obi*. For the feet, there is the white *tabi* sock and the slender *zori* slipper. These components are mixed and matched to reflect the wearer's taste.

In the Bay Area, one of the few stores to sell authentic kimonos is **Shige Antique Kimono** (1730 Geary Blvd. #203, 415/346-5567) in Japantown. Lined up against the wall of the small store are one-of-a-kind, vintage kimonos for men and women. The kimonos generally come in one-size-fits-all, but since the garment is a robe that is wrapped, and then held in place by the sash, it can adjust to all but plus-sizes. Most of the robes are made from hand-woven silk, with delicate flower and maple leaf motifs for young women, and starker designs for mature women and men. Customers can choose from a variety of silk *obi* sashes, which are often more beautiful than the kimonos themselves.

Shige Kimono also sells vintage wedding kimonos. Made from quilted material with bold colors (rich reds, oranges, purples) and designs (often with cranes), these kimonos are typically bought for display and decoration, rather than for wear. For those desiring something more casual, the store also sells the cotton *yukata*. Japanese still commonly wear *yukata* at night after soaking in the *ofuro,* a Japanese style bath.

Sari

In India, the sari is not just the national dress. Taking on an almost spiritual dimension, the sari has been a metaphor for the creation of the universe. As one folktale goes: "The sari . . . was born on the loom of a fanciful weaver. He dreamt of woman. The shimmer of her tears. The drape of her tumbling hair. The colors of her many moods. The softness of her touch. All these he wove together. He couldn't stop. . . . And when he was done . . . he sat back and smiled and smiled and smiled."

Indian clothing, loosely translated as sari, is estimated to be 5,000 years old. But the structure of today's sari most likely evolved about 2,000 years ago; its precursor was a skirt and veil ensemble depicted in sculptures from as early as the 1st century. Noor Jahan, the wife of Mughal emperor Jehangir, is often credited with combining the veil and skirt into one garment in the mid-1600s.

The typical sari is made from about six yards of material. It is draped over a petticoat-like undergarment and a short fitted shirt, called a *choli*, then wrapped and pleated around the waist, and finally draped over one shoulder. On a skillfully designed sari, the two parallel lengthwise edges are decorated with figurative images or symbols, while the *pallav*, the edge that drapes over the shoulder, expands on these motifs.

In the Bay Area, and in other cosmopolitan cities, the sari has become an elegant alternative to eveningwear. The flowing garment hides imperfections, giving all body types a graceful silhouette. While there are many shops that sell saris in San Francisco's surrounding areas, there is only one shop in the heart of the city, **Bombay Sari Palace** (548 Valencia St., 415/703-0978).

Bharti Parmar opened Bombay Bazaar with her husband in 1976. For years they sold food items from India, but so many customers asked where they could buy *saris* that Parmar opened a dress shop next to the grocery store in 1997. Bombay Sari Palace sells hundreds of one-of-a-kind saris imported from India. The silk materials are truly beautiful, decorated with appliqué, beading, and embroidery, on shear lemon yellow, translucent sand brown, or multicolored gray, orange, and red fabric. Bombay Sari Palace also sells *choli* suits (long, full skirts with *choli* and matching scarves), Punjabi suits (loose, short-sleeve dresses worn with scarves) and *kurtas* (loose long shirts for men). While the saris are one-size-fits-all, other garments may be altered at the shop. Parmar adds that no sari is complete without a *bindi*, also sold at the store. Placed between the eyebrows, the *bindi* signifies the third eye, controlling concentration attained through meditation, and symbolizing good fortune.

Fashion-Forward

For those wanting more modern wear, San Francisco boasts a number of shops that feature the contemporary designs of Asians and Asian Americans. Some of the clothes have a distinct Asian flavor, while others

GUMP'S

Founded in 1861, Gump's is a San Francisco institution, selling exclusive, high-quality items from around the world. Since the beginning, the Pacific Rim has been a featured theme, so it is fitting that a giant Buddha from the Qing dynasty stands at the center of this elegant store. Chinese American Robert Kuo has created some of the store's bestsellers. He is known for his hammered copper sculptures, among them snails, pigs, apples, and pears that stand about two feet tall. He has also crafted sleek Peking glass vases that are always in demand. The store also features Asian-inspired works by Alex Marshall and John Scott. Marshall's flat vases are Zen-like in their simplicity, as are Scott's hand-turned granite vessels. Jewelry is also plentiful at Gump's and there is no short supply of jade, coral, and pearl pieces.

Gump's is also known as a purveyor of fine antiques. Along with blue-and-white porcelain from China's Ming Dynasty and from Japan's Edo period, there are fine lacquer goods, chests, boxes and trays, as well as Celedon plates. But by far the most popular items are the Buddhist sculptures from 18th-and 19th-century Thailand and Cambodia. With their intricate carving and pure Eastern aesthetics, it's no wonder why. 135 Post St., San Francisco; 800/766-7628.

are done in cutting-edge styles preferred by fashionistas today.

There is no hipper shopping spot in San Francisco than Hayes Valley, bordered by the Van Ness performing arts district and the Western Addition. Among the area's fashion-forward shops and boutiques is **Azalea** (411 Hayes St., 415/861-9888), owned by Catherine Chow and Corina Nurimba, both Cornell graduates. Chow, who emigrated from Taiwan, and Nurimba, who hails from Indonesia, opened this chic little shopping space in the fall of 2003.

For girls who favor *Sex and the City* style, Azalea offers unique designer clothing, handpicked by Chow and Nurimba, who travel extensively throughout the United States, Europe, and Asia for styles that can't be found at department stores. Among the Asian designs are Beatrix Ong shoes from London, couture dresses by local Colleen Quen, and mod skirt-and-blouse ensembles by Kim Bui under the label DUC Kim Bui. The store also features jewelry by upcoming Asian American designers, such as Joyce Chou, whose fruit-inspired pieces are among Azalea's bestsellers. Other favorites: one-of-a-kind silk scarves and Jelly Kelly bags, shaped like Hermes's Birkin handbags, except crafted from malleable plastic. After browsing and buying, shoppers can treat themselves to a manicure or pedicure at the store's nail bar, which uses all-natural, organic products.

For more classic clothing with a modern edge, head straight to **Sunhee Moon** (142 Fillmore St., 415/355-1800) in the lower Haight district. Bringing to mind the style of Audrey Hepburn and Grace Kelly, Moon's beautiful clothing is masterfully designed and crafted from luxurious yet durable fabrics that provide an easy fit. Among her favorite materials are combed jersey and man-made suede, which she says sway with the body. Rather than embellishing her designs, Moon says she strips them down to create clean, elegant lines. Her stretch lavender blouse can be dressed up or down, perfect for jeans or dress slacks. And unlike the boxy, pleated skirts that require a perfect figure, Moon's version skims and slenderizes the body.

It's no surprise that Moon is inspired by European and Western design. Born in the United States, she graduated from UC Berkeley, then studied art history in Italy. After returning, she focused her energy on fashion and was given an advance from Barney's to start her own clothing line. Today, her designs are sold at Barney's New York and Los Angeles, M.A.C, and at boutiques in Japan. Luckily, San Franciscans and visitors to the city can find all of her latest clothing in one store.

For those who favor a more downtown urban style, **Nissa,** (3610 19th St., 415/865-0969) with its small, bare-bones wholesale store in the heart of the Mission district, is a must. Nissa, which means "woman" in Arabic, is owned by Ivy Chan, Umay Mohammed, and Shinobu Sering, who design all of the clothes in the line. While their aesthetic can be described as slacker-girl chic, Asian inspiration is also evident. Their clothing has included a kimono-style dress tied with an obi sash, and a sweater patterned after an Indian kurta. Sering, who emigrated from Japan, is particularly interested in clothes worn by Japanese blue-collar workers. Her loose black *tobi* pants, which cinch around the calf and ankle with attached leg warmers, are similar to those worn by Japanese carpenters (called *tobi* in slang). Nissa also features kitschy imports from Asia, such as cutesy hair clips from Indonesia, plastic turtle coin purses, and reproductions of old Japanese liquor-store bags that can be used as purses.

At the other end of the fashion spectrum is **Cicada Fashion & Art Gallery** (547 Sutter St., 415/398-4000), owned by Monique Zhang. In the '70s, Zhang was a protégé of Sandra Sakata, whose groundbreaking shop Obiko pioneered the philosophy of fashion as art. Today Zhang continues that tradition, creating one-of-a-kind bridal gowns and couture dresses—from a hand-painted silk organza dress robe to a shantung silk *cheongsam* embellished with delicate appliqués.

BEAUTY

Ancient beauty secrets are no longer so secret. Take, for example, **Ayoma LifeSpa** (355 Santana Row, 408/551-0010), recently opened in San Jose's newest luxury shopping district. Owned by Reenita Malhotra, Ayoma provides facials and massage therapies based on the 5,000 year-old traditional Indian medicine system, known as Ayurveda. It is based on five elements—space, fire, water, earth and air—which combine into three doshas—vata, pitta, and kapha.

Each person has a different dosha composition. Distress manifests when one or more dosha is unbalanced. It is believed that with proper diet and massage with special oils, pastes, and herbs, equilibrium can be achieved. At Ayoma, each client's dosha levels are determined through a questionnaire and a short consultation with a therapist.

Malhotra, who graduated from Williams College and then earned her doctorate in *Ayurveda* medicine in India, says she grew up following Ayurvedic principles. She performs more in-depth consultations for those looking for a lifestyle change, but says that anyone just longing for a few hours of relaxation will benefit from Ayoma's treatments. In addition to massage therapies, Ayoma offers the Mukhralepa facial, which is traditionally given to a bride on her wedding day to cleanse and nourish the skin, and the more aggressive, deep-cleansing Soundarya facial that eliminates toxins.

Threading is another tradition from South Asia. The ancient hair removal technique involves rolling a twisted cotton thread along the surface of the face, lassoing a hair, then lifting it from the follicle. Though it sounds a little crude, the method is still favored by women in India, Pakistan, the Middle East, and Vietnam, and it is finding new devotees in the United States. Most commonly used to shape eyebrows, it can also clean up unwanted hair on the upper lip, chin and cheeks. Hair typically grows back within three to eight weeks.

At **Cinta** (23 Grant Ave., 2nd floor, 415/989-1000), a full service beauty salon in downtown San Francisco, Ann Tran specializes in threading. She says the method is gentle and thorough, removing even the tiniest hairs. Many of her clients, both men and women, have gotten glycolic acid treatments or micro-dermabrasion, leaving their skin too sensitive for waxing, but perfect for threading.

Cinta also offers *mehndi*, a form of henna body painting developed in India 5,000 years ago. While still used in Hindu and Islamic cultures to decorate the hands and feet of brides, in the United States it can be applied as a temporary and safer alternative to tattooing. Henna paste is patterned onto the skin and left there to form a stain, which lasts up to three weeks.

In more recent times, Asia has developed cutting-edge beauty treatments. In Korea, Taiwan and Japan, permanent makeup is all the rage. Kana Bruno has brought these methods to San Francisco at her studio **Venus Permanent Makeup** (166 Geary St., Ste. 900, 415/398-1500), located in Union Square. Bruno uses a fine-tipped needle, rather than a tattoo gun, to apply lip, eye, and eyebrow liner for a natural look. Also popular is the eyelash permanent, which gives clients a thick, curly lash look that lasts for about eight weeks.

For hair, one of the trendiest techniques is the Japanese straight perm, or Thermal Reconditioning, which can transform the frizziest locks into a straight, shiny mane. The process, which takes anywhere from three to five hours, consists of a soy-based solution, heat, and special irons that won't damage or dry out the hair. It lasts for about six months.

In San Francisco, one of the few salons that specializes in the treatment is **Dekko** (1325 Indiana St., 415/285-8848), co-owned by native San Franciscan Jill Nishimura and U.K.-born Jules Chan. The loft-style salon, located in San Francisco's trendy Potrero Hill neighborhood, also provides haircuts by hair designers who have worked for some of the city's top salons, including Vidal Sassoon and Architects and Heroes, as well as for MTV. It is recommended that prospective clients book reservations at least a week in advance.

Manicures and pedicures were considered luxuries 30 years ago. Thanks to Asian Americans, particularly immigrants from Southeast Asia, that's no longer the case. Today, small shops that offer affordable treatments are abundant in San Francisco, as well as most other major cities. The trend started in the '80s, when Vietnamese Americans began opening salons in large numbers in Southern California. By the late '90s, it was estimated that Vietnamese Americans owned half of the nation's nail salons.

Even San Francisco's elite favors these no-nonsense salons. The city's first lady, Kimberly Guilfoyle Newsom, is a regular at **Elegant Nails** (1688 Lombard St., 415/441-7177), located in the Marina, where she gets her nails manicured by Triss Tran. Supervisor Fiona Ma favors **Golden Nails** (1432 California St., 415/775-1033), which Seak Muy Chan opened 16 years ago after escaping from Cambodia's Khmer Rouge regime. Chan says she decided on this line of work because her English wasn't good enough to get an office job; today she can't stop talking, and is known for keeping her clients laughing. Providing soothing manicures and fun conversation, Chan will sometimes suggest a game of cards to favored customers—to be played after their nail polish has dried, of course.

JEWELRY

For 5,000 years, the Chinese have treasured jade, or *yu*. It is said that when a scholar asked Confucius (551–479 B.C.) why men value jade, he replied: "It's gentle, smooth, glossy appearance suggests charity of the heart; its fine close texture and hardness suggest wisdom; it is firm and yet does not wound, suggesting duty to one's neighbor; it hangs down as though sinking, suggesting ceremony; struck, it gives a clear note, long drawn out, dying gradually away and suggesting music; its flaws do not hide its excellences, nor do its excellences hide its flaws, suggesting loyalty; it gains our confidence, suggesting truth; its spirituality is like the bright rainbow, suggesting the heavens above; its energy is manifested in hill and stream, suggesting the earth below; as an article of regalia it suggests the exemplification of that to which there is nothing in the world of equal value and thereby is Tao itself."

In ancient China, *yu* was soft, nephrite jade, which was often carved into utensils that were buried with the dead. It was believed that the stone would prevent the body from decay. More recently, *yu* includes a harder stone, jadite, which travelers began bringing to China from Burma in the 13th century. Today, jadite is more popular and valuable than nephrite, and is used to make necklaces, bracelets, and pendants, the most popular of which is donut-shaped, symbolizing longevity. While nephrite is known for its glossy texture, the best jadite has a rich, even tone, whether bright lavender or emerald green.

Jade Galore (1000 Stockton St., 415/982-4863) provides some of the best jade pieces available in San Francisco. The red-carpeted showroom situated in the heart of Chinatown has been in business for 30 years and has a solid reputation. Clients can expect honest prices and high quality service.

All of the store's jade jewelry is made from jadite imported from Burma, which is then crafted in China and Hong Kong. Jade Galore sells traditional Chinese pieces and items carved for the American market, such as Christian cross pendants. The store is also known for its 24-karat gold jewelry, including bangle bracelets and medallion pendants, some embossed with Chinese characters or Chinese zodiac animals.

Rosalina Tran Lydster designs more modern jewelry that is also luxurious. Her high-end creations, priced from $1,500 to $70,000, range from a pearl, gold, and diamond leaf brooch that transforms into a pendant, to a diamond and sapphire elephant ring from her animal fantasy collection. Sold exclusively under the Jewelry by Rosalina label at **Neiman Marcus** San Francisco (150 Stockton St., 415/362-3900), Newport Beach, and Las Vegas, each design is replicated no more than 10 times. Lydster takes pride in giving her clients unique jewelry that reflects their personalities. Her clients include actresses Ali Landry, Angie Harmon, and rapper Lil' Kim. Yuan Yuan Tan, a principal dancer with the San Francisco Ballet, has even modeled for the company.

Lydster follows in the footsteps of her parents. Her mother, Hai Vo, was a revered jewelry designer in Vietnam during the 1960s, creating pieces for the first lady and other Saigon socialites. After escaping the Communists and emigrating to the United States, her parents opened a jewelry shop in Sunnyvale, California. Vo still designs for some of her old clients, who live as far away as Paris. When she and Lydster travel together, they always stop by jewelry stores. "People say, 'Why are you looking at other people's stuff?'" Lydster says. "But that's not what it's about. It's about people's talent. I love jewelry. I consider it like artwork."

JAPANESE CERAMICS

In Japan, porcelain, pottery, and earthenware are known as *yaki.* The earliest *yaki,* in the form of earthenware, dates back 12,000 years ago to the Jomon period. However, today's ceramics owe more to the porcelain introduced to

Japan by Korean artisans in the 7th century. One master craftsman in particular, Ri Sampei, is considered the father of Japanese porcelain.

In the 16th century, it was the Chinese who influenced *yaki*, with the introduction of the tea ceremony and the development of porcelain-ware to accompany the art form. Early tea ceremony sets were elaborate in style, but soon a more austere aesthetic was preferred, with Korean kitchenware and Japanese peasant-wares much in use. This simple, spare design now defines the Japanese folk style.

More ornate porcelain, also inspired by the Chinese, has also been a mainstay of Japanese ceramics. Such pieces, most famously produced in Arita on Kyushu Island, have sold both domestically and to the West since the 17th century. Today, Japanese porcelain is known as Imari, which is the port near Arita.

In San Francisco, locals shop at **Sanko** (1758 Buchanan St., 415/922-8331) in Japantown. In business for 22 years, the no-frills store stocks a huge collection of imports—sashimi and sushi plates, rice bowls, sake and tea sets, presentation dishes and vases—from soothing earthenware to classic blue and white. For more discerning shoppers, art dealer **James Singer** (by appointment only, 415/789-1871) sells contemporary Japanese ceramics that are museum quality. In business for 30 years, Singer mainly sold Buddhist antiquities until three years ago when he was struck by a celadon porcelain piece by Fukami Sueharu. His collection for sale includes Mihara Ken's geometric-patterned earthenware vase, and Nagae Shigekazu's graceful vessel drizzled with blue-and-white liquid porcelain.

Japan's ceramics are the best in the world, according to Singer. "Japan is known for adopting and improving upon creations from the outside world, and that's true for ceramics," he says. "They have inherited a rich tradition and have the knowledge acquired over thousands of years. There is also an abundant availability of training programs, so they are very proficient. And there is a demand in clientele; the Japanese are sensitive to the ceramic tradition."

SHOPPING

Antiques

Dragon House. Chinatown's well-established shop specializes in antique Chinese porcelain and ceramics. It also carries ivory carvings and jewelry. 455 Grant Ave., San Francisco; 415/421-3693.

Evelyn's Antique Chinese Furniture. Evelyn's specializes in antique furniture from mainland China, with pieces ranging from the 17th to 20th centuries. There are even pieces made from huang huali wood, yellow flowering pear, one of the most collected woods in world. Furniture can cost anywhere from $1,500 and $7,000, and it's possible to have it custom-made in China. 381 Hayes St., San Francisco; 415/255-1815.

Ever Arts Antique Furniture. Chinese furniture. 1782 Union St., San Francisco; 415/776-7582.

Fumiki. Fumiki specializes in Asian antiques from 17th to 20th centuries, including Japanese tansu, screens, porcelain works, and even 19th-century bronze Buddhas. The store also carries contemporary chests and other modern furnishings. 272 Sutter St., San Francisco; 415/362-6677. 789 Santa Cruz Ave., Menlo Park; 650/321-4583.

Guillermina. While some praise its stock of Japanese and Korean furniture, its diverse offerings also includes furniture, teapots and gifts from countries such as Burma, the Himalayas, Indonesia, China, Philippines and Sri Lanka. 1099 W. Richmond Ave., Point Richmond; 510/237-0036, www.guillermina.com.

Nakura Tansu Gallery. For about 25 years, owner Tomo Nakura has been traveling regularly to Japan to fine one-of-a-kind pieces, including antiques and vintage home furnishings. 110 West Harris Ave., South San Francisco; 650/588-6115, www.Nakura.com.

Orientations. For more than 30 years, Orientations has specialized in importing art, home furnishings, and garden sculpture from China, Japan, Korea, and Southeast Asia. 195 De Haro St., San Francisco; 415/255.8277, www.orientations.us.

Peking Arts & Antiques. This isn't the usual Chinese trinket shop. Peking Arts sells collectibles from the Han Dynasty, Ming Dynasty, and more, including terra cotta statues, porcelain figures, snuff bottles, and jade statues. There are also 19th-century paintings from mainland China, Korea, and Japan. 333 Sutter St., San Francisco; 415/433-6780.

Xanadu Gallery. Elegant with a spectacular swirling staircase, the gallery stocks up on Indian and South East Asian items, from small decorative goods to furniture to Buddha figures. 140 Maiden Lane, San Francisco; 415/392-9999, and 871 Santa Cruz Ave., Menlo Park; 650/329-9999, www.xanadugallery.us.

The Zentner Collection. Its 35,000-square feet facility offers eclectic Chinese, Japanese, some southeast Asian and Burmese goods. Specialties include furniture, decorative items, Buddhism ceramics, and bronzes. 5757 Horton-Landregan St., Emeryville; 510/653-5181; www.zentnercollection.com.

Big Pagoda. 310 Sutter St., San Francisco; 415/298-8881.

Forgotten Shanghai. 1301 17th St., San Francisco; 415/701-7707, www.forgottenshanghai.com.

Genji Antiques. 22 Peace Plaza, Ste. 190, San Francisco; 415/931-1616.

Han Palace Antiques & Art Center. 1201 Powell St., San Francisco; 415/788-0628, www.hanpalace.com.

Kiku Japanese Antiques. 1420 Sutter St., San Francisco; 415/346-8629.

Narumi Japanese Antiques. 1902B Fillmore St., San Francisco; 415/346-8629.

Traditional Fashions

Sakura Sakura. Sakura Sakura takes traditional Japanese fabrics and designs and caters its wares to Western sensibilities. Japanese *obis* and kimono sashes are made into wall hangings, and *shibori* is made into silk scarves. 1737 Post St. #363, Kintetsu Mall, Japan Center, San Francisco; 415/922-9744.

Shige Kimono. Shige Kimono offers a full line of vintage, hand-painted, and silk-embroidered kimonos as well as cotton *yukatas* (lightweight summer kimonos), silk brocade *obis* (sashes worn with kimonos), and other kimono accessories. Some kimonos date from the 1920s and '30s, but the majority were made in the 1950s and '60s. 1730 Geary Blvd. #203, Kinokuniya Bldg., Japan Center, San Francisco; 415/346-5567.

Asian Renaissance. 662 Grant Ave., San Francisco; 415/397-1897.

Bombay Sari Palace. 548 Valencia St., San Francisco; 415/703-0978.

China Gem Full. 910 Stockton St. #8, San Francisco; 415/395-9292, www.ebizeasy.com/gemfull.

Krishna's Silk House. 512 Revival Terrace, Fremont; 510/796-5252, www.krishnasilks.com.

Sari Palace. 1000 University Ave., Berkeley; 510/841-7274.

Thousand Cranes. 1803 Fourth St., Berkeley; 510/849-0501.

Contemporary Fashions

Cicada Fashion & Art Gallery. Could just as easily be called "Fashion as Art." Cicada offers one-of-a-kind wedding and couture gowns. 547 Sutter St., San Francisco; 415/398-4000.

Nissa. A small wholesale store in the heart of the Mission District offering owner-designed fashions and imported fashion accessories. 3610 19th St., San Francisco; 415/865-0969.

Sunhee Moon : Emphasis is on simplicity at this designer-owned fashion boutique. Moon's creations are trendy, yet elegant and clean-cut. The fabrics are form fitting. Moon's clothes have been featured at Barney's New York. 142 Fillmore St., San Francisco; 415/355-1800, www.sunheemoon.com.

Anarkali Boutique. 2845 S. White Rd., San Jose; 408/531-1824.

Harajuku Boutique. 22 Peace Plaza, Ste. 511, Miyako Mall, Japan Center, San Francisco; 415/567-9233.

K&A Boutique. 783 Clay St. and 802 Stockton St., San Francisco; 415/982-8886.

Masterpiele. 619 Broadway, San Francisco; 415/392-3938.

Mei Qing Fashion. 1143 Grant Ave., San Francisco; 415/812-9219.

Nikko Fashion Store. 862 Clay St., San Francisco; 415/986-8613.

The Omodaka. 1737 Post St., Ste. 11B, San Francisco; 415/921-0505.

Treasure. 863 Clay St., San Francisco; 415/576-1282.

Spas

Kabuki Hot Springs and Spa. For a heavy dose of relaxation and pampering, Kabuki Hot Springs provides the perfect escape. The center offers the serenity of Japanese communal baths as well as more than 18 spa treatment rooms. Treatments include the Bliss Massage with Private Bath: which includes a soak in a Japanese Furo tub followed by a 50 minute Swedish or Shiatsu massage. Ayurvedic healing treatments are offered as well acupuncture and body wraps. Women and men are admitted on separate days to the baths, except for the coed Tuesday baths. 1750 Geary Blvd., San Francisco; 415/922-6000, www.kabukisprings.com.

Novella Spa & Imports. Novella is a retreat set in the middle of the Union Street shopping district. Several treatments are based on an Indonesian theme, such as the Javanese Beauty Ritual, including body exfoliation, a massage, and a body wrap. Also the Balinese Boreh is a skin-smoothing massage and body wrap. There are also Southeast Asian goods for sale. 2238 Union St., San Francisco; 415/673-1929.

Watercourse Way. Open since 1980, Watercourse Way features natural healing and rejuvenating therapies, including private tub rooms with steam or sauna, various types of massage, and skin care. One of the premier spa facilities in the Bay Area. 165 Channing Ave., Palo Alto; 650/462-2000, www.watercourseway.com.

International Orange Spa Yoga Lounge. 2044 Fillmore St., 2nd Floor, San Francisco; 415/563-5000, www.internationalorange.com.

Piedmont Springs Spa. 3939 Piedmont Ave., Oakland; 510-652-9191, www.piedmontsprings.com.

Spa Fusion. Located inside the Hilton Hotel. 333 O'Farrell St., San Francisco; 415/923-5014, www.spafusion.com.

Spa Seven. 2358 Pine St., San Francisco; 415/775-6546, www.spaseven .com.

Therapeia. 1801 Bush St. #27, San Francisco; 415/885-4450, www. etherapeia.com.

True Spa. 750 Kearny St., San Francisco, 415/399-9700.

Furniture and Home Furnishings

Asakichi. Asakichi carries some Japanese antiques as well as newer reproductions of cabinets, *tansu* chests, and the like. Ceramics, handmade paper, and zodiac incense holders are just a few items available.1730 Geary Blvd., #150, Kinokuniya Bldg., Japan Center, San Francisco; 415/921-2147.

Asiantique. In business in Berkeley since 1988, Asiantique specializes in antiques and reproductions from Asia, mainly Indonesia and Tibet. Home furnishings can also be made to order in several sizes and color finishes, and custom furniture to the customer's exact specifications is also available. 801 Delaware Ave., Berkeley; 510/528-8087, and 1036 Ashby Ave., Berkeley; 510/843-7515, www.asiantique.citymax.com.

Berkeley Mills. Berkeley Mills designs and builds-to-order hardwood furniture inspired by Arts and Crafts, Japanese, and Frank Lloyd Wright styles. Furniture melds East and West, balancing design and function. 2830 Seventh St., Berkeley; 510/549-2854, www.berkeleymills.com.

Dandelion. Established in 1968, Dandelion offers an extensive collection of traditional and contemporary designs for the home. Browse the unique selection of Japanese ceramic dinnerware, sake sets and pours, bronzewear, and bamboo craft. 55 Potrero Ave., San Francisco; 415/436-9500.

Suma. Suma presents handpicked home furnishings and other housewares, imported mostly from Thailand. The exquisite array of items are purchased by shop owner Marjorie Dial, who is willing to take special custom orders before her buying trips. 1224 9th Ave., San Francisco; 415/759-7862, www.sumaimports.com.

Toko Imports. Toko sells imported housewares, with a large percentage imported from the Philippines. Most are fashioned from recycled materials into attractive works of art. 1314 Grant Ave., San Francisco; 415/397-2323.

A Touch of Asia. This Cow Hollow boutique specializes in jewelry, antiques, and paintings. 1784 Union St., San Francisco; 415/474-3115.

The Wok Shop. In the heart of Chinatown for 33 years, The Wok Shop is a family-owned business specializing in hard-to-find Asian cooking utensils. The friendly staff are very knowledgeable. 718 Grant Ave., San Francisco; 415/989-3797, www.wokshop.com.

Zinc Details. The furnishings collection at Zinc Details takes its cue from

Japanese and Scandinavian designs, creating an eclectic mix with the store's own line of dinnerware, lighting, and other accessories. 1905 Fillmore St., San Francisco; 415/776-2100, and 1842 Fourth St., Berkeley; 510/540-8296, www.zincdetails.com.

Asian Image. 662 Grant Ave., San Francisco; 415/397-1897, and 800 Grant Ave., San Francisco; 415/398-2602.

City of Hong Kong. 519 Grant Ave., San Francisco; 415/982-1818.

Momen Futon. 1772 Union St., San Francisco; 415/922-7424.

Murasaki. 419 Water St., Oakland; 510/891-9929, www.murasakijacklondon.com.

Phoenix Gallery. 3391 Sacramento St., San Francisco; 415/749-0304, www.phoenixgallery.com.

Relin. 597 Grant Ave., San Francisco; 415/362-3785, www.relinsf.com.

Shiki. Japan Center, Kintetsu Building, 1737 Post St., San Francisco; 415/563-4550.

Townhouse Living. 1825 Post St., San Francisco; 415/563-1417.

Ying Shun Arts & Handicrafts. 833 Washington St., San Francisco; 415/983-0839.

Rugs

Afghan Treasures. Located in the heart of Union Square, Afghan Treasures features authentic hand woven Afghan and Iranian rugs and kelims, as well as furniture and other antiques. 976 Market St., San Francisco; 415/202-0193.

Jalili International. First founded in the city of Marand in Persia (Iran) in 1880. Over the course of the 20th century satellite offices have opened in London, Brussels, Dusseldorf, Hamburg, and Venlo (Holland). The San

Francisco office was established in 1979, and is managed by Kambiz Jalili, the fourth generation in this family business. Jalili offers a very large inventory of antique and semi-antique rugs and tapestries, and an extensive selection of contemporary rugs, India, Pakistan, Turkey, Egypt, Romania, Nepal, Tibet, and China. San Francisco Design Center, 101 Henry Adams St., Galleria Ste. 355, San Francisco; 415/788-3377, www.jalilirugs.com.

Kashmir Heritage. Offering hand-made and knotted Kashmiri carpets of the highest quality. Made on cotton or silk foundations with piles of silk, wool, mohair, cashmere or goat hair—some including a weave of silver or gold threads—all the carpets at Kashmir Heritage are inspected by the All India Silk Board prior to export. 310 Geary St., San Francisco; 415/839-4077. Other locations: Kashmir Royal Collection, 335 Powell St., San Francisco; 415/296-9012. Kashmir Gallery: 246 Powell St., San Francisco; 415/296-8148, www.kashmirheritage.com.

Nomad Rugs. Antique, traditional, and contemporary Middle Eastern and Central Asian rugs and kilims. 3775 24th St., San Francisco; 415/401-8833, www.nomadrugs.com.

Turkmen Collection. A very rich collection of authentic Afghan rugs. Services also include cleaning and repair. 500 University Ave., Palo Alto; 650/327-0668.

The Hatami Collection. 170 University Ave., Palo Alto; 650/321-6099.

Krimsa. 2190 Union St., San Francisco; 415/441-4321.

Magic Import Oriental Rugs. Little Kabul, 37468 Fremont Blvd., Fremont; 510/745-7691.

Peter Pap Oriental Rugs. 470 Jackson St., San Francisco; 888/581-6743, 415/956 3300, www.peterpap.com.

Sandra Whitman Gallery. 361 Oak St., San Francisco; 415/437-2402, www.sanfranciscoantiquedealers.com/sandrawhitman.

Tony Kitz Oriental Carpetry. 2843 Clay St, San Francisco; 415/346-2100.

Bookstores

Arkipelago Philippine Books. Dedicated to providing literary products from Southeast Asia, especially from the Philippines, to correct misinterpretations of Asian peoples & cultures in the United States. Arkipelago is also in search of authors or self-publishers to produce and distribute their books through their book production services. 953 Mission St., San Francisco; 415/777-0108, www.arkipelagobooks.com.

Eastwind Books & Arts. Founded in 1979, Eastwind Books & Arts houses one of the most extensive selections of Chinese language and Chinese-related books in the U.S. Publications hail from North America and Greater China. 1435 Stockton St., San Francisco; 415/772-5877, www.eastwindsf.com.

Eastwind Books of Berkeley. Formerly affiliated with the San Francisco store, this joint is owned by UC Berkeley professors, and it shows in the selection's intellectual breadth. Politics, health, ethnic studies, martial arts, pop culture and a nice selection of children's books are efficiently crammed in this relatively small space. 2066 University Ave., Berkeley; 510/548-2350, www.ewbb.com.

Kinokuniya Bookstore. Kinokuniya Bookstore boasts the country's largest selection of Japanese language books and books about Asia. Taking up a massive space in Japan Center, the sprawling book center offers an array of books on Japanese culture, food, and history. Guest appearances by authors and other events are held on occasion. 1581 Webster St., Kinokuniya Bldg., San Francisco; 415/567-7625, www.kinokuniya.com.

Rumi Book Store. Specializes in books on the history of Afghanistan, plus a collection of music and videos on Islam and the Middle East. The bookstore of course offers poetry, as well as books for children and families. 4050B Peralta Blvd., Little Kabul, Fremont; 510/744-3692, www.rumibookstore .com.

China Books & Periodicals. 2929 24th St., San Francisco; 415/282-2994, www.chinabooks.com.

Salve Regina Books & Gifts. 728 Pacific Ave. #115, San Francisco; 415/989-6279, www.salvereginabooks.com.

Sino-American Books & Arts Co. 751 Jackson St., San Francisco; 415/421-3345.

Tree of Life Bookshop. 1146 University Ave., San Jose; 408/283-0221, www.csecenter.org.

Zen Center Bookstore. 300 Page St., San Francisco; 415/255-6524, www.sfzc.org.

THE ARTS

P ROXIMITY AND POPULATION HAVE PUT CALI-
fornia at the forefront of Asian and emerging Asian American art. Its
western shores complete the geopolitical circle known as the Pacific Rim,
and in the San Francisco Bay Area, the Chinese, Japanese, Korean,
Pilipino, and Afghan diaspora account for some of the largest overseas
communities outside of the native countries.

While San Francisco may outnumber the East Coast in Asian and
Asian American residents, its size and history combine to make a smaller-
scale arts scene. Even though the Asian American population is twice as
large as Manhattan's, the city needs the additional mass of Oakland,
Berkeley, and San Jose to match the sheer size of New York City. Its New
World history lags 200 years behind New York, but its Pacific migrations,
which swelled after the late 1960s when the United States finally rolled
back its exclusionary acts, have created a modern Pan-Asian culture found
nowhere else in the world.

What has emerged is a dichotomy of art appreciation. One half is
steeped in a reverence for ancient civilizations and their high craftsmanship,
advanced design, and spiritual wisdom. The other half stems from a politically informed modernism acknowledging a unique American identity. The

two may not always overlap in museums and galleries, but the duality benefits art patrons who seek authenticity and identity.

These parallel veins can be traced back to San Francisco's topsy-turvy start. Railroads and agricultural bounty summoned thousands of workers from China, Japan, India, and the Philippines. At first, the West was more preoccupied with raw gold than polished artifacts, and encounters with Asia tended to be strictly on a working—and segregated—basis.

That separation continued as the nouveau riche soon sought to display material wealth. In the town built by fortune-hunters, a commercial store—not a museum—educated San Franciscans, and later the Western world, about Asian art.

In the mid-1800s, following Commodore Matthew Perry's foray into Meiji Japan the East Coast mania for Japanese products spread slowly to the West. Before then, Chinatown merchants sold porcelain, ivory, and jade mainly to their neighbors, although a few curious outsiders did venture into this quarter. One frequent visitor was Abe Gump, son of Solomon, cofounder of the famous store with his brother Gus.

In those early days, Gump's cluttered shelves reflected the preference for glittering, heavy European goods. Not until after the 1906 earthquake and fire, which destroyed the original storefront, and the takeover by the second Gump generation, did the shop's famous "Oriental Room" rise, first decorated with an altar rescued from a Chinatown Buddhist temple. Ironically, Chinatown storeowners, having lost their treasures in the conflagration, opted to stock up on cheaper goods. Gump eagerly stepped into the void, and even employed Chinatown sales techniques of hiding choice selections behind the counter, reserving them for suitable buyers. Soon a new Post Street locale re-created a Far East fantasyland on its second floor, drawing buyers, tourists, and dignitaries from throughout the world.

Gump promoted local artists, like famed watercolorist Chiura Obata, but its international glory lay in its phenomenal wares, including wood-panel Pilipino screens, possessions looted from the Imperial Palace after the 1911 overthrow of the Manchus, and Khmer sculptures from Cambodia's Angkor Thom. Gump stocked civic spaces (the Buddha in Golden Gate Park's Japanese Tea Garden), loaned out exhibits (the old Chinese Museum of Art in San Francisco), and seeded other great collections (Minneapolis's Walker Art Gallery and the Seattle Art Museum). Some goods have come full circle—Chicago millionaire Avery Brundage acquired pieces that have become part of the collection bequeathed to the Asian Art Museum.

Traditional wood-block prints, modern watercolors, and large sculptures came under the sphere of Japanese influence, from artists such as Obata and Isamu Noguchi. Later migratory patterns introduced Pilipino wood carvings and Indian statuary. The late 20th century appreciation for folk and tribal arts extends to goods from Tibet and Nepal—an appreciation propelled, in typical Bay Area fashion, by political awareness.

GALLERIES

The vocabulary for overseas Asian art has expanded from the familiar triumvirate of India, China, and Japan. Shifting political allegiances, new migration patterns, and the Western embrace of Asian spiritual concepts tell just a part of the changing portrait.

Today, ceramics and jade continue to enchant non-Asian collectors, with a special emphasis on snuff bottles. Asian and Asian American patrons more familiar with traditional arts favor paintings and calligraphy. In the last decade, the craze has been directed towards sacred arts and religious icons (Tibetan arts and all Buddhas in general). More recently, Korean celadon has become a popular collectible.

Gump's glory days are long past, but other galleries of repute have stepped in. **Xanadu Gallery** (140 Maiden Ln., 415/392-9999) in San Francisco and Santa Cruz stocks Indian and Southeast Asian items, especially Buddhas. Chinatown, otherwise swamped in tourist trinkets, boasts **Dragon House** (455 Grant Ave., 415/421-3693) as a leader in antique

DONG KINGMAN

Award-winning Dong Kingman (1911–2000) became a part of the movement known as the California Style School of Painting. Born Dong Muy Shu in Oakland, he moved to Hong Kong with his family at age five. Ironically, his adopted surname "King Man," a phonetic translation for "Scenery Composition," came from his days in Hong Kong, when he showed an early interest in art. He studied calligraphy and watercolor, and enrolled in the Fox Morgan Art School after he returned to Oakland in 1929.

Despite the Depression, Kingman worked as a newsboy and dishwasher before his career began to take off. A 1936 San Francisco solo exhibition featuring his blend of Chinese and Western sensibilities brought him to national attention. His scenes depicted San Francisco's urban vibe, and a 1937 exhibit moved an art critic to declare Kingman, with a somewhat tempered effusiveness, "San Francisco's number-one watercolorist at the present moment." His work as a WPA project artist cemented his national fame.

Kingman once explained, "I am Oriental when I paint trees and landscapes, but Occidental when I paint buildings, ships, or three-dimensional subjects with sunlight and shadow."

After World War II, Kingman taught at Columbia University and Hunter College in New York for a decade before eventually returning to San

Chinese porcelain and ceramics. Private dealers throughout the Bay Area deal in larger antiquities and specialized collections. Auctions and shows are another source for Asian antiquities, from the classic Butterfield auctions to the biennial San Francisco Arts of Pacific Asia Show.

Contemporary art galleries with a specialty in Asian American art are a rare sight in San Francisco, an ironic development given the prevalence of Asian-influenced design in industrial and home decor goods. The dot-com fallout of 2000 adversely affected the patronage of art centers in general. Collectors who want contemporary art usually go to private dealers, such as **Wylie Wong** (by appointment only, 415/626-1014), who also serves as the curator for the Chinese Cultural Center in San Francisco.

More often, Asian American artists are integrated into consciously

Francisco, where he taught at the Academy College of Art. He also did film work, working as a technical advisor and providing title background art for movies like *55 Days in Peking*, *The Flower Drum Song*, and *Lost Horizons*. In 1976 he even produced a short film, *Hong Kong Dong*, which won Outstanding Achievement Award for Best Short Film at the 1976 San Francisco International Film Festival.

Appointed a cultural ambassador in the 1950s, his role as a unifying force was impressively underscored in a 1981 exhibit of his works in Beijing, the first American one-man show after diplomatic relations resumed between the United States and China. His distinctive style captured the San Francisco cityscape, from murals at the Bank of California to a 1967 book written by *San Francisco Chronicle* columnist Herb Caen, *San Francisco: City on Golden Hills*.

"Dong Kingman in San Francisco" served as the centerpiece exhibit for the revamped Chinese Historical Society of America and Museum. A 2002–2003 retrospective of his seven-decade career, "Dong Kingman: Watercolor Master," toured the world, with stops in Beijing, Hong Kong, and Shanghai. His work continues to be exhibited in American and international museums.

multi-cultural and multi-disciplinary organizations such as the **Yerba Buena Center for the Arts** (701 Mission St., 415/978-ARTS or 415/978-2787). Small galleries like **Pro Arts** in Oakland also promote the message of multicultural art.

WORKSHOPS

On a grassroots level, the stalwart **Kearny Street Workshop** (934 Brannan St., 415/503-0520) has showcased up-and-coming Asian American artists since 1972. Kearny Street Workshop's pan-Asian emphasis parallels its multidisciplinary approach to the arts, which has included holding classes, grooming writers (Jessica Hagedorn, Gemmy Lim), promoting artists, and jumpstarting the Asian American Jazz Festival (which was handed over to

Asian Arts Improv). Since 1999, Kearny Street Workshop's largest venture has been APAture, an annual expo featuring works of 100 Bay Area artists from the ages of 18 to 35.

Kearny Street Workshop's 30-odd year existence encapsulates nearly the entire political history of the Asian American movement. It originally was founded in 1972 at the old International Hotel to promote local art from Chinatown. Kearny Street Workshop later opened the Jackson Street Gallery in the former space of the infamous Hungry I, the burlesque joint and performing venue for acts like Phyllis Diller, Barbra Streisand, and Bette Midler. In 1977, the hotel owners evicted the center and the elderly low-income Pilipino and Chinese tenants. The evictions spurred mostly insular Chinatown and Manilatown inhabitants into a show of public protest that launched modern Asian American activism. (Ultimately the tenants lost out and, in a cruel twist of irony, the hotel was razed and never rebuilt. As of print time, a mixed-use facility is still in the planning stages with the Housing and Urban Development federal program.) Since then, Kearny Street Workshop has moved six times—a reflection of artists' nomadic status in the chaotic San Francisco market—but its journeys have picked up a diverse following along the way. Priced out of its last location—dot-com epicenter South Park in 2000—it currently resides in the **SomArts Cultural Center.**

MUSEUMS

The undisputed one-stop resource is the **Asian Art Museum** (200 Larkin St., 415/581-3500), which left its cramped wing of the de Young Museum in Golden Gate Park in 2000 and opened in the former San Francisco Main Library in 2003.

The **Chinese Culture Center** (750 Kearny St., 415/986-1822), on the third floor of the Holiday Inn at Chinatown's edge maintains a link between the homeland and its diaspora through exhibits, concerts, and martial arts and Cantonese opera classes. Besides historical exhibits, such as *Chinese of America: 1786-1980*, the Center also covers pop culture from the past (*101 Heroes of Shui Hu Zhuan: Shiwan Ceramics and Paintings*) and present (*Bruce Lee*). One of its more popular offerings is its Chinatown Walks.

A few blocks away is the **Chinese Historical Society of America and Learning Center** (965 Clay St., 415/391-1188). Besides a permanent overview of Chinese American history, the society hosts changing exhibits featuring contemporary artists, such as watercolorist Dong Kingman and Hollywood illustrators Wah Ming Chang and Tyrus Wong.

Outside San Francisco and a stone's throw from Oakland's Chinatown, the **Oakland Museum of California** (1000 10th St., 510/238-2200), has on occasion hosted exhibits ranging from the rare *Imperial Treasures of China* to a retrospective on local sculptor Ruth Asawa. Its conscientious multi-cultural focus highlights Latino, African American, and Asian American local life, historic ritual, and traditional celebration. The **Berkeley Art Museum** (2625 Durant Ave. and 2575 Bancroft Way, 510/642-0808), two blocks from the University of California Berkeley campus, holds a store of more than 13,000 objects, which include the Jean and Francis Marshall collections of Indian miniatures and some Chinese paintings from the collections of Professor Emeritus James Cahill and his family. **The Pacific Film Archive,** the museum's twin in the area of motion pictures, contains the largest collection of Japanese movies outside of Japan.

Another educational powerhouse, Stanford University, boasts the **Iris and B. Gerald Cantor Visual Center for the Arts** (328 Lomita, 650/723-4177). Notable for its August Rodin Sculpture Garden, the spacious contemporary array of galleries counts Asian art among its many collections. The impetus for Asian art came from the desire of Leland Stanford Jr. to bring back treasures from China and Japan. He died of typhoid fever at 15 before he could accomplish this, and his mother acquired Japanese, Chinese, and Korean works in his stead. Additions over the years have

ASIAN ART MUSEUM

The undisputed emperor of collections, the Asian Art Museum of San Francisco has become the absolute museum stop on the West Coast for an encyclopedic look into the arts and cultures of Asia. After years as an adjunct to the M.S. de Young Museum in Golden Gate Park, the museum moved to its new Civic Center home in 2003 with the help of a $15 million gift by Silicon Valley entrepreneur Chong-Moon Lee. The new Asian is now an institutional presence in San Francisco, situated across from City Hall.

The force behind the Asian Art Museum's beginnings was neither Asian nor San Franciscan; rather, it was Chicago millionaire Avery Brundage. At the request of Marjorie Walter Bessinger, Brundage bestowed part of his art collection to the city in 1959 on the condition that San Francisco would build a proper setting for it. A new wing of the de Young Museum devoted to the Brundage collection was opened seven years later. This wing was enhanced when Brundage gave a second gift in 1969 in an effort to make the Asian art wing the premiere center in the West. When Brundage died in 1975, he donated the last of his 7,700 works of Asian art to the museum.

The Museum was transformed from its former incarnation as the San Francisco Public Library by Italian architect Gae Aulenti, who is famed for

resulted in 4,000-plus objects, some of which date to the Neolithic period.

Over in San Jose, the tiny **Japanese American Museum of Santa Clara Valley** (535 N. 5th St., 408/294-3138) opens only a few hours a day, but provides an archival overview of the Central Valley pioneers and walking tours to the adjacent Japantown, one of only three in the United States, protected by the California Japantown Preservation Pilot Project.

ARCHITECTURE AND LANDSCAPE

In Japantown controversy still exists at the **Peace Plaza and Pagoda**, designed by Tokyo architect Yoshiro Taniguchi, thanks to "improvements" that have fiddled with the original design. The plaza, envisioned as a gathering place for celebrations, serves that purpose only a few times a year for events like the Cherry Blossom Festival. More often, the concrete layout adapting old spaces into new museums. The 29,000-square-feet exhibition space of the new Asian allows the museum to exhibit twice as much art as it could in its former home. At any one time, 2,500 of the museum's 15,000-piece collection is on display.

The flow of the museum reflects the movement of ideas and influences through Asia. Three themes—the spread of Buddhism, trade, and local beliefs and practices—guide the museum-goer's journey through the geography of Asia and the history of Asian art. Moving from room to room, visitors encounter masterworks from India, West Asia, Southeast Asia, the Himalayas, China, Korea, and Japan, while tracing the spread of ideas across these cultures. This geographic and historical journey is complemented by rotating contemporary art exhibitions presenting innovative works by Asian and Asian American artists.

The new space includes highlights such as the magnificent Jade Gallery, a traditional Japanese Tearoom with regular programs on the tea ceremony, a retail store full of unique items, and Café Asia, offering wonderful Asian-inspired selections. Plan on spending a day to absorb and appreciate the spectacular collections and setting.

serves as a thoroughfare to the indoor mall.

More successful is the Japantown pedestrian mall across the street, with the approachable scale of its storefronts and the quiet origami-inspired fountains by local architect Ruth Asawa.

Asawa has been pivotal not only in the art and architecture scene, but also in sustaining arts instruction at San Francisco elementary schools. Her works include the round cityscape in bronze near Union Square, the Mermaid Fountain at Ghirardelli Square, the Hyatt Fountain at Union Square, and the Japanese American Internment Memorial Sculpture at the San Jose Federal Building.

European training and Californian sensibilities have contributed much to the look of such buildings as the tile-topped **Chinese Culture Center,** formerly the Chinatown YWCA, designed by the famous Julia Morgan

CHIURA OBATA

Landscape and woodblock artist Chiura Obata forged new paths as one of the first Japanese artists in the United States, but his most memorable works may come from the tragic period of the Japanese internments in America. Hundreds of paintings and sketches preserved that period of confinement portraying both the cruel desolation and unexpected beauty of those desert camps.

Born in 1885 in Japan, Chiura Obata, at an early age, showed his skill with *sumi-e,* or brush paintings. In his teens he studied with leading Tokyo artists, then made his way to the Western world to broaden his art studies. He emigrated to San Francisco three years before the earthquake, and made sketches of the devastation for Japanese newspapers. Living in San Francisco's Japantown, he worked as an illustrator for Japanese publications, and also painted murals and works for department stores, such as the famous Lotus Room ceiling at Gump's. His great talent was in landscapes, including more than 100 paintings of Yosemite and the Sierras. From these paintings, he created 35 prize-winning colored woodblock prints in Japan.

In 1932, he began teaching at the UC Berkeley art department, and also opened a Berkeley studio where he and his wife Haruko taught classes in art

(who also did the Japantown YWCA). While the Asian Art Museum is housed in a decidedly Beaux Arts structure built in 1907 and revamped by Italian Gae Aulenti, architects Hellmuth, Obata & Kassabaum, LDA Architects, and Robert Wong Architect joined in adapting the neoclassical as a backdrop.

While its work will likely not be on any tourist route, the award-winning Asian Neighborhood Design reclaims space for low-income populations, originally working with predominantly Asian neighborhoods and then spreading to other areas. Its successful projects include the south of Market **Tutubi Park** (Tagalog for dragonfly), and the **Ashbury House** in the Haight-Ashbury district.

What truly thrives in temperate Northern California climes are the gardens. The tranquility of the **Japanese Tea Garden** (415/752-1171) has and *ikebana* (flower-arranging). His tenure was interrupted in 1942 when they, with thousands of other Japanese and Japanese Americans, were interned at the Tanforan Detention Center. There, the man who had helped found the East West Art Society (with Chinese, Russian, Japanese, and American artists) in the 1920s created an arts school which the 650-plus camp residents attended. After being released from a second relocation camp, Topaz, the Obatas moved to St. Louis until the military exclusion ban was lifted in 1945. He returned to Berkeley, and received a promotion to associate professor of art in 1948. Six years later, he became a citizen and retired as professor emeritus.

Exhibitions of his work continue to be showcased, from the Oakland Museum and the Smithsonian to the de Young Museum. The 1993 book, *Obata's Wilderness*, compiles his Yosemite paintings. In conjunction with a 2000 Berkeley Art Museum exhibit, Berkeley-based publisher Heyday Books released *Topaz Moon: Chiura Obata's Art of the Internment*, edited by his granddaughter Kimi Kodani Hill. The Sierra Nevada Wilderness Project and the Yosemite Fund host an online exhibit, "The Great Nature of Chiura Obata" on http://obata.wilderness.net.

survived since 1894, when Baron Makoto Hagiwara built a Japanese village for the World's Fair. A benevolent Buddha, dated about 1790, is the oldest artifact in the city's collection and was a gift from Gump's in 1943.

Going south to the Peninsula, the San Mateo **Japanese Garden in Central Park** (650/522-7440) was designed by Nagao Sakurai, a landscape artist for the Imperial Palace of Tokyo. **Japanese Friend Garden** (408/277-4191) in Kelly Park marks the bond between San Jose and sister city Okayama, and duplicates that Japanese town's famed Korakuen Park.

Finally, while a bit of a trek from San Francisco, the **Hakone Gardens** (408/741-4994) in Saratoga are exceptionally noteworthy. Oliver and Isabel Stine, inspired by the 1915 Pan-Pacific Exhibition, crafted this 15-acre paradise with the requisite Zen and tea gardens, bamboo, and koi pond. The reproduction of a 19th-century Kyoto tea merchant's home and shop, built by visiting Japanese artisans in the traditional no-nails method, came later in 1991.

PUBLIC ARTWORKS

Public art can be a lightning rod among artistically passionate San Franciscans, and time does not necessarily endear controversial works. For instance, while Chicagoans flaunt Picasso's horse-like vision of women, critics still lobby for the removal of the Embarcadero's *Vaillancourt Fountain* (years after the late San Francisco columnist Herb Caen stingingly compared the 1971 homage to industrial seamen to poop).

Nevertheless, sculpture in San Francisco indeed exists, with a number by significant Asian and Asian American artists. Japanese sculptors seem to have the edge with **International Airport's** abstract bronze figure by Japanese legend Isamu Noguchi, a 12-foot-high polished rectangular block by Seiji Kunishima, and a black granite peace monument in **Lincoln Park,** to commemorate the peace between the United States and Japan. The *Origami Fountain* by Japanese American architect and sculptor Ruth Asawa is one of Japantown's successes.

North Beach and Chinatown hold the most visible representations of Asian-themed art. Chinese American artist Al Wong created *Light Clouds,* a red-lanterned tipped glass awning for Fire Station No. 2, where North Beach and Chinatown meet.

Sculptures of important Asian historical figures include Zlatko Paunov's bronze rendition of Indian leader Mohandas K. Gandhi, who peers nearsightedly at the waterfront off of the Embarcadero (as a miscreant stole his spectacles). Italian sculptor Benjamino Bufano, whose broad animal shapes are a favorite in the city, crafted the statue of Dr. Sun Yat-Sen that stands at the border of North Beach and Chinatown.

THE ARTS

Museums

Angel Island Immigration Station Museum. Surrounded by controversy from its inception, the Angel Island Immigration station was officially put into operation in 1910, "processing" over 175,000 detainees over the next 30 years. Most visitors will want to see the numerous poems scratched into the walls of the detention cells by Chinese immigrants. Ferries travel to the island from Tiburon and San Francisco. Visit www.angelisland.org for visitor information.

Asian Art Museum of San Francisco. San Francisco's Asian Art Museum holds the distinction of being one of the largest art museums in the world devoted solely to Asian art. The building itself (formerly the main branch of the San Francisco library) is an attraction—reworked by architect Gae Aulenti, whose previous projects include Paris' Musee d'Orsay. The Asian's impressive holdings include more than 13,000 sculptures, paintings, and ceramics from 40 countries, including China, Korea, Iran, Turkey, Syria, India, Tibet, Nepal, Pakistan, India, Japan, Afghanistan, and Southeast Asia. 200 Larkin St., San Francisco; 415/581-3500, www.asianart.org.

Berkeley Art Museum. Aside from works by the likes of Pollock and Rothko, the museum features Buddhist mandalas, Chinese paintings, Indian miniatures, and other Asian art over five floors of galleries. 2626 Bancroft Way, Berkeley; 510/642-0808, www.bampfa.berkeley.edu.

Chinese Historical Society of America Museum and Learning Center. Housed in the former YWCA (designed by Julia Morgan), the center offers a modern, often scholarly take of Chinese-American history. Its exhibits feature the works of modern Asian American artists. Besides community classes, the museum is an important source of genealogical research. 965 Clay St., San Francisco; 415/391-1188, www.chsa.org.

Gadar Memorial House. Contact the India Consulate General to arrange a visit to browse the library of Hindi and English books on Indian culture and history. 5 Wood St., San Francisco; 415/668-0662, www.indianconsulate -sf.org.

Iris and B. Gerald Cantor Visual Center for the Arts at Stanford University. The 1989 Loma Prieta earthquake knocked this Center out of commission for 10 years, but its 1999 re-opening premiered an elegant, expanded space. Among its impressive permanent pieces is its Buck Jade collection. 328 Lomita Dr. and Museum Way, Palo Alto; 650/723-4177, www.stanford.edu/dept/ccva.

Japanese American Museum San Jose (JAMsj). This museum hosts some contemporary art exhibits, but mostly focuses on the history of Japanese Americans in San Jose and the Santa Clara Valley. Borne from a research project on early pioneers in the Valley, the museum is filled with historical photographs, private memoirs, and unpublished historical documents. Docents give walking tours of Japantown. 535 N. 5th St., San Jose; 408/294.3138, www.jamsj.org.

Oakland Museum of California. Devoted to the art, history, and natural sciences of California. Those interested in Asian cultures will want to visit the museum's Pacific Regional Ethnographic Collection—approximately 3,400 objects and photographs from Polynesia, Melanesia, Micronesia, Australia, the Philippines, and Indonesia. The Rabe Collection forms the centerpiece of the museum's Pacific region collections. It is notable both for its breadth and scope, but also for the quality of the associated documentation. 1000 Oak St, Oakland; 510/238-2200, www.museumca.org.

Pacific Film Archive. The film counterpart to the Berkeley Art Museum is an incredible cinematic resource, including a huge collection of Japanese films—the largest collection outside of Japan. 2625 Durant Ave., Berkeley; 510/642-0808; www.bampfa.berkeley.edu.

Pacific Heritage Museum. Located in a U.S. sub-treasury building, the museum houses a variety of temporary exhibits featuring works from places such as the National Palace Museum in Taipei and the Center for the Pacific Rim at the University of San Francisco. There is also a video room with films focusing on Chinese writing, calligraphy, painting, porcelain, and other traditional arts. 608 Commercial St., San Francisco; 415/362-4100.

Japanese American History Archives. 1840 Sutter St., San Francisco; 415/776-0661, www.amacord.com/fillmore/museum/jt/jaha/jaha.html.

Japanese Tea Garden. Located in Golden Gate Park on Tea Garden Dr. near the de Young museum (under construction). 415/752-4227.

Museum of Craft & Folk Art. Fort Mason Center, Landmark Building A, San Francisco; 415/775-0991.

San Francisco Museum of Modern Art. 151 3rd St., San Francisco; 415/357-4000, www.sfmoma.org.

San Jose Museum of Art. 110 S. Market St., San Jose; 408/294-2787, www.sjmusart.org.

Triton Museum of Art. 1505 Warburton Ave., Santa Clara; 408/247-3754.

Galleries

Dento. Dento, which means tradition in Japanese, is dedicated to preserving some of the traditional Japanese crafts that are dying out in today's modern Japanese society. Everything in this gallery is hand-crafted by somebody in Japan, often the last masters in various formats—whether it's whimsical clay dolls from a father and son team in Tokyo, the last family keeping that tradition, or detailed woodblock printing. There are also performances of classical Japanese dance on a small stage in back.1737 Post St., Ste. 365, San Francisco; 415/359-9570.

F. Dorian. This gallery exhibits a collection of objects from all over Asia, from Japan to Afghanistan. Some works include carved deities from China and painted window shutters from the yurts of nomadic tribes. 370 Hayes St., San Francisco; 415/861-3191, www.fdorian.com.

Freddie Fong Contemporary Art. Sharing a space with other galleries, this tiny space showcases modern, mostly black-and-white work. Phelan Building, 760 Market St. #258, San Francisco; 415/566-1910, www.freddiefong.com.

International Art Gallery. This gallery features antique Japanese woodblock prints from the Ukoyo-e period of art, which formed in the late 16th/early 17th century. There are also prints from the Shin Hanga period in the early 20th century, as well as contemporary works. Japan Center #203, 1581 Webster St., San Francisco; 415/567-4390, www.tokaidoarts.com.

Intersection for the Arts. The oldest alternative art space in the city, rising artists often debut here. The emphasis on diversity covers not only the artists themselves, but the offerings, which range from music to poetry to art. 446 Valencia St., San Francisco; 415/626-2787, www.theintersection.org.

LIMN Gallery. The popular LIMN furniture store also owns a 4,000-plus square-foot gallery that features Chinese contemporary art from the Bay Area and from all over the world. Exhibits rotate every couple of months. 292 Townsend St., San Francisco; 415/977-1300.

Michael Leu Fine Arts Gallery. Cat lovers will find an array of amusing caricatures to choose from at the Michael Leu gallery. Other themes include women and landscapes, all done in bold colors, whether it's an oil painting, watercolor, or work in mixed media. 611 Post St., San Francisco; 415/345-1988, www.michaelleu.com.

ProArts Gallery. In Old Oakland, adjacent to Chinatown, the 3,000 square-foot nonprofit gallery hosts multicultural exhibits and special events. 461 Ninth St., Oakland; 510/763-4361, www.proartsgallery.org.

Takada Gallery. The works at Takada Gallery at Union Square tend to focus on minimalist and abstract art from Japan. Most ofthe art is either paintings or works on paper. 251 Post St., 6th floor, San Francisco; 415/956-5288, www.takadagallery.com.

Togonon Gallery. This contemporary art gallery opened in 1994, and since then explores culture and meaning through exhibitions of emerging and established West Coast artists. Ethnicity is explored more in the context of the American experience. 1821 Powell St., San Francisco; 415/291-9255, www.togonongallery.com.

TriangleGallery. Owner Jack Van Hiele has exhibited contemporary Asian and Asian American artists, as well as local artists for more than a quarter-century. 47 Kearny St., San Francisco; 415/392-1686.

T.Z. SHIOTA Oriental Objects of Art. Run by the Shiota family for more than a century, this gallery specializes in Japanese prints. 3131 Fillmore St., San Francisco; 415/929-7979, www.tzshiotagallery.com.

Xanadu Gallery. Housed in San Francisco's only Frank Lloyd Wright building, Xanadu Gallery is worth a visit just for the Guggenheim-style interior itself. A circular, spiraling walkway connects two floors of colorful folk art from all reaches of the world, including antique Vietnamese porcelain jarlets, and 3rd century A.D. Bodhisattva statues from Pakistan. 140 Maiden Ln., San Francisco; 415/392-9999.

Yerba Buena Center for the Arts. Somewhere between a museum, community center and gallery, the center covers a broad range of visual and performing arts. Its artist-in-residence program, exhibits, and concept as "idea house" take on a multicultural bent. 701 Mission St., San Francisco; 415/978-ARTS, www.yerbabuena.org.

Baxter Chang Patri Fine Art. Located inside the Hotel Nikko. 222 Mason St., San Francisco; 415/397-2000, www.baxterchangpatri.com.

Kee Fung Ng Gallery. 757 Grant Ave., San Francisco; 415/434-1844.

Shakris Fine Asian Works of Art. 954 Bush St., San Francisco; 415/929-0280.

Willits Center Gallery. 3755 Washington Blvd., Fremont; 510/979-5600, www.willitscenter.com.

Architecture and Landscape

Asian Art Museum. George Kelham, 1917. Remodeled by Gale Aulenti, with LDA Architects, Robert Wong and Hellmuth, Obata & Kassabaum, 2003. The renovations opened up the interior of the classic Beaux Arts frame with an indoor court open to natural lighting. The main staircase and grand hall have been retained, while a series of interior walls painted in monochrome colors ranging from gray to jade makes the 29,000 square feet of gallery space intimate and accessible. The most obviously "Asian" space is the tiny and charming Betty Bogart contemplative alcove. An interesting bit of lineage: HOK founding partner Gyo Obata is son of artist and UC Berkeley professor Chiura Obata. 200 Larkin St., San Francisco.

Bank of Canton building. A teller who remembers your name is a rare commodity nowadays. Back in 1894, when the pagoda building housed the Chinese Telephone Exchange, 20 female operators not only memorized telephone subscribers' names (identifying a person by a number was considered rude), but also their addresses and occupations in the case of folks with the same name. They also spoke five dialects as well as English. The exchange closed in 1949 with the advent of rotary dial phones, and the Bank of Canton purchased and restored the building in 1960. The building was also home to San Francisco's first newspaper, *The California Star.* 701 Grant Ave., San Francisco.

Chinese Six Companies. The 1908 building still houses the benevolent society, a union of family and clan organizations to govern Chinatown life and protect its interest in the outside world. 843 Stockton St., San Francisco.

Nam Kue School. Founded by the Fook Yum Benevolent Society and designed by Charles Rogers in 1925, the school provided a place to teach Chinese culture and language—unlike the nearby Commodore Stockton School, which banned Chinese on its premises. 765 Sacramento St., San Francisco.

Gum Moon Residence. One of three Chinatown buildings designed by Julia Morgan in a Florentine villa style, this 1912 edifice served as a shelter for Chinese girls sold into slavery and prostitution. Later, the home included an orphanage and then a kindergarten for children excluded from public schools because of the Chinese Exclusion Act. It continues to provide transitional housing for Asian women. Morgan also designed the Donaldina Cameron House, at 920 Sacramento St., in 1908, and the former Chinatown YWCA, at 940 Powell St., in 1932. 940 Washington St., San Francisco.

Hakone Japanese Tea Garden. The oldest Japanese-style residential gardens in the Western hemisphere, Hakone Gardens covers 18 acres with hillside arrangements, historic buildings, multi-tiered waterfalls and koi ponds, strolling gardens, unique lanterns, and stonework. 21000 Big Basin Way, Saratoga; 408/741-4994, www.hakone.com.

Hayward Japanese Gardens. Designed by Kimura Kimio in 1980, this public space in Hayward features three acres of native California plants arranged in traditional Japanese style, plus a koi pond and teahouse. 22373 N. 3rd St., Hayward; 510/881-6700.

Japanese Friendship Garden in Kelly Park. The "friendship" denotes the relationship between San Jose and sister city Okayama. The seven-acre park was modeled after that Japanese city's Korakuen Park. Its open spaces differ from traditional Japanese gardens, but it's still stocked with koi ponds, streams, a waterfall, and teahouse. 1300 Senter Rd., San Jose; 408/277-4191, www.sjparks.org.

Japanese Tea Garden. Four acres long, this is the oldest Japanese garden in California. Designed by Baron Makoto Hagiwara as a Japanese Village for the 1894 California Mid-Winter Exposition, it still retains the Moon Bridge, tea house and pool from the original construction. Tea Garden and Martin Luther King Jr. Drives, Golden Gate Park, San Francisco; 415/752-1171.

Nihonmanchi/Japan Center. Minoru Yamasaki, 1968. Three blocks and five acres in size, the Japan Center comprises two malls and the Radisson Miyako hotel and its open courtyards. Tokyo architect Yoshiro Taniguchi designed the Peace Plaza and five-story pagoda, which has since undergone some changes. The wooden drum tower (*yaguro*) and copper-roofed walkway bridging the malls are of architectural interest, although the building exteriors themselves, modeled after the Shoji school of architecture, are unexceptional. A notable treat is local artist Ruth Asawa's origami fountains, made of fieldstone, with tri-level seating and brick floor. 1737 Post St., San Francisco.

Old St. Mary's. With its mission to educate the Chinese about Catholicism, the church certainly benefited from their labor. The 1853 Gothic revival church, the first cathedral in California and registered historic landmark, had its granite quarried and cut in China, and the bricks were brought around Cape Horn. Chinese laborers put together the building, which destroyed in the 1906 earthquake and rebuilt three years later. Across the street at St. Mary's Square stands the 12-foot steel-and-rose granite statue of Sun Yat Sen, by sculptor Benjamino Bufano. 660 California St., San Francisco.

Oriental Warehouse. This 1868 San Francisco landmark had been a bonded warehouse that stored merchandise from Asia. Two fires in 1988 and

1994 and the 1989 Loma Prieta earthquake battered it. In 1997, rehabilitation turned it into an award-winning residential housing structure with 66 units. 650 First St., San Francisco.

Portsmouth Square. The gathering place for pigeons and elderly men playing checkers during the day, and the Chinatown markets at night, Portsmouth Square was originally the plaza for the Spanish colonial port town of Yerba Buena. Architects Clement Chen/Warnecke & Assoc. created this opens pace in 1971. 750 Kearny St., San Francisco.

San Mateo Japanese Garden in Central Park. Designed by Nagao Sakurai, former chief landscape architect at Japan's Imperial Palace, in 1966, this one-acre retreat offers a granite pagoda (donated by San Mateo sister city Toyonaka), teahouse, lanterns, bamboo groves, rare plants, and a koi pond. East 5th St., San Mateo; 650/522-7440, www.ci.sanmateo.ca.us /dept/parks/locations/teagarden.html.

The Sing Chong and Sing Fat buildings. After the devastation of the 1906 earthquake, the Sing Chong building was one of the first structures in San Francisco to be rebuilt. Architectural firm Ross and Burgren designed both buildings in 1908. California St. and Grant Ave., San Francisco.

Arts Organizations

3rd I SF. Presents independent filmmakers from Bangladesh, Bhutan, India, Nepal, The Maldives, Pakistan, Sri Lanka, Tibet, and other South Asian countries. 3rd I offers these artists film screenings, filmmaking courses, networking resources, and a distribution channel for the South Asian-American film community. 992 Valencia St., San Francisco; www.thirdi.org.

Asian American Women Artists Association. Located at the Kearny Street Workshop at SomArts. 934 Brannan St., San Francisco; www .aawaaart.com.

Asian Improv Arts. A promoter of visual and performing Asian American arts, the group oversees the Asian American Jazz Festival, Asian Pacific American Arts & Heritage Festival, and serves as a contact for the California Asian American and Pacific Islander Arts Network, a state-wide alliance of community, arts, and performing groups. 1375 Sutter St., San Francisco; 415/353-5732, www.asianimprov.com.

Association for Viet Arts. Dedicated since 1991 to the advancement of Vietnamese American artists, AVA promotes visual, performing, and literary arts. Projects include traditional folk music concerts, poetry readings, multimedia performances, painting exhibits, and cultural workshops. P. O. Box 90088, San Jose; www.vietarts.org.

Chinese Culture Center. The center offers a variety of cultural events, including exhibitions of traditional and contemporary art, performances of Chinese Opera and dance, classes in Chinese language, painting and floral design, publications, tours, artists workshops, and craft fairs. The center also donates its facilities to the Chinatown Community Arts Program. 750 Kearny St., 3rd Floor, San Francisco; 415/986-1822, www.c-c-c.org.

EKTA. EKTA relies solely on community funding to promote the artistic endeavors of South Asians in sharing their literature, music,and visual arts, and in staging theatre and dance presentations. P.O. Box 2302, Berkeley; www.ektaonline.org.

Ikenobo Ikebana Society of America. Founded in 1970, the society arranges workshops by visiting professors from their Kyoto-based headquarters and provides information and assistance to the general public on the subject of traditional Japanese flower arranging. 1737 Post St., #385, Kintetsu Mall, Japan Center, San Francisco; 415/567-1011.

Japanese Cultural and Community Center of Northern California. In the heart of Japantown, the center covers the spectrum in teaching traditional practices, including Japanese vegetarian cooking, martial arts, ikebana, shibori, kirakiraboshi choirs (Japanese children's song), and taiko (drumming). 1840 Sutter St., San Francisco; 415/567-5505; www.jcccnc .org.

Kearny Street Workshop. Kearny Street is the oldest multidisciplinary Asian Pacific American arts organization in the United States, working to preserve and inspire cultural connection within the Asian community, as well as give an outlet to local artists and performers. Exhibitions and events are often held at the SomArts space, the workshop's home. 934 Brannan St., San Francisco; 415/503.0520, www.kearnystreet.org.

KoreanYouth Cultural Center. The non profit organization teaches traditional Korean dance, drumming and song, including *pungmul*, *minyo* and *talchum*. The youth groups have performed at fairs, festivals, and the Ethnic Dance Festival. The center hosts an annual arts festival of its own in the fall. 4216 Telegraph Ave., Oakland; 510/652-4964; www.kycc.net.

Locus. Locus is an all-volunteer organization of Asian American artists and arts supporters that helps present the music, theatre, performing, literary, and visual arts of the Asian Pacific American community. Its main function is to provide physical space for performers to develop, rehearse, and display their works. Locus also hosts performances and events. Locus shares space with the Galeria de la Raza. 2857 24th St., San Francisco; 415/826-8009, www.locusarts.org.

National Japanese American Historical Society. The Historical Society specializes in exhibits touching on Japanese American culture and history and publishes a quarterly magazine, *Nikkei Heritage*. 1684 Post St., San Francisco; 415/921-5007, www.njahs.org.

Pacific Bridge. Beth Graves and Geoffry Dorn connect contemporary Southeast Asian artists with galleries, buyers, and other artists. Pacific Bridge maintains a residency program and curates exhibitions in leading Bay Area art spaces. 510/654-3212, www.asianartnow.com.

Yuki Teikei Haiku Society. Founded in San Jose in 1975,the society fosters the art of Haiku writing in English and has grown to an international organization of about 90 poets. The Society hosts monthly haiku writing and study meetings, publishes a bimonthly work/study journal, *Geppo*, and holds an annual haiku retreat on the Monterey Peninsula. www.youngleaves.org.

American School of Japanese Arts. 2000 Los Olivos, Santa Rosa; 707/537-9507.

Sogetsu Ikebana. 15040 Deniterera Creek Rd., San Jose; 408/259-5784.

Theater

Asian American Theater Company. The theater company celebrated its 30th anniversary in 2004. Although hit hard by the dotcom crash and other factors, the company continues to support new playwrights. It hosts its shows at the SomArts Theater at 934 Brannan St. The Asian American Theater Company was established in 1973 to develop and present original works of theater by, for, and about Americans of Asian and Pacific Islander descent. The company hosts a variety of productions. 690 5th St., Ste. 211, San Francisco; 415/543-5738, www.asianamericantheater.org.

Bindlestiff Studio. Bindlestiff Studio, touted as the first Filipino American theater in the country, presents Filipino American culture and the arts through concerts, theater, readings, as well as public workshops. The studio encourages experimentation with multimedia sources such as film and music, as well as visual and literary arts. Currently located in a temporary space on Natoma Alley, across the street from their old residence at 185 6th St., San Francisco; 415/974-1167, www.bindlestiffstudio.org.

Eth-Noh-Tec. Performs throughout the United States and abroad with several storytelling theater programs, workshops and residencies. They mix music, theater, dance, and the spoken word. 977 South Van Ness Ave.,

San Francisco; 415/282-8705, www.ethnohtec.org.

Naatak. Originally established by Stanford and UC Berkeley students, Naatak presents Indian theater and independent film to Bay Area audiences. The group operates under a highly charitable and supportive set of operating guidelines. 510/795-2726, www.naatak.com.

Teatro ng Tanan. Loosely translated as "Theater for the people," Teatro ng Tanan strives to promote a better understanding of Pilipino culture through its presentations, and to support developing new writers and directors. 415/974-1384.

Music and Dance

Academy of Hawaiian Arts. In 2002, Mark Keali'i Ho'omalu disbanded his award-winning dance troupe, Na Mele Hula Ohana, and opened this academy in Monterey, with a division in Oakland. The Kumu Hula (lead instructor) concentrates on seminars and his original work, some of which was featured in the Disney film *Lilo and Stitch*. His academy still offers hula lessons. 10700 MacArthur Blvd., Ste. 4, Oakland; 510/635-2160, www.academyofhawaiianarts.com.

Ali Akbar College of Music. To call either the school or its master, Ali Akbar Khan, an institution would be an understatement. Students learn to play the classical music of North India from internationally recognized sarode maestro Akbar Khan and the tabla maestro Swapan Chaudhuri. The facility also includes a concert hall. 215 West End Ave., San Rafael; 415/454-6264, www.aacm.org.

Alleluia Panis Dance Theater. The award-winning dance theater artist, who has received awards from organizations such as the Rockefeller Foundation and the National Endowment for the Arts, fuses modern movement, tribal anthropology, and fighting arts. 474 Faxon Ave., San Francisco; 415/239-0249, www.kularts.org.

Cirrus Dance & Arts. Aside from its performances, Cirrus offers classes in traditional Chinese dance and art, such as Chinese brush painting. 1600 Saratoga Ave., San Jose; 408/871-1234, www.cirrusdance.com.

Chitresh Das Dance Co and Chhandam School of Kathak Dance. The dance company is an internationally renowned representative of the Kathak style of Indian classical dance and performs all over the world. The Chandam school was established in 1980, and offers training in dance, tabla (drumming), and singing. The training and performance is quite vigorous as some routines can take two hours. 32 Saint Charles Ave., San Francisco; 415/499-1601, www.kathak.org.

Clarion Music Center. Clarion offers occasional workshops on varied world music instruments including the traditional Chinese souna, erhu, and huqin. 816 Sacramento St., San Francisco; www.clarionmusic.com.

Gamelan Sekar Jaya. Founded in 1979, GSJ is a nonprofit volunteer organization dedicated to the study and presentation of traditional and contemporary Balinese performing arts. The ensemble has been recognized as the "finest Balinese gamelan outside of Indonesia," and works under the direction of Balinese performing artists from the faculty of STSI Denpasar (the National Art Institute of Bali). In 1985, 1992, and again in 1995, the Governor of Bali personally invited Gamelan Sekar Jaya to undertake concert tours to Bali and Java. 6485 Conlon Ave., El Cerrito; 510/237-6849, www.gsj.org.

Ghungroo Dance Academy. This one of a kind Indian Ethnic Folk Dance Academy was established in 1992 with the goal of introducing the cultural heritage and folk dances of India to an American audience and to Indo-Americans curious about their own culture. GDA specializes in Bhangra and traditional folk dances, and the fusion of these traditional styles with modern hip-hop dance. The Academy hosts musical dance drama presentations featuring the senior students of the Academy. Their annual production showcases the dancers and their various styles. Classes are also offered through

GDA for beginning, intermediate, and advanced students. Locations in Fremont, Dublin, and Berkeley; 510/758-4117, www.ghungroodance.com.

Korean Youth Cultural Center. Aimed at political and cultural preservation, the center teaches Korean drumming (pungmul), folk singing (minyo), and Korean mask and dance (talchum). Its performing group, Hanmadang, produces annual Autumn and Spring festivals and also performs at other local festivals. 4216 Telegraph Ave., Oakland; 510/652-4964, www.kycc.net.

Lily Cai Dance Academy. Cai dance company emerged out of classes Lily Cai taught to Chinese students at Galileo High School in San Francisco in the mid-1980s. The academy performs Chinese classical and folk dances, including those performed by the country's 50-plus government-classified minority groups. Groups from the academy have even performed at Grateful Dead concerts. Fort Mason Center, Landmark Building C-353, San Francisco; 415/474-4829, www.ccpsf.org.

NaLei Hulu I Ka Wekiu. Founded by Patrick Makuakane in 1985, this *halau* hosts an annual performance at the Palace of Fine Arts. About 40 dancers make up the performance group, but hula students number in the hundreds. Besides the modern twist on hula, the school also holds occasional seminars in language, history, and Hawaiian arts and crafts. 1527 20th St., San Francisco; 415/647-3040, www.naleihulu.org.

Northern California Music and Art Center. Begun by Korean American musicians in 1971, the center teaches classical music. 3120 Geary Blvd., San Francisco; 415/668-5999, www.geocities.com/ncmacc.

Peony Performing Arts. Founder Xiaomu Houwas trained at the Beijing Dance Academy and became the principal dancer with the prestigious China Oriental Song & Dance Ensemble. Grounded in traditional Chinese classical and folk dance, she and her sister Sabrina Shuang Hou, a Kunqu Opera singer, run the center. 4000 Balboa St., San Francisco; 650/359-7223, www.houarts.org.

San Francisco Taiko Dojo. This world renowned taiko academy offers drumming classes and produces the annual International Taiko Festival in Berkeley. SFTD drummers perform at local events and festivals and at concerts around the world. 1581 Webster St., Ste. 200, San Francisco; 415/928-2456, www.taikodojo.org.

San Jose Taiko. Founded over 30 years ago, SJT is one of the premier taiko companies in the country. Regulars at the International Taiko Festival, they stage concerts and attend festivals all over the world. P.O. Box 26895, San Jose; 408/293-9344, www.taiko.org.

Shri Krupa Dance Company. Presenting the classical Indian dance form *Bharatanatyam* in and around the Bay Area. 408/293-5206, www.shrikrupa.org.

Wings of the Hundred Viet Dance Company. This unique company specializes in creating dance presentations that portray the myths, legends, and historic events of Viet Nam. 408/277-0524, www.geocities.com /~wingsof100viet.

Abhinaya Dance Company of San Jose. 19 N. 2nd St., Ste. 102, San Jose; 408/983-0491, www.abhinaya.org.

Afghan Cultural Music Center. 37415 Fremont Blvd., Fremont; 510/792-4746.

Exploring Music, Chinese Music Center. 814 Clement St., San Francisco; 415/831-2500.

Kaisahan of San Jose. Filipino folk dance and music. 19 N. 2nd St., Ste. 102, San Jose; 408/298-3787, www.kaisahan.org.

Kariyushi Kai Music & Dance Company. Classical Okinawan music and dance. 650/941-6714, www.kariyushikai.org.

LIKHA Pilipino Folk Ensemble. 555 John Muir Dr. #B412, San Francisco; 415/452-0834, www.likha.org.

Arts Classes

Ali Akbar College of Music. Students learn to play the classical music of North India on the instrument of their choice, Indian or non-Indian. There is training in both raga (melody) and tala (percussion). Students learn from masters Ali Akbar Khan and Swapan Chaudhuri, 215 West End Ave., San Rafael; 415/454-6264, www.aacm.org.

Chinese Culture Center of San Francisco. Situated inside a Holiday Inn, the center hosts exhibits, but also teaches classes in Mandarin, Cantonese opera, painting, kung fu, and Wing Chun. Docents conduct the Chinese Heritage Walk on Wednesdays and Sundays. 750 Kearny St., Third Floor, San Francisco; 415/986-1822, www.c-c-c.org.

Joseph Fine Art School & Gallery. Classes are offered in Chinese brush painting, calligraphy, ceramics, cartoon, and sketch work. The gallery also sets up student exhibitions at the end of each semester. 125 Clement St., San Francisco; 415/387-7138.

Kala Art Institute. Co-founded in 1974 by Archana Horsting and Yuzo Nakano, the West Berkeley institute is an urban, multicultural printmaking workshop for local and international artists, especially those from Pacific Rim countries. The 8,500-square-foot facility includes a shared workspace with professional printmaking and digital media equipment, art library, exhibition gallery, print archive, and consignment sales department. About 100 classes and workshops are offered to the public every year. 1060 Heinz Ave., Berkeley; 510/549-2977, www.kala.org.

Kearny Street Workshop. This multi-disciplinary venue used to host the Asian American Jazz Festival, but now concentrates on young artistic talent in its annual APAture festival. The workshops offered are primarily in writing, although KSW hosts many readings and exhibits as well. 934 Brannan St., San Francisco; 415/503-0520, www.kearnystreet.org.

Japanese Cultural Arts Center. Offers traditional Japanese arts and calligraphy workshops for adults and children, plus martial arts. The workshops are held at various locations in Berkeley and Albany. 510/524-9283, www.kiaikido.org/JCAC.

Stylers Art Gallery. This small gallery offers classes in Chinese calligraphy, brush painting, and other traditional Chinese arts. 661 Jackson St., San Francisco; 415/788-8639.

Wafuki Ikebana. Promoting itself as providing a less restrictive approach to traditional Japanese flower arranging, the organization offers classes in the Wafu School of Ikebana—taught by certified Wafu School instructors. 408/252-6833, www.wafu-ikebana.org.

Chinese American Cultural Center. 1269 Forgewood Ave., Sunnyvale; 408/747-0394.

East Bay Bonsai Society. Lakeside Garden Center, 666 Bellevue Ave., Oakland; 510/482-8428, www.GSBF-Bonsai.org.

Jyoti Kala Mandir College of Classical Indian Arts. 1034 Delaware St., Berkeley; 510/486-9851.

Temescal Arts Center. 511 48th St., Oakland; 510/923-1074, www.temescalartscenter.org.

Public Art

Visitors will find a plethora of public art on display in the Bay Area, much of it with historical subject matter, while other displays take a more abstract approach. From murals depicting episodes from a country's history to garden installations of carved stones and bronze statues of famous religious leaders, the Bay Area's public art offerings reflect the diversity and creativity of its residents.

Ang Lipini Lapu Lapu Mural. Translated as "The Descendants of Lapu Lapu," this mural, painted in 1984 by Johanna Poethig, Vic Clemente, and

Prescio Tabios, depicts heroes of the Philippine Revolution and other historic figures. San Lorenzo Ruiz Center, 50 Rizal St., San Francisco.

Five Carved Stones, 2000. This granite stone sculpture by Marcia Donahue resembles two smiling moons, two peaches, and a persimmon. The elements are incorporated into the park landscape and are meant to function for sitting, as well as adding to the beauty of the park. Chinatown Park (Woh Hei Yuen Park), Powell St. between Jackson and John Sts., San Francisco.

Ghandi statue. This bronze statue at the Embarcadero Ferry Building was a gift from the Indian Council for Cultural Relations headed by the Vice President of India in 1988. Embarcadero, San Francisco.

Lakas Sambayan/People Power Mural. Painted by Johanna Poethig, Vic Clemente, and Prescio Tabios in 1986 to commemorate the overthrow of Ferdinand Marcos. 300 Alemany Blvd., San Francisco.

Light Clouds. Based on an 11th century Chinese art form that depicts clouds and water as dragons, this award-winning installation features eleven ceramic fritted glass panels and four Plexiglass lanterns, which cast sinuous dragon/cloud shadows onto the facade of Fire Station #2 when the sun is overhead. Al Wong, 1994. 1340 Powell St., San Francisco.

Photos of People from the Neighborhood. This installation features photos of people from the Chinatown/North Beach neighborhood, enlarged and displayed on the wall of the North Beach Parking Garage. Inside the garage the artists painted a different fortune in each of the parking spaces. John Rubin and Harrell Fletcher, 2002. North Beach Parking Garage, 735 Vallejo St., San Francisco.

Speaking Stones. Designed to reflect the uniqueness of the local community, this project created a garden of meandering paths with lines of poetry carved into rocks, seat walls, walkways, and floors. On either side of the street entrances to the courtyard are two large colored octagons inspired by the *Bagwa* mirror used in Fung Shui. Seyed Alavi, 2000. Richmond Recreation Center, 251 18th Ave., San Francisco.

Take Root. Artist Rene Young constructed illuminated signage in English and Chinese. Backlit copper panels feature poetry by community writers. Rene Young, 1996. Chinatown Branch Library, Reading Room. 1135 Powell St., San Francisco.

Tectonic Melange. This 26-foot diameter medallion was created by inlaying Chinese calligraphic characters in black granite into a lighter colored granite. The writing is based on a poem by Tang Dynasty (650–676 B.C.E.) poet Wang Bo, "This Land's splendor spills from Heaven's treasure, its remarkable people thrive on Earth's bounty." Lampo Leong, 2000. Chinatown Park (Woh Hei Yuen Park), Powell St. between Jackson and John Sts., San Francisco.

Untitled. Cast-concrete animal figures based on the Chinese zodiac serve as climbing and sliding structures for the physical development of pre-school aged children. Mary Fuller, 1984. Portsmouth Square (Tot Lot, lower level), Clay and Kearny Sts., San Francisco.

DIVERSIONS

The incredible diversity of Asian and Asian American populations in the Bay Area is equaled only by their phenomenal integration into Bay Area culture. Traditional Chinese and Japanese neighborhoods are now dotted with Korean restaurants, Cambodian grocery stores, Vietnamese jewelry stores, and Indian markets. This overlapping diversity extends to playtime as well, with the last remaining "Chinese" movie house playing mainstream movies and hosting ethnic film festivals, while Korean karaoke bars are frequented by young, hip Asians of all backgrounds, and Japanese theater spaces workshop Pilipino plays.

The multigenerational nature of Bay Area Asian immigrants and Asian American natives is reflected in the way traditions are upheld and innovations evolve. World master musician Ali Akbar Khan teaches North Indian classical music in Marin County, while Pilipino American DJ Q-Bert has long led the San Francisco spinning scene.

Traditional pastimes also enjoy wide participation. Asian sports take to the water as teams race in dragon boats on Lake Merced and at Oakland's Jack London Square, or in Hawaiian outriggers in choppy bay waters or in Alameda's estuary. Year-round, martial arts studios train residents in Pilipino *escrima*, Indonesian *penjak silat*, Muy Thai kickboxing, and various iterations of Chinese kung fu, Korean martial arts, and Japanese combative sports. *Tai chi* practitioners make familiar early-morning figures at Golden Gate Park's Panhandle or near the bandshell. Churches and temples play host to religious and cultural celebrations on almost a weekly basis. Young children showcase their talents learned in the many Indian dance schools in southern Alameda County and the South Bay. At Christmastime, Pilipinos in Daly City put on plays commemorating the Passion.

CLUBBING

The days of glamorous Chinese nightclubs and underground opium dens may be behind us, but clubbing is still the way of the nightlife. In requisite black (and outerwear in leather, please), Asian Americans stand in line to get into the hot nightclubs. Naming the clubs is a risky business, considering how fast the turnover can be. Besides, the crowd follows the promoters: Synergy, Abzolute Wild, and Drink Club for East Asian crowds, and Ecstasy, Wicked, and 8th Dimension for South Asian *Desi* club-hoppers.

Favorite San Francisco venues include **111 Minna** (415/974-1719), **Bambuddha** (601 Eddy St., 415/885-5088), **SakeLab** (492-498 Broadway, 415/837-0228), **Whispers** (535 Florida St., 415/252-9442), old-timer **DNA Lounge** (375 11th St., 415/626-1409), and the **Bellagio.** The last isn't the Vegas club, but a Korean American hangout where you "rent" a table, pay for the food and drinks, and—if you spot a girl you like (or, less common, a guy)—the waiter acts as an intermediary to ask about their availability and "book" them.

The gay scene also has primarily Asian venues, with **AsiaSF** (201 9th St., 415/255-2742) as the most visible. A top-rated restaurant, AsiaSF features transvestite divas warbling away on a red runway. Gay or gay-friendly nightclubs with their share of Asian American male clientele have popped up in the South Bay as well, including **King of Clubs** (893 Leong Dr., 650/968-6366) in Mountain View.

MUSIC

Mass popular culture may not have caught up with accurate minority representation, but bigwig music producers and Hollywood tycoons who want a cue would do well to spend a night cruising San Francisco and beyond. The Bay Area smolders with talent in spoken word, music, and theater. For nearly two decades, spinning has become the province of Pilipino American DJs, like world champion Q-Bert, MixMaster Mike, and Apollo (the Invisibl Skratch Piklz). The transition to hip-hop and rap has been natural, with Rome Diggy and Raw Soul or Rosa Lee. One of the hottest hip-hop artists and producers to have come along is Lyrics Born, half-Japanese, half-Caucasian Tom Shimura. The Berkeley native (born in Japan) has performed locally at Bimbo's 365. South Asians have started their own fusion DJ mix, like the innovative Dhamaal crew, who mix multi-media, spinning, and sometimes live *tabla* (traditional Indian drums). Check out www.desiparty.com for information on more events.

Local independent music talent gets promoted during the annual summer **piNoisePop** (www.pinoisepop.cjb.net) festival, showcasing Pilipino bands, and the larger **Asian American Arts and Heritage Festival** (www.aaartsalliance.org) in May, which features a variety of musical disciplines and ethnic groups.

San Francisco Asian cultures keep their traditions alive as well. San Francisco's **Gamelan Sekar Jaya** (www.gsj.org) performs classic Indonesian orchestral music locally on a regular basis. San Rafael, just across the Golden Gate Bridge, is the unlikely Marin County home for one of the leading Indian music schools in the world, **Ali Akbar College of Music** (215 West End Ave., 415/454-6264). Chinese opera—especially Cantonese, which experienced a rebirth in the 1980s—boasts fantastic costuming, elaborate make-up, classical lyrics, and occasional martial acrobats that make for a memorable evening. The **Chinese Culture Center of San Francisco** (750 Kearny St., 415/986-1822) teaches the Cantonese version, while **Peony Performing Arts** (4000 Balboa St., 650/359-7223) trains locals in the mainland China tradition.

Ties to the homeland extend to pop culture as well. While the likes of Britney Spears may command American mainstream reviews and coverage, ethnic communities attend huge "underground" concerts at venues like the Henry J. Kaiser Center in Oakland and Bill Graham Civic Auditorium in San Francisco. These include megapop stars from China, India, Hong Kong, the Philippines, Taiwan, and Vietnam. Concert-goers are notified through garish posters at local mom-and-pop stores, small, community newspapers, and the watchful eyes of true fans.

DANCE

Dance is a major scene, from the high-energy *Punjabi Bhangra*, taught at Newark's **Ghungroo Dance Academy** (510/758-4117), to modern takes on Chinese dance. Professional companies like **Lily Cai Company** (www.ccpsf.org) put a modern twist on Chinese folk traditions. The acclaimed **Alleluia Panis Dance Theater** (474 Faxon Ave., 415/239-0249) revamps tribal movements and native martial arts into dazzling performances. Pacific Islander *Halaus* (hula dance companies) like Patrick Makuakane's **Na Lei Hulu I Ka Wekiu** (1527 20th St., 415/647-3040) in San Francisco and Mark Ho'omalu's **Academy of Hawaiian Arts** (10700 MacArthur Blvd., 510/635-2160) in Oakland tour the West Coast and compete in national competitions, once placed in the top five at a Hawaiian competition. The **Pacific Islanders Cultural Association** (www.pica-org.org) sponsors the annual two-day **Aloha Festival** in Chrissy Field. The annual **Ia 'Oe E Ka La Hula Festival,** and its renowned international competitions, takes place mid-fall at the Alameda County Fairgrounds in Pleasanton.

THEATER

The twin impact of the dot-com bust and the terrorist attacks of 9-11, permanently altered the landscape of the arts. Closure, consolidation, and collaboration proved no exception among Asian American arts companies.

Companies like **Teatro ng Tanan** (415/974-1384) are teetering on the edge. Stalwarts like San Francisco's **Kearny Street Workshop** (934 Brannan St., 415/503-0520) and the **Asian American Theater Company** (www .asianamericantheater.org) have persisted since the 1970s, but age doesn't always mean growth. The first continues to be devoted to youth and the surrounding community, while the second has been living a nomadic existence since its peak in the mid-'90s. The economic realities of the technology bust may have forced artists to consider combining visions, but the shocking repercussions of 9-11 have made partnerships that much more reassuring.

When it comes to theater, duality defines the arts: immigrant identity and the Asian American experience clash at times, but both maintain a strong sense of political consciousness. Bucking Broadway's tragic take in musical crowd-pleasers like *Madame Butterfly* and *Miss Saigon*, playwrights like Philip Kan Gotanda and Brenda Wong Aoki address modern subject matter in the context of the Asian American cultural experience.

LITERARY SCENE

A recent Bureau of Labor Statistics study proved once and for all that San Franciscans love their books. That Asian Americans have a significant voice in the local literary scene should come as no surprise. University of California, Berkeley professor Maxine Hong Kingston established an early Asian American voice with *Women Warriors*, and continues to publish, with her latest *Fifth Book of Peace*. Oakland-born Amy Tan learned to put the joy in *Joy Luck Club* by consulting a writing coach formerly based in the North Bay. Acclaimed author and East Bay resident Gail Tsukiyama frequently makes public appearances. The **Kearny Street Workshop** (934 Brannan St., 415/503-0520) offers writing classes to help burgeoning authors, and has promoted the likes of Jessica Hagedorn.

Nearly ever major bookstore hosts a wide variety of author readings. The University of San Francisco, through its **Pacific Rim Voices**

ANGEL ISLAND

The long history of Asian migration can still be seen in tourist attractions, state park encampments, and crumbling old towns. Outside of Chinatown and Japantown, Angel Island might be the most visible of these historical attractions. While comparisons to Ellis Island are highly overrated, it nevertheless deserves recognition as an immigration station for the nearly one million immigrants that passed through—or were denied passage—to "Gold Mountain," as California was called.

From 1910 through 1940, Japanese, Korean, Pilipino, Indian, and Chinese immigrants made their stop at Angel Island, answering questions from U.S. officials determined to uphold the various exclusion acts. The concept of paper sons and daughters emerged, as hopefuls claimed false blood relations to residents who had made it to the United States. Men and women were separated, and detainment could take months. Graffiti, if poems and yearnings of fear and slim hopes scratched in Chinese calligraphy can be called thus, serves as the historical document to this otherwise silent group.

and **Voices of Our Nation's Arts** programs, is a good source for talks by Asian American writers. Bookstores, catering specifically to Asian subject matter in both English and native languages, include Japantown's **Kinokuniya** (1581 Webster St., 415/567-7625), **Eastwind Books** (2066 University Ave., 510/548-2350) in Berkeley, and **Arkipelago Philippine Bookstore** (953 Mission St., 415/777-0108) in downtown San Francisco.

FILM

Sadly, the era of Chinatown movie theaters has passed on. The few Indian movie-houses which opened during the dot com heyday are mostly closed after the bust—the one notable exception being Fremont's **Naz 8 Cinemas** (39160 Paseo Padre Pkwy., 510/797-2000). But San Francisco is still a premiere place for Asian and Asian American films, thanks to NAATA (North

The island's role as the last point of entry ended after a fire gutted the administration building.

Today visitors ferry over to walk or bike its paths, picnic, and sometimes camp overnight at this small outcropping. About 5.5 miles in circumference, the island does have a "mountain": Mount Livermore's highest point is 780 feet and is a site for a Nike missile installation. Besides the immigration station and museum, other points of interest include Ayala Cove, Camp Reynolds, and Fort McDowell. Its older history reaches back into the days of the Coastal Miwok Indians, later becoming a hideout for whalers and pirates, a cattle ranch, and a strategic military spot for the Civil, Spanish-American, and first World wars.

Docents lead tours April through November, weather permitting. Tram tours with audio commentary run from March to November, while kayak tours, run by a private company, can go year-round. Dogs, roller skates, roller blades, skateboards, scooters, and wood fires are not allowed, but people can bring (or rent) bicycles and charcoal.

American Asian Telecommunications Alliance). Its **Asian American Film Festival** (www.naatanet.org) brings documentaries, feature films, and speakers from Asia. For a year-round trip into Asian cinema (if you don't try the many ethnic video stores), the **4-Star Movie Theater** (2200 Clement St., 415/666-3488) truly has a multicultural marquee, from mainstream American flicks to Asian mini-festivals.

CULTURE NIGHTS

The Bay Area's concentration of educational institutions fosters a huge setting for cultural exploration. From numerous campuses come a huge variety of cultural clubs and celebrations. Whether at private and pricey universities, state commuter schools, or community colleges, students often rediscover and showcase their heritage in cultural nights. UC Berkeley's **Vietnamese Student Association** (www.ocf.berkeley.edu/~vsa) and

INDUS (http://indus.berkeley.edu)—the largest Asian student organization—fill Zellerbach Hall with their annual shows.

FESTIVALS

From lunar New Year to Indian Independence Day, the celebrations never stop. San Francisco and Oakland Chinatowns—always reliable for nearly every American holiday—shut down to celebrate the lunar New Year. Street parades commemorate this and the Autumn Moon Festival during the fall harvest season.

The blossoming of cherry trees beckons thousands in Japan to witness spring's changes, akin to fall foliage tours but on a national scale. Here in the Bay Area, smaller scale observances happen in the San Francisco and San Jose Japantowns, with *mochi*-pounding and *taiko* drums providing an inevitable accompaniment to the event.

Indian Independence Day, which commemorates that country's freedom from England on August 15, 1947, is observed with much fanfare and parades in Fremont. *Pistahan* (the annual Pilipino American cultural festival) has swelled into a two-day affair complete with parades and a multi-arts fair in San Francisco.

Two more notable summer block parties include Japantown's Nihonmachi Fair and the Oakland Chinatown Street Fest. In the latter, a good four or five blocks are closed off—no mean feat this—and booths and stages are set up on the auto-free streets.

From May through November, Portsmouth Square in San Francisco Chinatown gives way to a carnival atmosphere with the Chinatown Night Market Fair. Complete with Ferris wheels and fortune-tellers, the outdoor street gathering showcases musical performances, martial arts, and other entertainment.

Pageantry is also a big part of Asian culture, with competitions for Miss Chinatown, Miss Asian America, Miss Cherry Blossom, and Miss India America. (In a run for equal opportunity is the Mr. India America contest.) These competitions—mainly for scholarships—don't have quite the same resonance as the ones in Asia, where a tiara serves as the homing beacon to the film and television industry. Instead, these queens and their runner-up consorts work hard year-round traveling to festivals, grand openings, and other events—and sometimes on their own dime.

DIVERSIONS

Bars

SAKE/SOJU BARS

Anzu at Hotel Nikko. This restaurant and bar, situated in the Hotel Nikko, sports a sake-cocktail list that incorporates just about every color under the sun. Anzu serves Nearly 60 sake cocktails, which the bar prefers to call sake martinis. 222 Mason St., San Francisco; 415/394-1111, www.hotelnikkosf.com.

Betelnut. A boisterous Union Street crowd can choose from three sake cocktails at the bar: the Bonsai Martini, the Sakarita and the Sake Colada. Betelnut also serves sake flights at the counter, giving customers a chance to taste a few of its premium sakes. There are a number of Asian beers on the menu as well as Pan Asian cuisine. 2030 Union St., San Francisco; 415/929-8855.

RoHan Lounge. RoHan specializes in the soju cocktail—a Korean liquor distilled from rice, barley and sweet potato. There are various brands that line the shelf over the crimson bar. RoHan is the only pure soju bar in the city, serving soju straight up, on the rocks, or in any of a dozen unique cocktails. 3089 Geary Blvd., San Francisco; 415/221-5095.

Sake Lab. Sake Lab offers more than 40 varieties of sake by the bottle, costing anywhere from about $10 to over $200. For amateurs, Sake Lab helps out with charts detailing the differences between the types of sakes.

498 Broadway St., San Francisco; 415/837-0228; www.sakelab.com.

Tsunami Sushi and Sake Bar. Beyond a half-dozen sake cocktails are served at the bar, Tsunami offers premium, rare sakes, and sake samplers. 1306 Fulton St., Ste. 351, San Francisco; 415/567-7664.

Ace Wasabi's Rock N Roll Sushi. 3339 Steiner, San Francisco; 415/567-4903; www.acewasabis.com.

Bacchus Wine and Sake Bar. 1954 Hyde St., San Francisco; 415/928-2633.

Blowfish Sushi. 2170 Bryant St., San Francisco; 415/285-FUGU.

Cafe Royal. 800 Post St., San Francisco; 415/441-4099.

Fly Bar. 762 Divisadero St., San Francisco; 415/931-4359.

Mas Sake. 2030 Lombard St., San Francisco; 415/440-1505;www.massake.com.

Midori Mushi Sushi and Sake Lounge. 465 Grove St., San Francisco; 415/503-1377.

Movida Lounge. 200 Fillmore St., San Francisco; 415/934-8637.

Ozumo. 161 Steuart St., San Francisco; 415/882-1333.

Ryoko's. 619 Taylor St., San Francisco; 415/775-1028.

Sake Bomb. 614 Pine St., San Francisco; 415/434-9840.

Sushi Groove South. 1516 Folsom St., San Francisco; 415/503-1950.

True Sake. 560 Hayes St., San Francisco; 415/355-9555, www.truesake.com. (See page 103 for more details.)

CLUBS

111 Minna Street. For the hipster who wants it all: this modern gallery hangs loose with house music, bar and artwork on display. The egalitarian approach and affordable rental policy often mean reflecting the diverse demands of the city. 111 Minna St., San Francisco; 415/974-1719, www.111minnagallery.com.

AsiaSF. AsiaSF takes the concept of dinner theater to another realm. Elegant drag queens are the entertainment, as is the wait staff. The menu is mostly California-Asian cuisine, while AsiaSF's signature drinks are named after the "ladies," such as Leilani's Chocolate Martini and Ginger's Sake Cosmo. The bar has an extensive sake selection. There are lip-synch performances by the "gender illusionists." Reservations are recommended, especially on weekends when the old-style nightclub can get crowded. 201 9th St. (at Howard), San Francisco; 415/255-ASIA (2742), www.asiasf.com.

Bambuddha. Even Buddha hangs out here—at least, a 20-foot reclining rooftop version. A hipster hangout in the equally hip Phoenix hotel, Bambuddha attracts lots of celebrities and up-and-coming UK musicians. The club selects from Filipino, Balinese and Thai aesthetics for the pan-Asian cuisine and indoor waterfalls. DJs spin an eclectic mix on the Funktion One sound system. 601 Eddy St., San Francisco; 415/885-5088, www.bambuddhalounge.com.

N Touch. This dance bar attracts a large crowd of Asian-Pacific Islander gay men. Music ranges from '70s dance to contemporary house. Monday is Karaoke night. 1548 Polk St., San Francisco; 415/441-8413, www.ntouchsf .com.

Yoshi's at Jack London Square. This combination Japanese restaurant, live jazz venue has become an institution in the Bay Area. Many of the biggest names in jazz music from around the globe have graced the stage at Yoshi's. The restaurant offers full meals as well as sushi snacks in the lounge. 510 Embarcadero West, Oakland; 510/238-9200, www.yoshis.com.

26 Mix. 3024 Mission St., San Francisco; 415/826-7378.

Blind Tiger. 787 Broadway, San Francisco; 415/788-4020.

Buddha Cocktail Lounge. 901 Grant Ave., San Francisco; 415/302-1792.

Cabana. 396 South 1st St., San Jose; 408/971-2262; www.cabanasanjose.com.

Club Six. 60 6th St., San Francisco; 415/863-1221.

Club 1028. 1028 Geary St., San Francisco; 415/567-7540.

Dragon Bar. 473 Broadway, San Francisco; 415/834-9383.

La'zeez-Asian Fusion Restaurant & Bar. 25 Mason St., San Francisco; 415/771-5503.

Li Po. 916 Grant St., San Francisco; 415/982-0072.

Romeo 5 Asian Art Cafe & Bar. 1581 Webster St., Ste. 210, San Francisco; 415/885-5108.

Shanghai 1930. 133 Steuart St., San Francisco; 415/896-5600.

Film

4-Star Movie Theater. As Chinatown theaters died across the country, this independent joint owned by Frank Lee in the Richmond District began showing first and second-run mainstream Hollywood films, Saturday midnight classics, kung fu films, imports straight from Hong Kong, and Asian mini-film festivals. 2200 Clement St., San Francisco; 415/666-3488; www.hkinsf.com.

Berkeley Art Museum/Pacific Film Archive. A counterpart to the UC Berkeley museum, this incredible cinematic resource includes a huge collection of Japanese films. It frequently focuses on international directors or themed showings, such as the UCLA-curated traveling "Heroic Grace: The Chinese Martial Arts Films" on classic Shaw Brothers productions. 2625 Durant Ave. and 2575 Bancroft Way, Berkeley; 510/642-0808; www.bampfa.berkeley.edu.

Dr. Martin Luther King Jr. Library. Downtown San Jose's new jewel, the main branch of the city's public library, houses an extensive collection of

Vietnamese language films, and books as well. In collaboration with the San Jose State University Library, it maintains the Asian American Center. 150 E. San Fernando St., San Jose; 408/808-2000, www.sjpl.lib.ca.us.

India Movie Center 6. Hindi and South Indian films, particularly Telugu, are the predominant fare of this multiplex. 1433 The Alameda, San Jose; 408/830-9999, www.imc6.com.

Naz8. The tech fall, and the return of Indian workers on H-1B visas, dashed the hopes of the first multicultural multiplex chain. One of two Fremont theaters closed, leaving Sunnyvale and a Southern California outlet remaining, and plans to open one in Texas remain. Primarily playing to an Indo-American audience, the theater screens movies from India, Pakistan, Afghanistan, Iran, China, Taiwan, Korea and the Philippines. 39160 Paseo Padre Parkway, Fremont; 510/797-2000, www.naz8.com.

Karaoke

Do-Re-Mi. Karaoke bars have proliferated since this first one opened in 1993. Private "song rooms" allow groups of college students and professionals to pass the evening with friends. Longtime local television news reporter Vic Lee has been known to belt out a few tunes here. 1604 Post St., San Francisco; 415/777-8884.

The Mint Karaoke Lounge. Rated by many the best Karaoke bar in the city, the Mint features a playlist of 5,000 pop tunes, as well as Spanish language hits. Though the Mint, which has been around since 1968, used to be a gay bar, the crowd these days is more mixed. 1942 Market St., San Francisco; 415/626-4726, www.themint.net.

Sonic Lounge. Though it's located in Japantown, Sonic is a combination Thai restaurant, Karaoke lounge and nightclub. The club draws clientele from around the globe, inspiring Sonic to offer Karaoke in five different languages, including English, all available on the main lounge floor as

well as in the private Karaoke rooms. 1705 Buchanan St., San Francisco;
415/929-9174.

7-Bamboo Cocktail Lounge. 162 East Jackson St., San Jose; 408/279-
9937.

The Alley. 3325 Grand Ave., Oakland; 510/444-8505.

Claran Lounge. 1251 Franklin Mall, Santa Clara; 408/248-4682.

Club Hong Kong. 517 Clement St., San Francisco; 415/668-1600.

Sachi Cocktail Lounge. 1581 Webster St., Ste. 207, San Francisco;
415/567-5866.

Tango Tango. 1550 California St., San Francisco; 415/775-0442.

Anime and Manga

Foothill Anime. Meets on the first Sunday of every month in building
5015 at Foothill College. 12345 El Monte Rd., Los Altos Hills; www
.foothill.anime.net.

Heroes Club. The Heroes Club is a Japanese anime collector's dream.
Aside from the Japanese action figures on hand, employees at the store act as
community builders, linking local artists to collectors in search of custom
designs or paintings. 840 Clement St., San Francisco; 415/387-4552.

Kimono My House. Still in its original location on the roof of a warehouse in Emeryville, Kimono My House has been in business for over 20
years, and was the first store in the United States devoted solely to
Japanese anime merchandise. Godzilla, Ultraman, and Transformers are
all here, as well as far more obscure characters sure to excite anime and
manga fans of all ages. 1424 62nd St., Emeryville; 510/654-4627;
www.kimonomyhousetoys.com

No-Name Anime. No-Name is the most prominent Japanese animation
club in the Bay Area. The group holds its meetings once a month at the

Santa Teresa Library. Library location: 290 International Circle, San Jose; 408/281-1879, www.nnanime.com.

Pow! Both rooms of this ultra hip cocktail lounge are filled with Japanimation cells, Playstations, and other video game paraphernalia. Japanimation is mixed with classic and independent cartoons while DJs spin house and hip-hop. The idea here is to suck down cocktails while getting sucked into the world of anime. 101 6th St., San Francisco; 415/278-0940.

Tsunami Anime. Meets weekly at San Jose State University Washington Square Hall, room 109. 1 Washington Sq., San Jose; www.studiokyuu .com/tsunami.

Collector's Universe & Anime. 3288 Pierce St, Richmond; 510/526-2639.

Nikaku Animart. 615 North 6th St., San Jose; 408/971-2822, www .nikaku.com.

The Place. 39120 Argonaut Way, PMB 816, Fremont; 510/794-5121.

Tokyo Motor Trenz. 1737 Post St. #10B, San Francisco; 415/922-6388.

Walking Tours

Chinese Cultural Center. Heritage walks offered several times a week, or by appointment. 750 Kearny St., San Francisco; 415/986-1822, www. c-c-c.org.

City Guides. Biweekly, free walking tours sponsored by the San Francisco Public Library. 100 Larkin St., San Francisco; 415/557-4266, www. sfcityguides.org.

Wok Wiz. A variety of culinary and historical tours, including "I Can't Believe I Ate My Way Through Chinatown," a walking cooking class. 654 Commercial St., San Francisco; 415/981-8989, www.wokwiz.com.

Sports

California Dragon Boat Association. The largest dragon boating organization in the Bay Area, CDBA organizes the Northern California International Dragon Boat Championships. Teams practice at four separate sites: Berkeley Marina, Alameda, Bair Island Aquatic Center in Redwood City, and Lake Merced in San Francisco. 268 Bush St. #888, San Francisco; www.cdba.org.

International Dragon Boat Association. Founded in 1996, the non-profit focuses on community-building, cultural preservation and youth activities. It hosts the August Jack London Square festival in Oakland. 844 Prospect Ave., Oakland; 510/452-4272, www.edragons.org.

Northern California Outrigger Canoe Association. With 2,000 members and growing, the association has been around since 1977. On both a spectator and participant level, the biggest draw hereabouts is the Aloha Festival, usually the first weekend in August in San Francisco. An annual membership of $100 to $300 is usually enough to get you into deep waters. www.ncoca.com.

San Francisco Bay Area Dragon Boat Racing Club. Oriented towards competition, the team offers free lessons on Saturday mornings in Foster City. Check the website for most updated contact information. www.bayareadragons.com.

Festivals

JANUARY

Chinese New Year. Chinatown streets are alight with a colorful procession of floats as well as Chinese puppets, lion dancers, marching bands, Miss Chinatown USA pageant winners, and Gum Lung, a 201-foot, block-long dragon. The parade runs from Market and Second streets to Kearny Street and Columbus Avenue. 415/982-3000, www.chineseparade.com.

Tet Festival. Hosted by the Coalition of Nationalist Vietnamese Organizations of Northern California, this lunar new year festival features costume and talent contests, carnival rides, business booths, martial arts demonstrations, live music, and food. Santa Clara County Fairgrounds, 344 Tully Rd., San Jose; 408/295-9210.

Vietnamese Spring Festival. A free event to celebrate the lunar new year, the festival highlights Vietnamese culture and arts, family activities, live performances, and food from around the world. The parade on Market St. includes diverse community organizations, multicultural music, and colorful floats. 408/292-8283, www.vsfsanjose.com.

Vietnamese Tet Festival. The Lunar New Year, or Vietnamese Tet Festival, lures thousands annually, offering Vietnamese food, dancing and music in the streets. Larkin Street at Geary. 415/351-1038, www.vietccsf .org/newyear_eng.htm.

FEBRUARY

San Francisco Arts of Pacific Asia Show. Eighty international dealers display rare and antique objects, as well as contemporary art from throughout Asia. Festival Pavilion, Fort Mason. 415/674-7283, www.caskeylees.com.

MARCH

Morgan Hill Haru Matsuri. Spring Festival that includes the Northern California Taiko Expo. 408-779-9009, www.mhbcc.org/hmatsuri.htm.

San Francisco International Asian American Film Festival. 415/255-4299, www.naatanet.org/calendar/sfiaaff.

APRIL

Cupertino Cherry Blossom Festival. Cupertino Memorial Park on Stevens Creek Blvd., 408/257-7424.

Northern California Cherry Blossom Festival. This spring celebration is held when the cherry trees first blossom. Amid the festivities are martial arts demonstrations, music, Japanese crafts booths, as well as a parade. Japantown, Grant Ave. between California and Pacific Sts, San Francisco; 415/563-2313, www.nccbf.org.

MAY

Nikkei Matsuri: Japanese American Cultural Festival. Annual event held in San Jose's Japantown. www.nikkeimatsuri.org.

JUNE

Chinatown Night Market. The Market takes place in Chinatown's Portsmouth Square from June to October, with nearly 100 booths, including food, Chinese handicrafts, and artworks such as calligraphy. 415/397-8000, www.sanfranciscochinatown.com.

Ethnic Dance Festival. Palace of Fine Arts Theatre, Bay and Lyon Sts., San Francisco; 415/474-3914.

Fiesta Filipina. The biggest Filipino Festival in America celebrates Independence Day with rides, traditional foods, a crafts fair, and live entertainment. Civic Center Plaza, San Francisco; 650/871-6647, www .fiestafilipina.com.

JULY

Chinese Summer Festival. Presented in part by the Chinese Historical and Cultural Project. San Jose History Park, 408/366-0688, www. chcp.org.

San Francisco Obon Festival. San Francisco Buddhist Church. 1881 Pine St., 415/776-3158, www.bcsfweb.org.

San Jose Obon Festival. "The Festival of Gratitude," commemorates the story of Mogallana (Mokuren in Japanese), one of ten disciples of Shakyamun. While in deep meditation Mokuren saw his mother suffering in the hell of hungry spirits and asked the Buddha how he could help her. The Buddha instructed him to care for his fellow monks and his community, freeing both his mother and himself. His joy and gratitude were so great that he began to dance. The Obon Festival is San Jose Japantown's largest cultural event. 408/294-3138, www.jamsj.org.

AUGUST

Festival of India. Two day festival in Fremont celebrating India's independence from the British. www.fiaonline.org.

Nihonmachi Street Fair. In Japantown and the Japantown Center, San Francisco. 415/771-9861, www.nihonmachistreetfair.org.

Oakland Chinatown StreetFest. This is the largest Asian festival in the Bay Area. It covers 10 city blocks and draws upward of 100,000 people. Over 200 vendors participate and there are cultural performances, food booths, as well as artisans on hand. Oakland's Chinatown. 510/893-8939, www.oaklandchinatownstreetfest.com.

Pistahan. Celebration of Filipino arts, culture, and cuisine with attractions, displays, crafts, entertainment and food held annually at Yerba Buena Gardens. 415/543-1718.

SEPTEMBER

Alameda Noodlefest. At Noodlefest, attendees can taste Korean chap chae and udon noodles, Filipino pancit, Japanese somen, and of course Chinese chow mein. The food is prepared by members of the Bay Area's

Asian Pacific Islander community. Buena Vista Methodist Church, 2311 Buena Vista Ave., Alameda; 510/522-2688.

Chinese Moon Festival. Overfelt Gardens, 2145 McKee Road at Educational Park Dr., San Jose, in the Chinese Cultural Garden. 408/251-3323, chineseculturalgarden.com.

Filipino Heritage Festival. Plaza de Cesar Chavez Park, San Jose; 408/259-2164, www.geocities.com/fahap.

PiNoisePop. Annual Filipino-youth music and pop culture festival. www.pinoisepop.cjb.net.

San Francisco Chinatown Autumn Moon Festival. Also called the Mid-Autumn Festival, the celebration, which dates back over 1,000 years, marks the end of the summer harvest and provides an occasion to give thanks for the bounty of the land. Presented by the Chinatown Merchants association. 667 Grant Ave., San Francisco; 415/982-6306, www.moonfestival.org.

OCTOBER

Ia Oe E Ka La Hula Festival. Presented by The Kumu Hula Association of Northern California. www.kumuhulaassociation.com.

DECEMBER

Asian Art Museum's New Year's Bell Ringing. Visitors are encouraged to ring a 2100-lb., 16th-century bronze bell in observance of an ancient Japanese New Year's tradition. Asian Art Museum, San Francisco. 415/581-4400.

Hmong International New Year Festival. A weeklong festival beginning in late December and ending in January, Hmong from around the world join the local community to celebrate the holiday with traditional song, dance, games, contests, and food. The 2004 event saw over 100,000 attendees. Held at the Fresno Fairgrounds on Kings Canyon Rd. 559/252-8782, www.hmongnewyearusa.org.

HEALTH
AND fITNESS

SAN FRANCISCO'S CHINATOWN IS FAMOUS THE world over for the morning scene in Portsmouth Square, where Chinese men and women can be seen practicing the graceful movements of health-enhancing *tai chi*. From the square up Clay Street to the corner of Waverly Place, a maze of placards in English and Chinese advertise acupuncturists, herbalists, massage parlors, and other traditional Chinese health services.

But while Chinatown is representative of the Bay Area's adoption of Eastern health and fitness practices, it is just a small part of the picture. A quick glance through the San Francisco Yellow Pages reveals a page and a half of listings for "yoga," two pages for "acupuncturists," and four for "martial arts." Equally telling is the number of Bay Area Acupuncturists who are members of the United California Practitioners of Chinese Medicine (UCPCM), a professional association: almost 300.

Successive waves of Asian immigration to the Bay Area account for most of the success that traditional health practices enjoy in the Bay Area—most have gravitated towards a style of healthcare and fitness that they understand and in which practitioners speak their native language. But it's hard to discount liberal Bay Area attitudes towards health and fitness when considering this success—the region is known for its stress on tolerance and alternative lifestyles. Non-Asian Bay Area residents have adopted alternatives to Western medicine and fitness earlier than residents in most other parts of the United States. This interest over the last decade has gone mainstream, particularly as Western research increasingly finds merit in Eastern approaches and as the Bay Area's aging baby-boomers search for ways to improve their quality of life. Even traditionally Western-oriented health centers, like Stanford University Medical Center in Palo Alto and California Pacific Medical Center (CPMC) in San Francisco now offer alternative medicine programs. A number of the area's institutions of higher learning have also embraced the trend. The University of California San Francisco (UCSF), for instance, has established an integrative medicine clinic and offers its medical students opportunities to study alternative healthcare.

With so many acupuncturists, yoga instructors, and martial arts masters hanging up their shingles in the Bay Area, it's not always easy to discern the accomplished practitioners and instructors from the less experienced ones. Beware of folks who have not been practicing long or whose credentials are unimpressive. While everyone has to start somewhere, when it comes to taking herbs, which can harm your health if mixed or dosed incorrectly, make sure the person administering them is a genuine professional. In the pages that follow, you'll find explanations of the great eastern traditions most available in the Bay Area, and some leads on practitioners and instructors.

TRADITIONAL CHINESE MEDICINE

For over 2,000 years doctors of Traditional Chinese Medicine, or TCM, have not only been diagnosing and healing patients, but also preventing illness and disease. A belief in the principle of opposing forces (*yin* and *yang*) is at the core of TCM. When applied to healthcare, it means that good health results when your *yin* and *yang* are in balance—illness occurs when they are not. To reach equilibrium your "vital energy," or *qi*, must be able to

GOING MAINSTREAM

Perhaps nothing suggests how widely accepted and respected Asian-style health and fitness have become in the Bay Area than the fact that a number of major hospitals and universities now have medical centers where Western and Eastern practices converge. Down in the South Bay, the Stanford University Medical Center, which is closely affiliated with Stanford University School of Medicine, has set up the **Stanford Center for Integrative Medicine,** which offers treatments like acupuncture, medical *qigong*, and *shiatsu*. It especially focuses on helping patients who are suffering from chronic medical conditions.

In San Francisco, the **University of California San Francisco's (UCSF) Osher Center for Integrative Medicine** has a traditional Chinese medical practice and, in collaboration with the **American College of Traditional Chinese Medicine (ACTCM)** in San Francisco, provides first and second year medical students a program to learn more about traditional Chinese medicine.

The **Institute for Health and Healing at the California Pacific Medical Center (CPMC),** meanwhile, offers a host of Asian health treatments. Ayurvedic clinician Reenita Malholtra, for example, teaches a class called Living Ayurveda, and offers ayurvedic lifestyle and nutrition consultations. Other practitioners perform ayurvedic treatments like Mukhralepa, which rejuvenates the skin, and Hastha-bhyanga, which rejuvenates the feet and hands. The institute also offers *qigong* therapy, traditional Thai massage, *shiatsu*, and classes in yoga, tai chi, and *qigong.*

flow unhindered through your body along invisible energy pathways, known as meridians. When one or more pathways are blocked or there is too much or too little *qi* running through them, a person becomes ill. Lifestyle, emotions, and environment can all disrupt the flow of *qi*. So, besides asking about symptoms and giving a physical examination, TCM practitioners may ask about emotional and lifestyle habits. During the examination they will probably check the six pulses on each wrist and ask to see the patient's tongue, noting its color and texture. They may also check skin, hair, eyes, voice, and other body parts for signs of disharmony. The detection of any malady may result in the prescription of one or more of the following treatments.

Herbal medicine: A concoction of herbs with medicinal properties, which the practitioner may adjust with each visit. Herbs are traditionally brewed like a tea but some doctors now offer them in capsule form.

Acupuncture: The sticking of fine metal needles into the skin at places where meridians come closest to the skin.

Deep tissue massage: Known as *tuina*, or acupressure, it is like acupuncture, except the practitioner uses fingers and hands instead of needles.

Cupping: The placement of glass or bamboo cups on the skin to create suction, which affects the flow of *qi* and blood.

Moxibustion: The burning of a stick or cone of a pungent herb called mugwort near the problem area.

TCM's aim is to treat underlying conditions rather than just outward symptoms. Patients should expect to visit a practitioner regularly over the course of several months, depending on the particular problem. TCM tends to work slowly and is not for those seeking a quick fix—with regular visits a practitioner will come to better understand the patient's body, and the more effective the treatment will be.

TCM practitioners in California are licensed as "acupuncturists," though acupuncture itself is just one of many types of treatment within traditional Chinese medicine. Many TCM practitioners advertise themselves first and foremost as acupuncturists, though the good ones are normally well versed in other treatments as well.

Practitioners

For long years of experience plus a pleasant bedside manner, 58-year-old **Dr. Lip** (1806 38th St., 415/566-5310) may be the man to see in San Francisco—he certainly is for the countless patients from Hong Kong,

Taiwan, and mainland China who regularly make their way up the steep staircase to his office on a residential street in the Sunset district. The son of an herbalist, Dr. Lip has been practicing TCM since 1966, first in Hong Kong and then in San Francisco, starting in 1980. He also has extensive experience in traditional Chinese-style bone setting, having worked as the team doctor for the Hong Kong Rangers Football Club for three years in the 1970s.

Upon arrival at Dr. Lip's office, patients are greeted from behind the counter by Mrs. Lip, who speaks with patients in Cantonese, Mandarin, and sometimes English, while busily filling prescriptions from the walls of herb drawers behind the counter. Like any doctor's office, patients sign in and take a seat in the waiting area. The cost of Dr. Lip's treatments can be high—a two-week supply of herbs can cost 50 dollars. But consider the case of Mr. Jung—a patient-turned-assistant who first started seeing Dr. Lip when he was in his sixties and suffering from sciatica, sinusitis, heart disease, asthma, and gout. Now 74, he is the picture of health, and continues to drink Dr. Lip's herbs twice a week. "Dr. Lip saved my life," he proclaims, as he fills another prescription.

Sandra Zheng (not her real name) had her first child through in-vitro fertilization (IVF) when she was 36 years old. Desiring more children a few years later, she underwent another IVF at a well-regarded fertility clinic in San Francisco—it failed twice over the course of two years. Her doctor suggested that while undergoing the procedure a last time, the 40-year-old consider acupuncture treatments with Angela Wu at **Wu's Healing Center** (1014 Clement St., 415/752-0170), and today she and her husband are the proud parents of twins.

Dr. Wu's fertility program is intensive. She suggests women start seeing her for weekly acupuncture or acupressure treatments 3-6 months before they want to get pregnant or start IVF treatment. She prescribes herbs and asks patients to follow a special diet. Treatment intensifies during the actual IVF cycle, including home acupuncture treatments. After

TRADITIONAL CHINESE MEDICINE IN CALIFORNIA

Waves of Chinese people immigrated to California in the mid-19th century. Some came to work on the railroads that would soon crisscross the United States. Others flocked here to seek their fortune in the California Gold Rush. But whatever their motivation, they would inevitably get sick, creating demand here for the healing arts of their homeland.

Prejudice, arrogance, and ignorance kept traditional Chinese medicine from spreading beyond the Chinese population for many years. Indeed, for much of the 20th century, acupuncturists could be arrested in California for performing their trade. It was not until the 1970s that attitudes began to change. Thanks to practitioners' and patients' lobbying efforts, the California Board of Medical Examiners finally legalized the industry in 1975—albeit with caveats: Acupuncturists had to be referred to patients by a doctor, dentist, podiatrist, or chiropractor. The state lifted these restrictions in 1978, when it also made acupuncture treatments eligible for Medi-Cal reimbursement and approved the industry as a certified healthcare profession.

Of course, traditional Chinese medicine involves much more than just acupuncture. Without the ability to prescribe herbs, offer specific types of massage, and perform moxibustion and cupping, Chinese medicine practitioners were stymied in their efforts to treat patients. The state rectified this situation in 1980 when it expanded the scope of legitimate practice for acupuncturists. Eight years later the profession received another big boost when the state passed legislation that included acupuncturists as "physicians" in California's Workers Compensation system.

conception, she recommends acupuncture treatments twice weekly during the first trimester and once a week during the last 6-8 weeks of pregnancy. Weekly treatments ideally continue for three months after birth to hasten recovery and encourage successful pregnancies in the future.

Located in the heart of San Francisco's Chinatown at the intersection of Clay Street and Waverly Place, **Tong Fong** (101 Waverly Pl., 415/296-

7591) looks like a typical Chinese retail pharmacy, selling items like herb cookers and acupuncture needles. Dr. Zeng, with 40 years of experience, and his son Dennis, have an office and treatment room in the back of the store. In China, patients traditionally look for doctors with a long family history of practicing Chinese medicine. The Zengs certainly qualify—the elder Zeng's father and grandfather were both TCM doctors in China.

A reputable pharmacist from the Kowloon side in Hong Kong, the elder Dr. Tam moved his **Dana Oriental Market** (800 California St. #120, 650/969-2034) to Mountain View in the South Bay in 1987. His son has since taken over the operation, and while he does not practice TCM himself, there are three doctors on staff treating mostly Chinese clients. The shop, which is located in a modern three-story building, is both a pharmacy and a market selling videos, groceries, and cell phones.

1-2-3 Acupuncture (4546 El Camino Real, #206, 650/949-2339), located in Los Altos in the South Bay, specializes in the treatment and management of neck and upper back pain and related problems. Led by **Helen Liu,** who practiced at the China Academy of TCM in Beijing, the clinic is also the office of Certified Massage Therapist Michael Xu, for patients needing traditional Chinese deep tissue massage.

For those wanting to study TCM but who are unable to study in Asia, the Bay Area offers a number of schools specializing in the field. To become a licensed practitioner, make sure to choose a program authorized by the state of California to grant your chosen degree. **The American College of Traditional Chinese Medicine** (455 Arkansas St., 415/282-7600) in San Francisco is one of the most well established schools on the West Coast. ACTCM first began offering instruction in 1981, educating students through a rigorous four-year program beginning with biology and chemistry and leading into local TCM internships. The **Academy of Chinese Culture & Health Services** (1601 Clay St., 510/763-7787) in Oakland has also been educating TCM practitioners since 1981, and allows full-time students to complete its four-year professional degree program in three years. The same holds true in the South Bay at the **University of East-West Medicine** (970 W. El Camino Real, 408/733-1878) in Sunnyvale, which was founded in 1997 by TCM practitioner Ying Qiu Wang.

AYURVEDIC MEDICINE

Ayurveda is an ancient Indian healing tradition integrating mind, body, and spirit. Although less well known than traditional Chinese medicine, ayurvedic medicine has risen in popularity over the last decade thanks to holistic-healing guru Deepak Chopra. Meaning "the science of life" in Sanskrit, *ayurveda* emphasizes the prevention of disease and is primarily a "wellness" or "healing" system. Practitioners help patients create a lifestyle that is in balance with the cycles of nature so that disease takes care of itself. Ayurvedic medicine teaches that each person's body is made up of three energies, known as *doshas*, but in different proportions. Ill health strikes when an individual's *doshas* are out of balance with their predetermined "body type." To rebalance them, an ayurvedic practitioner might tell you to be most active at a certain time of day or to eat more of one thing and less of another. They might also prescribe herbal remedies, massage, detoxification, and/or yoga.

Compared to TCM, ayurveda is in its infancy, both in popularity and comprehension by the public. It is not yet a licensed profession, nor is there a recognized scope of practice for ayurvedic practitioners in California. The **California Association of Ayurvedic Medicine** (800/292-4882), a non-profit professional organization located in Foster City, is working to improve public knowledge and acceptance of their practices.

One of the most respected ayurvedic practitioners in the Bay Area is sari-clad **Pratichi Mathur** (1111 W. El Camino Real #109, 800/924-6815) in Sunnyvale. Descended from a long line of *vedic* healers and a student of a top Indian authority on ayurveda, she arrived from India in 1998 with the goal of bringing authentic ayurveda to the United States. She takes appointments in Sunnyvale, Oakland, and San Francisco.

BARBARA BERNIE

Forty years ago traditional Chinese medicine practitioners could be prosecuted for performing acupuncture on a patient in California. Now traditional Chinese medicine is a flourishing healthcare profession. Key among the people who struggled to legitimize traditional Chinese medicine in California in the 1970s and 1980s was San Francisco resident Barbara Bernie.

A model and interior designer during the first half of her working life, she went on to become a licensed acupuncturist, Chairperson of California's Acupuncture Licensing Examination Sub-Committee, and a consultant to the California State Acupuncture Committee, where she worked to establish high standards and regulations for schools and professionals. As founder of the American Foundation of Traditional Chinese Medicine (AFTCM), she promoted the exchange of knowledge between the People's Republic of China and the United States, organizing foreign acupuncturists to study in China and co-sponsoring conferences. She helped hospitals develop their acupuncture programs and healthcare professionals understand traditional Chinese medicine's healing powers.

Now Bernie is elderly and ailing. But her efforts and those of other pioneers like her were instrumental in making traditional Chinese medicine in the Bay Area the respected profession that it is today. Says longtime San Francisco resident and Hong Kong native Cindy Yu about Bernie: "She is one of those people who makes you believe that there are real angels/Bodhisattvas on earth."

Years of experience and an understanding of western medicine characterize **Dr. Jay Apte**. She received a degree in medicine and surgery in India in 1973 and a Master's degree in pharmacology in the United States in 1990, and opened her first clinic in Houston, Texas in 1987. Now with clinics in San Francisco and Fremont as well, her services include body type analysis, ayurvedic diet and lifestyle counseling, vegetarian cooking classes, and weekly support groups. She is also the founder of **Ayurveda Institute of America (AIA)** (561 Pilgrim Dr., Ste. B, 650/341-8400) in Foster City.

CHINESE BONE-SETTING

The next time you break a leg, dislocate a shoulder, or sprain an ankle, you might want to consider seeing a practitioner skilled in the ancient art of Chinese bone-setting. A subfield of Chinese therapeutic massage, or *tuina*, it involves manipulation to realign bones, ligaments, and muscles. Instead of putting a plaster caste on your broken leg, as in western medicine, a Chinese bone-setter applies an herbal patch and places a thin board along the damaged limb to help it heal. The practitioner then checks the injury regularly to adjust the herbal patch's tightness as swelling decreases. Depending on the seriousness of your problem, this could entail daily visits to the doctor for two to three weeks or more. While more time consuming than Western bone-setting methods, it has a big advantage: A plaster cast stays the same size no matter how much an injury's swelling has subsided, whereas the herbal patch allows for fine-tuning and, arguably, better support.

Probably the most well known and well-marketed school in the area, however, is the **California College of Ayurveda** (117A E. Main St., 866/541-6699), founded and directed by **Dr. Marc Halperin.** The school is headquartered in Grass Valley, but has opened branches in San Francisco, San Jose, and Seal Beach. Students graduate with the title of Clinical Ayurvedic Specialist (C.A.S.).

ASIAN BODYWORK AND THERAPEUTIC MASSAGE

Massage is an integral part of Asian-style healthcare. Based on ancient Chinese medical theories regarding the flow of *qi*, Asian massage focuses on helping the body heal itself by balancing and unblocking energy movement through the body—whereas Western massage focuses on relaxation.

People from all over the Bay Area travel to San Rafael, in Marin County, for a session with *tuina* expert and TCM practitioner **Rocky Wang** (1299 4th St., Ste. 406, 415/258-9199), who specializes in injury and pain treatment. Many patients come to him after all other treatments have failed. Friendly and responsive, Wang arrived in the United States nine years ago after working in China for eight years as an orthopedic surgeon practicing both Western and Chinese medicine. He also taught traditional Chinese medicine for seven years at the American Center for Traditional Chinese Medicine (ACTCM) in San Francisco. His appointments normally last 45 minutes to an hour and involve a health check, some acupuncture, and then massage and stretching, and herbal prescriptions as needed.

Korean *sukido* therapy practitioner **Yokey Kim** (1610 Post St. #205, 415/921-2003), a 64-year-old native of Korea, works with his daughter out of a small, second-floor office in San Francisco's Japantown neighborhood practicing his own unique acupressure technique. After studying many healing methods in Korea, including acupuncture, shiatsu, and yoga, he developed a technique that utilizes the entire hand, as opposed to the "point-pressure" style of other techniques, which mostly utilizes the thumb. Dr. Kim has been practicing acupressure for 32 years.

Many Japanese people in San Francisco go to **Sain-Saine** (415/292-3542) inside the Japan Center Miyako Mall in Japantown, for *anma*, which has its roots in China some 1,300 years ago. Its literal meaning is "massage," or "massage practitioner," in Japanese. Sain-Saine's Japanese-speaking therapists massage, rub, press, and hit your body, and if you're in a hurry, they offer a 15-minute special.

Authentic Japanese *shiatsu*, literally "finger massage," a type of *anma* relying on finger pressure, was systematized early in the 20th century, but relies on many of the same principles as older Japanese massage techniques. **Fuji Shiatsu** (1721 Buchanan Mall, 415/346-4484) in San Francisco's Japantown features a number of licensed practitioners, two of whom were trained in Japan. Ask for Michiko and Naomi for the massage clinic's most authentic *shiatsu*. For *shiatsu* in a serene spa setting, the posh **Kabuki Springs & Spa** (415/922-6000) is located right in Japantown, in the Japan Center. Tomo and Yoshio, both trained in Japan, have been practicing

JAPANESE ACUPUNCTURE

Certified acupuncturist Kei Kurotani compares the difference between Chinese and Japanese acupuncture to the difference between dim sum and sushi: "Asian taste but different," he quips cheerily at his 10th floor office in downtown San Francisco. He uses thinner needles than in traditional Chinese acupuncture—as thin as a cat hair—and inserts them less deeply. He applies moxibustion directly on the skin without burning it, using his fingertips to adjust the heat. Kurotani, who studied both Chinese and Japanese acupuncture in Japan, practiced in Tokyo and Burma before arriving in the United States five years ago. His mostly Japanese clientele seek relief from irritability, anxiety attacks, and stress-related asthma, as well as gynecological problems, HIV/AIDS, and cancer. "I can't cure HIV or cancer," he says, but following his treatments, which seek to balance the immune system, patients "can have a better appetite and quality of life."

shiatsu there for over 20 years. Kabuki also offers a couple of different types of ayurvedic massage, including *shirodara*, a treatment utilizing warm, herbalized oil poured over the forehead.

MARTIAL ARTS

Closely tied to traditional Chinese medicine, the Chinese internal martial arts, like *tai chi* or *qigong*, use mind, breath, and movement to strengthen, unblock, or calm internal energy, or *qi*. Qigong and *tai chi* exercises are helpful in the treatment of conditions like high blood pressure, arthritis, and depression, and are believed to slow the aging process. They also increase flexibility and strengthen muscles.

In China, martial arts are often practiced outdoors in the morning, and the tradition lives on in the Bay Area. *Tai chi* aficionados gather daily in front of the **Lake Merritt Bart Station** in Oakland starting at around 7:00 in the morning for two to three hours. On weekends, Golden Gate Park is a beehive of activity. **Golden Gate Park Tai Chi Class** meets at Spreckels

Lake at 36th Avenue and Fulton Street on Saturdays and Sundays, starting at 6:30 in the morning for advanced students and 8:30 for everyone else. The group focuses mostly on the highly popular Yang style *tai chi*, taught by Grand Master **Bill Chin,** but instruction is also available in Chen style from Master **Frank Soon.** On Sunday mornings at 9:30 in the park at 6th Avenue and Fulton, **Liping Julia Zhu** (415/355-0888) teaches Taiyi Swimming Dragon Chuan, a mixture of *qigong, tai chi,* and dance. She and her students normally grab a bite to eat at a nearby Chinese restaurant following the hour-long class. For high-quality indoor study during the week, **Martin Inn** of the **Inner Research Institute** (www.iritaichi.net) offers Yang-style *tai chi* classes to all levels on 8th Street in San Francisco. Beginner courses start every four months.

Of the more aggressive martial art forms, *kung-fu, tae kwon do, karate,* and *aikido* are the most common. **Tat Wong Kung Fu Academy** (www.tatwong.com), with branches in San Francisco, San Mateo, and Concord, is especially popular. Founded by Master **Tat-Mau Wong**, a Hong Kong native, who has been practicing martial arts since 1963, the academy teaches the powerful and practical Choy Lay Fut style, which emphasizes fast and powerful stance transitions coordinated with devastating punching and kicking combinations. Many parents in San Francisco prefer to send their children for instruction in the throws and attacks of *aikido.* The **Aikido Center** (www.pacificaikido.org) in Japantown, which also has a branch in Mountain View, offers instruction in the "principle of circular motion," which effectively teaches students to manipulate an opponents own energy, or *qi,* against them. The center also offers Zen meditation on Friday evenings at 5:30. For those wanting to study *shorinji kempo,* the **World Shorinji Kempo Organization** (www.geocities.com/sfshorinji) has established branches in San Francisco's Japantown and San Jose. *Shorinji kempo,* utilizing punches, kicks, throws, pins, and locks, was developed by a Japanese government agent stationed in China in the 1930s and 1940s. The experienced **Master Atsushi Muraoka,** meanwhile, teaches a combination of *karate* and *shorinji kempo* at his **Ken Zen Do** (1529 South B St., 650/341-4142) school in San Mateo. He encourages students to "practice hard with a smile."

Hwa Rang Kwan (www.hwarangkwan.com) in San Francisco, San Rafael, and Redwood City is the oldest Korean martial arts school on the West Coast. It's best known for classes in tae kwon do, a discipline involving strong, quick strikes with both the hands and feet. **Master D. K. Shin,** with 47 years experience, has personally trained all instructors.

YOGA

It's hard to find a neighborhood in the Bay Area that does not have a place for practicing yoga. First developed in India as an aspect of *ayurvedic* medicine, yoga has, over the last 10 years, boomed in popularity in the United States. As much a mental and spiritual practice as a physical one, yoga involves meditation, breath control, and specific body postures called *asanas.* The practice of yoga relieves physical and mental tension and can help to avoid physical injury as well. Breath control, or *pranayama,* improves health by increasing the flow of vital energy. There are numerous different styles of yoga practiced today. The most popular in the Bay Area are the following.

Hatha: Focuses on holding traditional postures using accurate alignment.

Iyengar: Based on the teachings of B. K. S. Iyengar, is hatha yoga but with an emphasis on the precise alignment of muscles, joints, and bones. Students generally hold poses for a longer time than in other branches of yoga and use various props to help align their bodies.

Ashtanga: Based on the teachings of K. Pattabhi Jois, is also hatha yoga but with an emphasis on continuous movement from one posture to the next, and breath synchronization.

For some of the best Iyengar instructors in San Francisco, serious students often go to the **Iyengar Yoga Institute** (2404 27th Ave., 415/753-

0909). The first Iyengar institute in the United States, it offers a rigorous instructor training program on top of the regular classes. Many of the instructors at the institute have traveled to India to study with Mr. Iyengar himself. **Ramanand Patel,** who has been studying yoga seriously since 1968, is a leading instructor worldwide and one of the institute's most popular teachers. He teaches at a number of yoga studios in San Francisco, Marin, and the East Bay, and offers workshops internationally, so check out his whereabouts at www.yogirama.com.

For Iyengar guided by personal intuition, there's no instructor more popular than **Rodney Yee,** codirector at **Piedmont Yoga** 4125 Piedmont Ave., 510/652-3336) in Oakland. In fact, *Organic Style Magazine* referred to Yee, who has become something of a celebrity, as America's most popular yogi. Yee is also a respected instructor of other yoga teachers and has taught many of the other instructors at Piedmont Yoga.

Ben Thomas, of the highly recommended **California Yoga Center** (570 Showers Dr. #5, 650/947-9642,) in Mountain View, generally starts his Iyengar classes by choosing one small part of the body for students to focus on when doing postures that day, then spends time correcting both beginning and advanced students, always in an amiable manner. Thomas is usually instructing classes at the California Yoga Center, but for a complete list of locations, check out his website at www.thomasyoga.com.

Ashtanga students head to Mill Valley for classes at **YogaStudio** (www.yogastudiomillvalley.com) with **John Berlinsky,** who studied with Mr. Jois in Mysore, India. YogaStudio, with branches in both Larkspur Landing and Mill Valley, offers instruction in a wide variety of yoga styles at various levels in an attractive setting. The cost for classes at this popular, well-run studio is on the high side of the Bay Area spectrum.

HEALTH AND FITNESS

Traditional Herb and Health Food Shops

Great China Herb Co. This shop offers a massive wall of fresh Chinese herbs and carries everything from ginseng to dried scallops. The shop first opened in 1922, and the current owners still use the same set of cabinets to store the herbs. There is a Chinese doctor at the store for those feeling ill. 857 Washington St., San Francisco; 415/982-2195.

Pharmaca Integrative Pharmacy. This shop is filled with aisles upon aisles of nutritional supplements, herbs, homeopathic remedies, and natural body care products, as well as stacks of natural healing books. Pharmaca also hosts occasional evening lectures by herbalists, nutritionists, homeopaths, and the like. 925 Cole St., San Francisco; 415/661-1216. Other location: 1744 Solano Ave., Berkeley; 510/526-2452.

Superior Trading Company. This herb company boasts the largest house of Oriental herbs and ginseng, with imports from China, Korea, and Hong Kong. 837 Washington St., San Francisco; 415/982-8722; www.superiortrading.com.

Vinh Khang Herb & Ginseng. This small shop is packed with hundreds of drawers full of herbs. The shop's claim to fame came when actress Julia Roberts walked in to film a portion of *Dying Young*, but mostly this shop has become popular via word of mouth. 512 Clement St., San Francisco; 415/752-8336.

Alpha Health Foods Herbs & Acupuncture Clinic. 3100 Coolidge Ave., Oakland; 510/465-7410.

American Chinese Natural Herbs. 2449 Alvin Ave., San Jose; 408/532-6982.

Chinese Herb Co. 918 Clement St., San Francisco; 415/387-1892.

Kee Cheung Co. 718 Pacific Ave., San Francisco; 415/397-6888.

Lhasa Karnak Herb Co. 1938 Shattuck Ave., Berkeley; 510/548-0372. 2513 Telegraph Ave., Berkeley; 510/548-0380.

San Francisco Herb & Natural Food Co. 47444 Kato Rd., Fremont; 510/770-1215, www.herbspicetea.com.

The Scarlet Sage Herb Co. 1173 Valencia St., San Francisco; 415/821-0997, www.scarletsageherb.com.

Tran's Trading Co. 849 Washington St., San Francisco; 415/788-0110.

Wan Hua Co. 665 Jackson St., San Francisco; 415/398-5471.

Yau Hing Co. 831 Grant Ave., San Francisco; 415/989-0620.

Ying Wai Chinese Herb Store. 320 10th St. #134 Oakland; 510/832-1128.

Acupuncture, Herbalists, Other Practitioners

1-2-3 Acupuncture and Health Center in the South Bay specializes in traditional Chinese medicine to help patients with pain-related problems. **Helen Liu**, who practiced previously at the China Academy of TCM in Beijing, is the lead practitioner there. 4546 El Camino Real, Ste. 206, Los Altos; 650/949-2339, www.123acupuncture.com.

American College of Traditional Chinese Medicine. Aside from taking classes, the college runs a community clinic using acupuncture and Chinese herbs to treat upper respiratory problems, immune deficiency, gastro-intestinal troubles, cardio-vascular and musculo-skeletal problems, among other ailments. 450 Connecticut St., San Francisco; 415/282-7600 (college); 415/282-9603 (clinic).

Angela Wu, who runs **Wu's Healing Center** in San Francisco, is the person to see if you are having trouble having a baby. She uses herbs, acupuncture, and other TCM approaches to help patients conceive naturally and with the help of Western assisted reproduction techniques. 1014 Clement St., San Francisco; 415/752-0170, www.wushealingcenter.com.

Carl Hangee-Bauer, ND, L.Ac, SOMA Acupuncture and Chinese Health Clinic. Services offered include acupuncture, naturopathic medicine, Western and Chinese herbal medicines, and nutritional counseling. 1615 20th St., San Francisco; 415/643-6600, www.somaacupuncture.com.

Chi Nei Tsang Institute. Chi Nei Tsang is a holistic approach to massage therapy with its origins in Chinese Taoism. It integrates the physical, mental, emotional, and spiritual aspects of individuals. Practitioners are trained in Chi-Kung and work mainly on the abdomen with deep, gentle touch, to train internal organs to work more efficiently. 2812 Telegraph Ave., Berkeley; 800/495-7797, 510/534-7697, www.cntcenter.com.

Dana Oriental Market was a venerable Chinese pharmacy in Hong Kong before moving to the South Bay in 1987. While the elder Dr. Tam no longer practices traditional Chinese medicine, three other practitioners are available to see patients. 800 California St. #120, Mountain View; 650/969-2034.

Dr. Jay Apte is a respected ayurvedic healer in the South Bay with many years of experience, starting with training in India in both western and ayurvedic medicine in the early 1970s. She has also founded a school, the **Ayurveda Institute of America (AIA)**, to teach ayurveda to doctors, nurses and others. Ayurveda Institute of America, 561 Pilgrim Drive, Suite B, Foster City; 650/341-8400; www.ayurvedainstitute.com.

Institute for Health and Healing is the integrative medicine clinic operated by **California Pacific Medical Center (CPMC)**. It offers a variety of Ayurvedic and TCM treatments. 2300 California St., San Francisco; 415/600-HEAL or 415/600-4325, www.cpmc.org/services/ihh.

Kei Kurotani offers patients suffering from a range of ailments Japanese-style acupuncture at his clinic in downtown San Francisco. The technique is known for its light touch and shallow insertion of extremely thin needles. Toshi Union Square Salon, 166 Geary St., Ste. 1000, San Francisco; 415/370-1757.

Medicine Buddha Healing Center. A blend of East Indian Ayurvedic Medicine, Chinese Medicine, and Tibetan Medicine. Treatments include Pancha Karma purification/cleansing massage, herbal remedies, dietary and nutrition counseling, and lifestyle health recommendations. 2427 McKinley Ave., Ste. 1, Berkeley; 510/843-0163; www.ayurveda-berkeley.com.

Osher Center for Integrative Medicine at UCSF has a traditional Chinese medicine practice and provides first and second year medical students a program to learn more about TCM and its relation to western medicine. 1701 Divisadero St., Ste. 150, San Francisco.

Peggy Arent is a highly popular acupuncturist and gifted healer specializing in the five-point method of acupuncture. Her practice attracts the "who's who" of San Francisco. Be sure to bring plenty of reading material as the wait can be long. 620 Euclid Ave., San Francisco; 415/221-5098.

Peter C. C. Lip offers four decades of experience in traditional Chinese medicine and a pleasant bedside manner at his clinic in San Francisco's Sunset District. He also is practiced in the art of Chinese bone-setting. His waiting room often fills up so be prepared to wait. 1806 38th St., San Francisco; 415/566-5310.

Pratichi Mathur, who hails from a long line of ayurvedic healers in India, is a respected ayurvedic specialist in the Bay Area and founder of the **Ganesha Institute.** She takes appointments in San Francisco, Berkeley and Sunnyvale. PMB 211, 1111 W. El Camino Real, Ste. 109, Sunnyvale; 800/924-6815.

Rocky Wang is a highly respected practitioner of traditional Chinese medicine operating in the North Bay and San Francisco. He specializes in treating patients suffering from chronic pain in their back, neck, knee, etc.

using a combination of herbs, acupuncture and *tuina*. 1299 Fourth St., Suite 406, San Rafael; 415/258-9199 and 3033 Clement St., San Francisco; 415/353-7700.

Stanford Center for Integrative Medicine, which is part of the Stanford University Medical Center and affiliated with Stanford University School of Medicine, offers acupuncture, medical qigong, shiatsu, and other Asian-inspired treatments. 300 Pasteur Dr., Stanford; 650/498-5566, www.scim.stanfordhospital.com.

Tung Fong Herbs Co., located in the heart of San Francisco's Chinatown, is both a Chinese retail pharmacy and a doctor's office. The elder Dr. Zeng boasts 40 years of experience. Prices are reasonable. 101 Waverly Place, San Francisco; 415/296-7591.

Usha Khosla, originally from India, is a noted ayurvedic specialist in the East Bay at the **Ayurveda Healing Center.** She is trained in both ayurvedic and Western medicine and has over 30 years of experience. 29621 Mission Blvd., Hayward; 510/727-9891.

Anne Angelone, MS, L.Ac.; Valencia Healing Arts Center. 1193 Valencia St., San Francisco; 415/647-6222.

DAAN Acupuncture and Chinese Herb Center. Dr. Lois Yen, Susan S. Yen, MSTCM, L.Ac. (acupuncture and health consultations). 614 Jackson St., San Francisco; 877/322-6168, 415/433-3277, www.daan.com.

Daniel Donner offers nutritional evaluations, acupuncture, homeopathy, and herbal medicine. Piedmont Avenue Clinic. 3927 Piedmont Ave., Oakland; 510/655-0555, www.piedmontaveclinic.com.

Dr. Bai Qing Deng (Acupuncturist and Herbalist). 775 Filbert St., San Francisco; 415/397-8139. Second location at 2288 Noriega St., San Francisco; 415/682-0293.

Fu Fu Acupuncture & Qi Gong Clinic. 5300 Geary Blvd., Ste. 315, San Francisco; 415/933-9993.

Japantown Acupuncture & Oriental Medicine. Yuko Gower L.Ac (acupuncturist and herbalist). Kinokuniya Building, 1581 Webster St., Ste. 245, San Francisco; 415/922-2100.

The Longevity Center of Classic Chinese Medicine. 4950 Hamilton Ave. Ste. 205, San Jose; Arnold E. Tayam: 408/374-3686; Shasta Tierra-Tayam: 408/712-4048, www.longevity-center.com.

Peninsula Holistic Health Center. 53 N. San Mateo Dr., Ste. B, San Mateo; 650/348-2764.

Raymond Cheung (Acupuncturist/Chiropractor). 2408 Lombard St., San Francisco; 415/928-3734.

Usha Khosla, Ayurveda Healing Center. 29261 Mission Blvd., Hayward; 510/727-9891.

Yongyi Wu, L.Ac. O.M.D DR.; Wu's Acupuncture Herbal Center. 835 Clay St., Ste. 102, San Francisco; 415/362-7276.

Martial Arts

Academy of Martial Arts Shotokan, Inc. The Academy, which has been teaching Shotokan Karate since 1989, focuses on balance and muscle control. AMAS is recognized by both the International Shotokan Karate Federation and the Japan Karate Association. Classes for children and adults, 2219-A Gellert Blvd., South San Francisco; 650/878-1177, www.bestkarate.com.

Aikido Center, under head instructor Hideki Shiohira, offers classes to all levels in Japanese aikido in both San Francisco and the South Bay. 1755 Laguna St., San Francisco; 415/921-5073 and 2560 Wyandotte Ave., Ste. A, Mountain View; 650/969-1731, www.pacificaikido.org.

Golden Gate Park Tai Chi Class meets on Saturday and Sunday mornings at Spreckels Lake in Golden Gate Park. Grand Master **Bill Chin**

teaches Yang style long form mostly, but Chen style is also offered. Spreckels Lake, 36th Ave. and Fulton St., Golden Gate Park, San Francisco.

Heart of the Mission Aikido. Heart of the Mission offers a new beginning class for adults every two months, taught by black-belt instructors. Students learn to move fluidly and to relax under pressure. The studio is geared to first-timers, as well as those just coming back to their Aikido practice. 565 3rd St. #309, San Francisco; 415/643-8407, www.heartaikido.com.

Hwa Rang Kwan. Hwa Rang Kwan, established in San Francisco in 1965 by Grandmaster D.K. Shin, holds the distinction as the oldest Korean martial arts center on the West Coast. The center teaches taekwando, hapkido, kickboxing, and kumdo at branches in San Rafael, San Francisco, and the peninsula. 371 5th St., San Francisco; 415/495-2025; 1739 Noriega St., San Francisco; 415/504-8778; 133 Roosevelt Ave., Redwood City; 650/369-5425; 933 D St., San Rafael; 415/457-3445, www.hwarangkwan.com.

Ken Zen Do USA, founded by Master **Atusushi Muraoka** in the South Bay, provides instruction in Ken Zen Do, which is a combination of full contact karate and shorinji kempo. 1529 South B St., San Mateo; 650/341-4142, www.kenzendo.com.

Martin Inn offers tai chi instruction to all levels of students at his **Inner Research Institute** in San Francisco. He focuses on Yang style short form. 301 8th St. # 260, San Francisco; 415/285-9408, www.iritaichi.org.

Taiyi Swimming Dragon Chuan, a mixture of tai chi, qi gong, and dancing taught by popular instructor Liping (Julia) Zhu. The group meets Sunday mornings at 6th Ave. and Fulton Street in Golden Gate Park at 9:30. 415/355-0888.

Tat Wong Kung Fu Academies, founded by Master **Tat-Mau Wong**, is a popular place to study Kung Fu in San Francisco, San Mateo and Concord. Wong, who has been involved in martial arts since the 1960s, specializes in the Choy Lei Fut style. 2901 Clement St., San Francisco;

415/752-5555. 53 43rd Ave., San Mateo; 650/341-9292. 5100 Clayton Rd. #A10, Concord; 925/288-0900, www.tatwong.com.

World Shorinji Kempo Organization. The San Francisco offers courses to all levels in this relatively new Japanese martial art form whose goal is to develop "healthy bodies, indomitable courage, and well-rounded character in order to make individuals capable of leading happy lives. At the same time the purpose is to nourish in them the courage and enthusiasm that will allow them to act aggressively to achieve a peacefully and prosperously ideal society, and to raise people well endowed with good judgment and a sense of justice who will serve as true leaders." Classes are held on the lower floor of the Sokoji Temple in Japantown at the corner of Laguna and Sutter St. http://wsko.econ-net.or.jp.

Yang's Martial Arts Academy offers instruction in the North Bay in traditional Korean royal court martial arts and in the traditional *Poomse* and *Kyroogi* forms of Tae Kwon Do from Grand Master **Soon Tae Yang**, a 9th degree black belt with over 45 years experience. 548 Magnolia Ave., Larkspur; 415/924-4366.

Academy of Tae Kwon Do. 3972 Washington Blvd., Fremont; 510/490-3636.

Evolving Body Mind Kung Fu Academy. 666 63rd St., Oakland; 510/658-3378, www.kungfu.net.

Lien-Ying Tai Chi Chuan Academy. 15 Walter U Lum Pl., San Francisco; 415/362-4180.

USA Martial Arts. 1029 Blossom Hill Rd., Ste. 8, San Jose; 408/448-1995, www.usama.00sports.com.

Bodywork

1-2-3 Acupuncture and Health Center in the South Bay specializes in pain management treatments, including Chinese *tuina*. Michael Xu is the certified massage therapist on staff. Wear loose clothing. 4546 El Camino Real, Ste. 206, Los Altos; 650/949-2339, www.123acupuncture.com.

Fuji Shiatsu in San Francisco's Japantown offers authentic shiatsu in a cozy setting. Masseuses Michiko and Naomi were both trained in Japan. 1721 Buchanan Mall, San Francisco; 415/346-4484.

Kabuki Springs & Spa is the place to go when you not only want a massage, but also want to pamper yourself. For an excellent Japanese shiatsu, ask for Tomo or Yoshio, who have over 20 years experience. Japan Center, 1750 Geary Blvd., San Francisco; 415/922-6000, www.kabukisprings.com.

Rocky Wang is a highly recommended traditional Chinese medicine practitioner operating in the North Bay and San Francisco. He is expert in Chinese *tuina,* among other treatments. 1299 4th St., Ste. 406, San Rafael; 415/258-9199, and 3033 Clement St., San Francisco; 415/353-7700.

Saine-Saine, located in the heart of San Francisco's Japantown, specializes in Japanese *anma*. For people with little time to spare, a 15-minute special is available. Japanese-speaking masseuses also offer reflexology. Miyako Mall, Japan Center, San Francisco; 415/292-3542.

Yokey Kim at **East West Chiropractic Center** (Kim's Body Design & Acupressure) practices Korean sukido therapy. With 32 years of practice, he is a master at relieving chronic pain. 1610 Post St. #205, San Francisco; 415/921-2003.

Yoga

Ben Thomas is a popular and experienced instructor of Iyengar style yoga at various spots around the South Bay. To find out where he is teaching at any given time, consult his website. www.thomasyoga.com.

The Breema Center. Offering traditional stretching classes and energy balancing. 6076 Claremont Ave., Oakland; 510/428-0937, www.breema .com.

California Yoga Center offers fine teachers and all levels of instruction in Iyengar style yoga, including pre-natal and classes for people with back problems. Meditation and pranayama workshops are also available. 570 Showers Dr., Ste. 5; Mountain View; 650/947-9642, www.californiayoga .com.

Funky Door Yoga teaches a routine of 26 poses which work the whole body in 90 minutes. The poses work synergistically and cumulatively to return the body to a balanced state, building energy, stamina, and flexibility. Incorporating strength, balance and "the tourniquet effect," which allows the stretching, squeezing and massaging of the internal organs. Bikram Choudhury brought his system to the United States in 1971 at the invitation of the American Medical Association. 186 Second St., San Francisco; 415/957-1088; 1334 Polk St., San Francisco; 415/673-8659; 1749 Waller St., San Francisco; 415/668-2227 and 2567 Shattuck Ave., Berkeley; 510/204-9642, www.funkydooryoga.com.

Iyengar Yoga Institute of San Francisco is known for excellent instruction at all levels in the Iyengar style and has a highly regarded teacher training course. Check out the bookstore. 2404 27th Ave., San Francisco; 415/753-0909, www.iyisf.org.

John Berlinsky is arguably the best instructor in the Bay Area for the ashtanga style of yoga. He teaches at **YogaStudio** in Mill Valley, which also has a lovely new studio in Larkspur Landing. 650 E. Blithedale Ave., Mill Valley; 415/380-8800 and 2207 Larkspur Landing Circle; Larkspur; www.yogastudiomillvalley.com.

Rodney Yee, a nationally recognized celebrity on the yoga circuit, teaches Iyengar style yoga at **Piedmont Yoga Studio**, where he is co-director.

Instructors graduate from his teacher training program well-trained. 4125 Piedmont Ave., Oakland; 510/652-3336, www.piedmontyoga.com.

Ramanand Patel is a highly regarded instructor of Iyengar style yoga teaching at various studios around the Bay Area. Check his website for times and locations. www.yogirama.com.

Rusty Wells teaches power yoga at **Yoga Flow Castro,** one of four studios under the Yoga Tree umbrella in San Francisco. His classes are so popular they can attract a hundred people at a time. Yoga Tree offers good instruction at various levels, locations, and in ashtanga, anusara, hatha, jivamukti, and Iyengar styles. Yoga Flow Castro; 97 Collingwood, San Francisco; 415/701-YOGA. Other Yoga Tree studios: 780 Stanyan St., San Francisco; 415/387-4707; 1234 Valencia St., San Francisco; 415/647-9707; 519 Hayes St., San Francisco; 415/626-9707, www.yogatreesf.com.

Zhi Dao Guan: The Taoist Center. Taoist meditation and martial arts. 3824 MacArthur Blvd., Oakland; 510/336-0129, www.thetaoistcenter.com.

7th Heaven. Ashtanga, kundalini, Iyengar, Vinyasa. 2820 Seventh St., Berkeley; 510/665-4300, www.7thHeavenyoga.com.

Berkeley Shambhala Center. 2288 Fulton St., Berkeley; 510/841-3242.

Elevation Pilates. 3425 Balboa St., San Francisco; 415/386-9008.

It's Yoga. Ashtanga, Pranayama, meditation. 848 Folsom St., San Francisco; 415/543-1970, www.itsyoga.net.

ReFormation Yoga & Pilates Studio. 1070 Lincoln Ave., San Jose; 408/993-9642.

Shambhala Meditation Center. 1630 Taraval St., San Francisco; 415/731-4426.

Siddha Yoga Meditation Center of San Jose. 4115 Jacksol Dr., San Jose; 408/559-1716.

Spirit Rock Meditation Center. 5000 Sir Francis Drake Blvd., Woodacre; 415/488-0164, www.spiritrock.org.

Yoga Mandala. 2807 Telegraph Ave., Berkeley; 510/486-1989, www.yoga-mandalastudio.com.

SPIRITUALITY
AND RELIGION

T HE HISTORY OF ASIAN RELIGIONS IN THE SAN Francisco Bay Area is the story of the fusion of ancient tradition with the native environment and people. In this land of rich, green, sweeping hills and wide Pacific vistas, the spiritual legacies of Tibet, Japan, India, and China have taken root and flourished in a way that is uniquely Californian.

Northern Californians are well known for embracing hybrid spiritualities and new religious movements. The Bay Area in particular is replete with opportunities for spiritual exploration. There are Buddhist temples from a variety of lineages, Hindu temples, Sufi *Zikrs*, Islamic mosques, and Asian Christian churches, among many others. Some emphasize traditional practices, for those who wish to follow the ways of the ancestors, while others teach some of the hybrids of spiritual practice that have found fertile ground in the West.

BUDDHISM

Buddhism was born in the 5th century A.D. with one man's realization of enlightenment. And though his life and circumstances may seem extraordinary, Buddhism teaches that the quality of *boddhicitta* (enlightened body and mind), which the Buddha embodied, is common to all human beings, whether they are a prince or a beggar, a politician or a housewife.

In the centuries that followed, Buddhism spread from India through Tibet, where it fused with the indigenous shamanic Bon tradition, and then outwards to China, where it took root as Mayahana Buddhism and Ch'an Buddhism. Almost a thousand years after the Buddha's passing, Buddhism came to Japan, where it took the face of various movements and sects, including Zen. It also spread to Southeast Asia, into what are modern-day Cambodia, Thailand, Vietnam, and Indonesia.

Buddhism made its way to America in the mid-19th century, when Japanese and Chinese teachers and immigrants began landing on these shores. A small number of texts from India and China were also arriving at this time. These texts were translated into English, and were soon discovered by the poets, artists, and intelligentsia of the day, such as American philosopher and Transcendentalist Henry David Thoreau, and Madame Blavatsky, the founder of the English-based Theosophical Society.

In the post-World War II era, Zen Buddhism became the unofficial muse for the Beat movement. Japanese teachers such as D. T. Suzuki, and western translators such as Alan Watts, made the teachings, ethos, and experience of Zen readily available to a wider audience. Beat artists like poet Allen Ginsberg and composer John Cage incorporated the Zen ethos into their art. In the 1950s, Jack Kerouac wrote the novel *Dharma Bums* about his friend, Pulitzer Prize-winning poet Gary Snyder, then a young Sinologist who became a resident (1956–65) at Ryosen-an, Daitokuji Kyoto, a temple restored and presided over by the American Buddhist Ruth Fuller-Sazaki.

In the mid-'60s, after the Chinese occupation of Tibet, the first Tibetan lamas began to come to America and Europe. In the last 50 years, Buddhism in its many forms has become an integral part of American culture and Bay Area life.

Certain teachings and practices of Buddhism have been consistent down through the centuries: An emphasis on the cultivation of compassion for all living creatures; the belief that *boddhicitta* (Buddha nature, awakened mind and heart) is the essence of all beings; that *bodhicitta* can be experienced through meditation; and that the embodiment of *bodhicitta* happens when we transcend the wheel of *samsara* (the cycle of life and death) while we are still alive, thus becoming enlightened.

The Bay Area has many opportunities for both the serious Buddhist practitioner and for those who are just curious. Sunday introductions, offered at many local centers, are a good place for the novice to learn basic methods of meditation, listen to a *dhar ma* speak, enjoy a cup of tea, and have a chance to meet members of the local *sangha* community.

The **San Francisco Zen Center** (300 Page St., 415/863-3136) is one of the largest *sanghas* (Buddhist communities) outside of Asia. The *sangha* includes **Green Gulch,** located in Marin, **Tassajara,** in the Ventana Headlands near Big Sur, and **City Center,** located at the corner of Page and Fell Streets in the city.

City Center, also known as Beginner's Mind Temple (*Hosshin-ji*), was established in 1969 by Shunryu Suzuki Roshi as a training center in the Soto Zen tradition. The much beloved Suzuki Roshi, famous for his book *Zen Mind, Beginner's Mind,* put a new face on the Soto tradition when he brought it to San Francisco in the midst of the exploding revolution of the '60s. The *Zendo* at City Center is spare and open. Meditation is done in the traditional Soto manner facing a blank white *shoji* screen, or, alternatively, facing a wall.

City Center offers opportunities for volunteer work-study that can be exchanged for classes, practice activities, fees, or tuition. Daily meditation, *zazen,* is held at 5:25 A.M. and 5:40 P.M. Monday through Friday and on Saturday mornings at 6:30 A.M. First-time practitioners of Zen are encouraged to attend the Saturday morning (8:45 A.M.) introduction to meditation and practice. Overnight accommodations and a vegetarian breakfast are offered to serious meditators for a reasonable price.

Nestled in a deep green valley which snakes dragon-like towards the misty coast of Muir Beach, the **Green Gulch Farm Zen Center** (1601

Shoreline Hwy., Sausalito; 415/383-3134), also known as Green Dragon Temple (Soryu-ji), is a long-standing Bay Area institution. The Center's emphasis is on the integration of meditation and ordinary work in the Japanese Soto Zen tradition. Individuals who come to stay here will have the opportunity to experience Zen practice in a day-to-day, moment-to-moment manner.

The Senior Dharma Instructor is Tenshin Zeb Anderson, who was initiated by Suzuki Roshi in 1970 as Tenshin Zenki ("Naturally Real, The Whole Works"). His *satsangs* embody a particular stillness and fullness of the moment that is simple and natural, yet infinitely deep.

The Center holds ongoing classes in Buddhist philosophy and practice. Ongoing retreats in Zendo meditation are also held, which range from one to seven days. There are opportunities for residential practice, as well as accommodations for short-term stays and a limited work-study program. On Sunday, a public program is offered, which includes *zazen* instruction, a lecture, tea, and a public lunch for a nominal fee.

If you cross the Richmond Bridge back into Albany (near Berkeley), you will find **The Community of Mindful Living** (850 Talbot Ave., 510/527-3751). CML supports the practice and teachings of mindful living offered by Vietnamese Zen Master and Nobel Peace Prize nominee Thich Nhat Hanh. "To be mindful means to dwell deeply in the present moment, to be aware of what is going on within and around us. Practicing mindfulness cultivates understanding, love, compassion, and joy."

Thich Nhat Hanh's teachings are for real life, both at the simplest level of day-to-day action and at the level of community and global action and service. In the 1960s it was Thich Nhat Hanh who persuaded Martin Luther King to oppose the Vietnam War. King subsequently nominated him for the Nobel Peace Prize. Thich Nhat Hanh's teachings are simple and his transmission is one of true peace—powerfully and undeniably. The Berkeley/Albany Center offers ongoing instruction, meditation retreats, and organizes events when Thich Nhat Hanh is in town.

Adyashanti is a local Zen teacher who is completely fresh, spontaneous, and not bound within the rigidity of a particular tradition. His *darshan* is at the **Open Gate Sangha** (408/236-2220). Adyashanti has the unique ability to truly touch a place of *boddhicitta* in the individual, no matter where they are in their spiritual unfolding. He is engaging, funny, humble, and contemporary, yet timeless. His *darshans* are attended by individuals of a variety of ethnicities and religious persuasions. The website has the latest schedule of intensives and weekly *darshans* held in the Bay Area: www.zen-satsang.org.

Tibetan Buddhism

Tibetan Buddhism truly began to move with vigor and purpose into the West when, in 1956, the current Dalai Lama and 80,000 other Tibetans and monks were exiled from Tibet. Within the next years, in tempo with the transformational period of the '60s in the West, young Tibetan teachers such as Tharthang Tulku, Chögyam Trunga Rimpoche, and Sogyal Rimpoche, as well as His Holiness the Dalai Lama, began to teach, share, and preserve their culture by spreading this living tradition into the West.

Much of contemporary American Tibetan Buddhism has grown up around these various *Rinpoches, Llamas* and *Tulkus,* teachers of various degrees and orders who have brought their traditions and teachings to the West. Thus, Tibetan Buddhism in the Bay Area is dominated by centers that focus on the work and teachings of a particular instructor and his or her lineage.

Situated in the Berkeley Hills, with sweeping views of the Bay, the **Nyingma Institute** (815 Highland Pl., 510/843-6812) is a quiet sanctuary of contemplative meditation and focused living, found through "skillful means." Founded by Tarthang Tulku, an accomplished Tibetan Lama who came to the United States in 1969, the Nyingma Institute in Berkeley is associated with the beautiful Odiyan Retreat in northern Sonoma County and Dharma Publishing, publisher and translator of many key Tibetan texts.

AVALOKITESHVARA

Tenzin Gyatso, the 14th Dalai Lama of Tibet, is believed by followers to be an emanation of Avalokiteshvara, the Buddha of Boundless Compassion. In the Buddhist pantheon Avalokiteshvara (or Chenrezig, Kaun Yin, and Kannon, as this Buddha is known in Tibet, China, and Japan, respectively) is an emanation of the Buddha, who upon reaching enlightenment vowed to continue working until all Beings were saved. After working for aeons the Buddha looked out and realized that there were still immense numbers of suffering beings to be saved. Seeing this, the Buddha became despondent and his head split into thousands of pieces. Avalokiteshvara is often visualized with eleven heads, and a thousand arms fanned out around him, thus representing the ability of this Buddha to work with a myriad of beings simultaneously: One body, many forms.

Thus it is said that Avalokiteshvara will take any form necessary, the Dalai Lama, a shop-boy, a grandmother, a teacher, or even a thief, in order to help all human beings develop compassion and obtain enlightenment. So as you walk down the street in the course of your normal day, don't be so quick to disregard the homeless person at your feet, or the frenetic businesswoman who passes by. Instead, look a little closer. With lucid eyes unobscured by *maya* (illusion) and an open heart you may find to your surprise the Buddha in disguise.

There are numerous ongoing classes and courses of study held at the Institute. The curriculum is a balance of Buddhist Philosophy and Psychology, Buddhist Texts, Skillful Means, Meditation, and *Kum Nye* (Tibetan relaxation exercises). **The Nyingma Institute** offers a work-study program where participants can stay as a resident for a period of six months. There are clean, shared rooms that offer beautiful views of the Bay or open onto the garden. Meals are delicious and vegetarian. The schedule is rigorous, however, integrating work, study, and meditation for up to 14 hours a day.

Perhaps one of the most thoughtful gifts the Nyingma Institute has given to the community is an exquisite rose garden with a tranquil lotus pond, a *stupa*, and one of the huge copper prayer wheels made especially by the Institute and kept in constant rotation to promote peace, harmony, and balance. Visitors are welcome to sit here, meditate, and escape from the frenetic to and fro of daily life. The staff at the Nyingma Institute are kind and dedicated: they embody what they teach. They are always open to questions from new visitors and are ready to suggest numerous opportunities for the curious to participate in volunteer work, ranging from tending the gardens to sewing prayer flags. Simple tasks give those interested a chance to experience the Institute's daily life. A variety of programs are held throughout the day on Sundays, including meditation, Tibetan chanting, and Kum Nye and Dharma Lectures from key teachers.

Other Buddhist Centers and Congregations

Set in the redwoods and rolling hills of West Marin, **Spirit Rock Meditation Center** (5000 Sir Francis Drake Blvd., Woodacre, 415/488-0164) is dedicated to the teachings of the Buddha as presented in the *Vipassana* tradition. *Vipassana*, which means "to see things as they really are," is one of India's most ancient techniques of meditation. It was practiced and taught by the Buddha. Spirit rock also promotes a diversity of backgrounds and ethnicities.

Spirit Rock is a true California hybrid: It was founded by two psychotherapists who had integrated Buddhism into their lives and work, Sylvia Boorstein and Jack Kornfield. Since its founding, Spirit Rock has grown into a central community center, offering ongoing classes and daylong and residential retreats. Featured speakers, presenters, and teachers are as diverse as the author Alice Walker and his Holiness the Dalai Lama.

The experience at Spirit Rock is one of quiet contemplation, aligned with the rhythms of nature and a strong sense of *sangha*, which

THE WAY OF TEA

The Way of Tea is a practice and art that developed in the 15th and 16th centuries in close conjunction with Zen. One of the gracious features of Green Gulch is a beautifully wrought traditional teahouse called **The Sowing the Moon Teahouse.** On select Sundays throughout the year, visitors can participate in a traditional tea ceremony under the direction of Christy Bartlett, Sensai Director of the Urasenke Foundation of California. The Urasenke School is one of the foremost lineages of tea-masters going back to Japan.

In the practice of *Chanyo* (the Way of Tea), the teahouse is accorded the status of sanctified space. According to the 18th-century tea-master and philosopher Shaku, upon entering the tearoom, "all discrimination between self and other vanishes, a spirit of gentleness prevails, so that peace may be attained when modesty, respect, purity, and tranquility are understood."

Those interested in pursuing further study in *Chanyo* can do so at the San Francisco–based **Urasenke Foundation.** Classes are small and conducted in both English and Japanese. The study of tea synthesizes fields as various as history, history of art, history of literature and intellectual thought, as well as cuisine, horticulture, and architecture, among other areas. Yet the focus of study is on the precise postures, movement and ritual which constitute the tea ceremony (www.urasenke.org).

strengthens the individual's practice. Schedules for ongoing programs and retreats are posted on the website.

Pine Street in San Francisco is home to the **San Francisco Buddhist Church** (1881 Pine St., 415/776-3158), the oldest *Jodo Shinsu* (Pureland) Buddhist Church in America. Founded in 1898, the Buddhist Churches of America serviced the growing Japanese population of the region. It was originally called a church instead of a temple to make the assimilation into 19th century San Francisco a little easier. *Jodu Shinsu,* or Shin Buddhism, is one of the major religions of Japan. Visitors entering the *hondo,* or main hall, will find a large, round, golden statue of Amida Buddha (Buddha of Infinite Wisdom and Compassion). On the roof is a quiet contemplation spot with a *stupa* that houses the Holy Relics of The Buddha. The Relics were a gift to the BCA by the Emperor of Siam (Thailand) in 1935. The church welcomes all visitors, and the staff is more than happy to answer questions. Services are held in both English and Japanese.

HINDUISM

Hinduism is a vast universe of numerous deities and the oldest living major spiritual tradition in the world. From it comes the saying "the many and the one," for as many faces and gods as there are in the Hindu pantheon, they are all seen to be One. This polytheistic religion works with vast *kalpas*, or cycles of time, a sense of inclusiveness and worlds within worlds, all co-existing. Hinduism has also developed some of the most sophisticated and precise "technologies of consciousness," systems which precisely map not only cosmologies, but also the "technology of the mind, body, and soul" which can be activated through *yoga*, meditation, knowledge, devotion, and *tantra* to realize an awakened consciousness in a material body. This factor has been part of Hinduism's appeal to many in the West.

For many native-born practitioners, Hinduism serves the same purpose many religions serve: It is a place where the passages of life—birth, death and marriage—are marked. It provides a foundation of ethics to live by. It gives a sense of community and lineage. It is a place where supplications for good fortune can be made and a recognition of the divine presence in life sanctified.

In the 20th century, Hindu missions began to flourish on American soil. In the 1920s, Yogananda founded the Self-Realization fellowship in Los Angeles. In 1933 Vivekananda and the Bengali saint Ramakrishna founded the Ramakrishna-Vivekananda Center of New York, and in 1933 the young Krishnamurti, philosopher and teacher of the Theosophical Soceity, settled in Ojai where he proceeded to inspire and transform many individuals. By the 1960s, increasing numbers of Americans were making the pilgrimage to India to find the spiritual awakening it was said to offer, and in the years that followed various teachers and gurus came to America, some beloved, others infamous.

With all of this apparent "discovery" of Hinduism in the West, it should be remembered that it is the ancient tradition of temple life that is the central facet of religious life for millions of Hindus. To walk into a traditional Hindu temple is to walk into an extravaganza, a sensory overload, where a panoply of deities—Siva, Vishnu, Krishna, Brahma, Laksmi, Hanuman, Rama, Sita, Parvati—all share space.

Today, in the Bay Area, a thriving Indian community flourishes, with one of the largest numbers of Hindu Temples in America. Located in Livermore, the site of U.C. Berkeley's research labs, is the **Livermore Siva-Visnu Temple** (1232 Arrowhead Ave., 925/449-6255), an impressive structure built to traditional North and South Indian specifications. It is one of the few Hindu temples in Northern California that offers comprehensive services for worship of Hindu deities (*Homas,* Asian *Abhishekas, Archanas,* etc). The temple has an abundant attendance with over 1,000 visitors a month, and as many as 10,000 visitors on special days, such as *Ganesha Chathurthi.* In the spirit of inclusiveness, individuals of all faiths are welcome. There are daily, weekly, and monthly *puja* schedules for visitors, and all major Hindu holidays are observed. The temple is open weekdays 9 A.M.–12 noon, and 6 A.M.–8 P.M., weekends and holidays 9 A.M.–8 P.M.

Located across from the Radio Shack on Union Street in downtown San Jose is the local center for **ISKCON (International Society for Krishna Consciousness)** (2990 Union St., 408/559-3197). Although the image of the robed, mad-dancing "Hare Krishna" may be the stereotype, many don't realize that the Krishna Consciousness movement goes back 5,000 years and is a denomination of the *Gaudiya Vaishnava* faith, a devotional tradition based on the teachings of the *Bhagavad Gita* and the *Bhagavat Purana (Srimad Bhagavatam). The Bhagavad Gita,* a part of the larger Hindu epic the *Mahabarata,* focuses on Krishna's discourse with the warrior prince Arjuna, and his teachings of the Nature of God and Love. Krishna has many faces and forms, from the Divine Beloved romantic lover of Rahdha and the 16,000 *gopis,* to the radiant child, to the form of a young man and counselor to Arjuna. In essence, Krishna is experienced and known to his followers as Divine Love. *Darshans* (the blessing of gods) are held daily at the San Jose ISKON Center in the morning and evening. Classes on the study of the *Bhagavad-gita* are also held on a weekly basis.

The Divine Mother and Bhakti Yoga

The worship of the Mother has a long and revered tradition in India. She is Mother India who nourishes and sustains. She is the mother who births humans into the world, the Beloved, and the sister. She is the goddess Lakshmi, goddess of abundance. She is Kali/Durga, Goddess of transformation and time. According to the Hindu tradition, the Mother can appear as an enlightened one in human form. Although this may seem strange, even extreme to some Western minds, such figures in India draw large followings and overflowings of devotion. In the Hindu tradition this devotion is called *bhakti* yoga, or the path of devotion, as opposed to *jnana* yoga, the path of knowledge, or *karma* yoga, the path of service. The Fourth Path of Hinduism, or *Adhyatma* yoga, is an integration of all three into what is called "The Science of Soul Union."

To experience a form of *bhakti* yoga without traveling to India, simply drop by the **M.A. Center** (10200 Crow Canyon Rd., 510/537-9417). Located in Castro Valley, down a long winding country road and past an equestrian stable, this is the home of **Ammachi** when she is in Northern California, as well as the site of her *darshans* and retreats, which draw thousands.

Mata Amritanandamayi, born in India's Kerala State in 1953, is revered as a modern-day incarnation of the Divine Mother. She is affectionately known as Ammachi, which means "Mother" in Malayalam (a South Indian dialect). What she gives appears simple: hundreds of thousands come to her (sometimes as many as 10,000 in one day) for . . . a hug. Perhaps the most well-attended of Ammachi's *darshans* is the *Devi Bhava,* or the worship of the Goddess in human form. Early in the evening *mantras* are chanted and ghee, flowers, and milk are offered to Ammachi, who wears garlands of flowers and an impressive headdress. The hall is filled to capacity, with hundreds waiting outside, and it becomes increasingly charged with energy as a continuous wave of *bhajans* (traditional songs in praise of God) are played with several harmoniums and expert singers.

What happens next is somewhat extraordinary, for in the next 14 hours up to 7,000 people come to rest their heads on Ammachi's breast, look in her eyes, have her whisper a *mantra* in their ear, and give them a big hug. As the hours pass, the hall becomes charged with indisputable waves of energy, *shakti,* the radiating energy of creation in its divine female essence. The daughter of Martin Luther King Jr. once sat as an honored guest at Ammachi's side.

It is almost noon the next day when the last of those who have come to see Ammachi will have laid their head on her breast to receive her blessing, and she will still be there, radiant, glowing, and somehow as fresh as when she first started 14 hours before.

ISLAM

Islam, which in Arabic is derived from *salaama,* has a twofold meaning: peace, and submission to God. Central to Islam is the teaching that one must intentionally and conscientiously surrender totally to the service and belief of Allah, the "One and Almighty God."

Islam was founded in the deserts of Arabia in the 6th century A.D. by the Prophet Mohammed, who was ordained with a vision, enrapturement, and "message of God." Within a short period the religion he established as

SALAT

An integral and obligatory part of the devout Muslim's daily worship is *salat*, or *'as-salât* in Arabic. Through *salat*, the prayers and supplications held five times daily, a person "communes with his Lord, the Creator and the Sustainer of the Universe." Before prayer is purification. Worshippers are asked to ensure that their faces, arms to the elbows, and feet to the ankles, are clean. Prayers are chanted in Arabic and are performed by kneeling towards Mecca (Qiblah). They are performed at dawn, *Salat Al-Fajr*; noon, *Salat Al-Zuhr*; afternoon, *Salat Al Asr*; sunset, *Salat Al Maghrib*; and evening, *Salat Al-Isha*. This marks out the hours of the day as the hours of God, creating a rhythmic pattern of contemplation of God from sunrise to sunset.

"God's Messenger" served as a politically unifying force amongst the numerous and diverse tribes of Arabia. Islam quickly spread, and in the centuries to come was embraced by numerous racial and ethnic groups: Persians, Turks, Africans, Indians, Pakistanis, Afghans, Chinese Malays, and Indonesians. It provided the cultural climate for the rich tradition of architecture, science, and literature that flourished for over seven centuries under the Ottomans. Today, Islam is the world's second largest religion, and continues to shape world events. The Bay Area is home to many mosques and places of Islamic worship for the adherent, the potential convert, or the curious.

Providing the Silicon Valley Muslim community with a variety of services and a strong community network for both the spiritual and worldly life is the **Muslim Community Association of San Francisco** (3003 Scott Blvd., Santa Clara, 408/970-0647). Here, congregational prayers and services are held for over 2,000 people. Educational programs are provided for both adult and school-age children, as well as for women and men. The MCASF's Outreach Services provide non-Muslims with a better understanding of Islam. Special programs are also provided for

Muslims who have just arrived in America. Programs are held in English, Arabic, Persian, and Urdu. Both of MCASF's locations are in Santa Clara. Updated times and services can be found at www.mca-sfba.org.

SUFISM

If we look at most of the world's religions, we see the interplay between orthodox, or conventional, teachings and mystical, or esoteric, teachings. The mystical or esoteric path is more concerned with the inner essence and inspiration of the religion than its political, social, or ethical implications. It is said that the similarity at the heart of these esoteric traditions is that they each lead to a universal state of being which is not defined by religion, ethnicity, or creed.

Sufism, whose etymology derives from the Greek *sophia* (for wisdom) and the Arabic *sof* for purity, developed within Islam in Iran, Arabia, India, and Spain. Its adherents were poets, dancers, mystics, holy men and women, individuals who were as often as not outside the conventions of normative society. In Sufism, it is held that the individual is in essence pure, and the Path, or *Tariqa*, is the reuniting with this purity through reuniting with the Divine Beloved.

Modern day Sufism brings together members of all different races and nationalities. It is said that "wisdom does not belong to any particular religion or race, but to the human race as a whole." Sufism has flourished in the Bay Area, producing both teachers and intergenerational families who participate in and give life to this age-old tradition.

There are a plethora of Sufi activities in the Bay Area which, in the spontaneous tradition of Sufism, are not necessarily bound to a building or temple. The best place to get information on both Sufism and Sufi activities from various paths is http://SufiSonoma.org. Self-described as "a loosely defined membership of people," Sufi Sonoma is the gateway into such activities as *Zikrs* (which in Arabic literally means "remembrance of the unity of all things"), where members gather together and chant, dance, or meditate. The site also lists the Dances of Universal Peace founded by Sufi Sam or Murshid Sam, a Rinzai Zen Master who had traveled and received transmission from masters around the world and was a student of Hazrat Inayat Khan. The Dances of Universal Peace have become a global phenomenon and have taken on a rich life of their own. The essence of Sufi practice is opening the heart to God and to the Divine Beloved in the form of other human beings. Be prepared for a joyful, transformative experience.

CHRISTIANITY

The history of Christianity in Asia stems back at least 17 centuries to the 4th century A.D., when the Roman Christian historian Arnobius recorded that Christianity had reached the land of the "silk people." Christian missionary inroads into China continued through the centuries, with many converts and churches built, but it never became a state religion in China.

Christianity reached Japan in the 16th century under Portuguese ministries. It was suppressed during the next few centuries but resurfaced at the end of the 19th century. There have been various cross-pollinations of Christianity in India over the years, notably by Portuguese Christian missionaries in Macao, present-day Goa. Christian populations have also developed in Indonesia, Thailand, Korea, and the Philippines, which today is predominantly Christian.

The tradition of a strong Asian Christian community has been a part of the Bay Area for the last century, with churches such as the **Westview Presbyterian Church** (118 First St., 831/724-6222) in Pajaro Valley, which began as a mission to Japanese immigrants in 1898, and still has an active Japanese congregation today.

Those who want to participate in a distinctly Asian-influenced Christian experience can choose from a variety of churches. The **First Chinese Baptist Church of San Francisco** (1 Waverly Pl., 415/362-4139), founded in 1880 and located in the heart of Chinatown, is a multi-generational, bilingual, bicultural church. It serves Chinese American nationals and recent immigrants. Services are held in both English and Cantonese. The church provides a full range of programs for families, youth, children, and couples.

On the Berkeley–Oakland border is the Korean Baptist Church **Berkland** (332 Alcatraz Ave., 510/652-0240). Founded in 1981, Berkland, a member of the Southern Baptist Convention, now has branches in such diverse regions as Beijing, Moscow, Tokyo, Seattle, and New York. The motto of the church is "to be the kind of church described in the Bible with applicable teaching, heart-felt worship, honest friendships, fervent prayer, and compassionate care for those in need." It offers a full range of services for all ages, and has locations in both Berkeley and San Francisco.

There are numerous other groups, such as the **Southbay Chinese Baptist Church** (448-454 Francis Dr., San Jose, 408/926-2621), which caters to a young crowd and serves as a focus of community, integrating worship and spirit with day-to-day life. Members of SCBC are Cantonese-speaking college students and young professionals from the Silicon Valley, who come together for worship, community, and social activities. Services are held in both English and Cantonese.

SPIRITUALITY AND RELIGION

Christian Congregations

Berkland Baptist Church. Founded in 1981 by Pastor Paul Kim and his wife, Berkland Baptist Church (BBC) is a member of the Southern Baptist Convention. Berkeley Sunday Service at 12:15 pm. San Francisco Sunday Service at 3:30 pm. 1690 21st Ave., San Francisco, and 332 Alcatraz Ave., Oakland; 510/652-0240, www.berkland.org.

Christ Episcopal Church Sei Ko Kai. Near Japantown, this Japanese Epispocal Church fosters a strong sense of community and congregation. Services are held in in both English and Japanese. 2140 Pierce St., San Francisco; 415/921-639, www.christepiscopalchurch.seikokai.org.

First Chinese Baptist Church. One of the oldest churches in the community, the First Chinese Baptist Church was organized in 1880, with the congregation settling into a building at the current location eight years later. The church at the site was destroyed in the 1906 earthquake and rebuilt in 1908. The church offers services as well as language classes. 15 Waverly Place, San Francisco; 415/362-4139, www.fcbc-sf.org.

Korean Central Presbyterian Church of San Francisco. Begun on October 4, 1992, as a college group ministry serving a small number of students, the KCPC now serves a large congregation of college students, young adults, and married couples. Outside of Sunday services, the church offers retreats, fundraisers, and socials. 6154-6160 Mission St., Daly City; 650/550-0071, www.sfkcpc.org.

Old St. Mary's Cathedral. Old St. Mary's is one of the most prominent buildings in the Chinatown area. The cathedral was built by Chinese laborers in 1854, using brick that was shipped around Cape Horn, and granite from China. Though the original was destroyed in the 1906 earthquake, the cathedral was rebuilt in 1909. 660 California St., San Francisco; 415/288-3800, www.oldsaintmarys.org.

San Francisco Korean United Methodist Congregation. "Becoming Christ-like through Worship, Outreach, and Nurturing." SFKUMC was established in 1904 by some of the earliest Korean immigrants to America. The Church strives to serve as a focal point of the Korean American community, and maintains a historical resource room containing photographs and documents covering its long history. Services are held in both English and Korean, and weekly Bible Fellowships are part of the offerings. 3030 Judah St., San Francisco; 415/759-1005, www.sfkumc.org.

Saint Patrick's Catholic Church. Tagalog masses are offered every first Sunday of the month at this predominantly Pilipino parish. Formerly an Irish American church, the church is a SF Historic Landmark whose entire pastoral staff is now Pilipino. 765 Mission St., San Francisco; 415/421-3730, www.stpatricksf.org.

St. Patrick's Proto-Cathedral Parish. Once the cathedral of San Jose, this historic church conducts mass daily in Vietnamese and serves as a central resource for the Bay Area's Vietnamese Catholic community. 389 E. Santa Clara St., San Jose; 408/294-8120.

St. Maria Goretti Church. A place of worship for Vietnamese Catholics, this church also maintains the Chapel of Vietnamese Martyrs on Singleton Rd. a few blocks away—a shrine to 117 followers killed during early anti-Catholic persecutions in Vietnam. 2980 Senter Rd., San Jose; 408/363-2300.

Southbay Chinese Baptist Church. A church of Cantonese speaking college students and young professionals who come together for worship. Services are held in both English and Cantonese. Cantonese Sunday School is also offered along with Young Couple and Youth Fellowships. 448-454 Francis Dr., San Jose; 408/926-2621, www.scbc.net.

Sunset Chinese Baptist Church. A congregation of overseas and American-born Chinese meeting as separate language worship services and fellowship. Cantonese and English Services. Prayer Teams available for your needs. 3635 Lawton St., San Francisco; 415/665-5550, www.members .christweb.com/scbcsf.

Wesley United Methodist Church. Founded in 1895 by pioneer Issei Christians, the Wesley United Methodist Church provides a place for worship, education, and fellowship to people from all over the Santa Clara Valley. The church sponsors a large number of annual events such as the New Year's Ozoni, the Shinnen Kai, the Nikkei Matsuri Japantown Community Festival and the Mochitsuki. Western style and religious events such as a ski trip, Easter breakfast, church picnic, family camp, as well as summer camps and a variety of sports tournaments and potlucks are also planned throughout the year. The church serves the community through participation in the ACTS for the Homeless and InnVisions programs which provide counseling, training, shelter, and child care for the homeless and needy. 566 Fifth St., San Jose; 408/296-0367.

Chinese Community Church. 1535 Jackson St., San Francisco; 415/771-0808.

Chinese Presbyterian Church of Oakland. 265 8th St., Oakland; 510/452-4963, www.oaklandcpc.presbychurch.org.

Cumberland Presbyterian Chinese Church. 865 Jackson St., San Francisco; 415/421-1624.

Filipino Christian Church. 505 South White Rd., San Jose; 408/926-6365, www.filipinochristianchurch.org.

First Chinese Southern Baptist Church. 1255 Hyde St., San Francisco; 415/775-4288.

First Filipino Baptist Church. 2801 Florence Ave., San Jose; 408/923-8492.

Presbyterian Church in Chinatown. 925 Stockton St., San Francisco; 415/392-1500.

San Jose First Vietnamese Church. 102 S. 21st St., San Jose; 408/998-1361.

Westview Presbyterian Church. 118 First St., Watsonville; 831/724-6222.

Buddhism

Berkeley Buddhist Temple. Started nearly 90 years ago, the Berkeley Buddhist Temple follows the Jodo-Shinshu form of Buddhism. The temple also hosts Dharma discussions and meditation sittings. 2121 Channing Way, Berkeley; 510/841-1356.

Buddhist Church of San Francisco. Founded in 1898, this church/temple is the United States oldest Jodo Shinshu (Pure Land) Buddhist Church belonging to the Buddhist Churches of America (BCA). The church welcomes all vistors and the staff are more than happy to answer any questions you may have. Services in English and Japanese. 1881 Pine St., San Francisco; 415/776-3158, www.bcsfweb.org.

Buddhas Universal Church. Standing five stories high, Buddhas Universal Church is the largest Buddhist church in the country. Built in 1961, the temple is a place of serenity for the largest Buddhist congregation in San Francisco. It also affords views over the whole city. 720 Washington St., San Francisco; 415/982-6116, bucsf.org/church.

Chua Duc Vien. Vietnamese Buddhists visit the Perfect Virtue Temple to pray, study, and walk in its serene gardens. The temple is open to the public, and on Sundays, the nuns serve vegetarian lunch. 2420 McLaughlin Ave., San Jose; 408/993-9158.

The Community of Mindful Living. CML supports the practice and teachings of mindfulness and mindful living offered by Vietnamese Zen Master and Pulitzer Prize Peace Nominee Thich Nhat Hanh. The Albany center, one of many in the Bay Area, organizes ongoing instruction and meditation retreats and organizes events when Thich Nhat Hanh is in town. 850 Talbot Ave., Albany; 510/527.3751, www.iamhome.org.

Green Gulch Center. Green Gulch, located in a beautiful meandering valley which overlooks the Pacific Ocean, is part of the San Francisco Zen Center *Sangha*. On Sunday, a public program is offered which includes azen instruction, a lecture, tea, and a public lunch for a nominal fee. Ongoing classes are held in Buddhist philosophy and practice. Ongoing retreats in azen meditation are also held, ranging from one to seven days. 1601 Shoreline Highway, Sausalito; 415/383-3134, www.sfzc.com.

Kong Chow Temple. This Taoist temple, founded in 1857, has some of the most colorful altars in the entire city. The green, red, and gold altars display representations of various gods. This fourth-floor location was built in 1977, and is also home to the Chinatown Post Office. 855 Stockton St., San Francisco; 415/788-1339.

Norras Temple. Norras Temple is the oldest Buddhist Temple in San Francisco, dating back more than 50 years. Featuring an altar made of wood imported from China, the temple is also adorned with symbols from Tibetan Buddhism. The temple itself was named after Tibet's Norras Buddhist Temple. 109 Waverly St., San Francisco; 415/362-1993.

Nyingma Institute. Founded by Tarthang Tulku, an accomplished Tibetan Lama who came to the United States in 1969, the Nyingma Institute in Berkeley offers ongoing classes and courses of study. The curriculum is a balance of Buddhist Philosophy and Psychology, Buddhist Texts, Skillful Means, Meditation, and *Kum Nye* (Tibetan relaxation excercises). Sunday programs, held throughout the day, feature lectures, Tibetan chanting, and meditation practice. For updated schedules check the website. 1815 Highland Pl., Berkeley; 510/843-6812, www.nyingmainstitute.com.

Open Gate Sangha. If you want to experience a Zen teacher who is completely fresh, spontaneous and not bound within the rigidity of a particular tradition, attend Adyashanti's *darsan*. Adyashanti has the unique ability to truly touch a place of *boddhicitta* in the individual, no matter what their path or where they may be at in their spiritual unfolding. The Website and phone contact have the latest schedule of intensives and weekly darshans which are held around the Bay Area. Los Gatos; 408/236-2220, www.zen-satsang.org.

RIGPA. A Tibetan word meaning "the innermost nature of the mind," *rigpa* is the name given to the work of Rigpa International founder Sogyal Rinpoche. His groundbreaking book, the *Tibetan Book of Living and Dying*, has become a classic work on Tibetan Religion in the West. The San Francisco Center offers ongoing retreats, events, and courses. 111 New Montgomery St. #403, San Francisco; 415/777-0052, www.rigpabayarea.org.

San Francisco Zen Center. The Zen Center was established in 1969 by Shunryu Suzuki Roshi as a training center in the Soto Zen tradition. It is one of the largest Buddhist *sanghas* outside Asia, and offers three separate practice centers: City Center in San Francisco; Green Gulch Farm in Marin County, and the Tassajara Zen Mountain Center—the first Zen training monastery in the West. There are opportunities for volunteer work/study which can be exchanged for classes, practice activities, fees, or tuition. Meditation practices are held daily, and overnight accommodations are offered for serious practiciners at a reasonable price. 300 Page St., San Francisco; 415/863-3136, www.sfzc.com.

San Jose Buddhist Church Betsuin. Founded in 1902, the San Jose Buddhist Church Betsuin is a temple of the Jodo Shinshu Nishi Hongwanji tradition of Buddhism. 640 North 5th St., San Jose; 408/293-9292, www.sjbetsuin.com.

Shambhala Center. Chögyam Trunga Rimpoche, one of the early translators of Tibetan Buddhism to the West, founded the Shambhala community of meditation centers in 1973. There several Shambhala Centers which service the Bay Area and offer ongoing training in meditation, study, and contemplative arts. The focus is on an integration with practice in daily life. In Berkeley an open house is held every Sunday from 9:00 am to 1:00 pm. Free meditation instruction between 9:30 am and 11 am, a *dharma* talk at 11:15, followed by tea and hospitality at noon. 2288 Fulton St., Berkeley; 510/841-6475. www.shambhala.org/center/berkeley.

Spirit Rock. Set in the redwoods and rolling hills of West Marin in Woodacre, Spirit Rock Meditation Center is dedicated to the teachings of the Buddha as presented in the Vipassana tradition, but also hosts a variety of Buddhist traditions and is dedicated to supporting ethnic and lineage diversity. Spirit Rock places a strong emphasis on *sangha* community and offers ongoing classes and daylong and residential retreats. Featured speakers, presenters, and teachers have included author Alice Walker and his Holiness the Dalai Lama. 5000 Sir Francis Drake Blvd., Woodacre; 415/488-0164, www. spiritrock.org.

Tassajara Zen Mountain Center. Tassajara Zen Mountain Center is a mountain retreat set in the rugged Ventana Wilderness. From September to April, Tassajara is closed to the public while the resident community immerses itself in the 1,000-year-old tradition of monastic zen training. From May through August, Tassajara opens its gates to welcome and serve guests from all over the world. Please keep in mind that reservations are absolutely required, even for day guests. 39171 Tassajara Rd., Carmel Valley; 831/659-2229, www.sfzc.org.

Tien Hou Temple. Perched three flights up, overlooking one of Chinatown's most colorful streets, sits the Tien Hou Temple, founded in 1852, which makes it the oldest Chinese temple in San Francisco. The inside is quite beautiful, with paper lanterns hanging from the ceiling, and a shrine to Tin Hou, the goddess of Heaven, encased in the gilded wood along one of the temple's walls. 125 Waverly Pl., San Francisco.

Berkeley Zen Center. 1931 Russell St., Berkeley; 510/845-2403.

Cao Dai Temple of San Jose. 947 S. Almaden Ave, San Jose; 408/286-4220.

Gold Mountain Sagely Monastery. 800 Sacramento St., San Francisco; 415/421-6117.

Konko Church of San Francisco. 1909 Bush St., San Francisco; 415/931-0453.

San Francisco Buddhist Center. 37 Bartlett St., San Francisco; 415/282-2018, www.sfbuddhistcenter.org.

Wat Buddhanusorn. 36054 Niles Blvd., Fremont; 510/790-2294.

Wat Mongkolratanaram. 1911 Russell St., Berkeley; 510/849-3419 or 510/540-9734.

Wat Nagara Dhamma (Wat Nakorntham). 3225 Lincoln Way, San Francisco; 415/665-7566.

Hinduism

Berkeley Vedanta Center. Swami Vivekananda founded the first American Vedanta Society in New York in 1895, and the second in San Francisco in 1900. Vedanta is the philosophy that evolved from the teachings of the Vedas—a collection of ancient Indian scriptures and the oldest religious writings that exist in the world. More generally, the term "Vedanta" includes not only the Vedas themselves but also the entire body of literature based on them. The Berkeley and San Jose Centers offer ongoing lectures and meditation classes. Interviews with the resident Swami are encouraged prior to enrollment, and are available by appointment. Berkeley Center, 2455 Bowditch St., Berkeley; 510/848-8862; San Jose Center, 1376 Mariposa Ave., San Jose; 408/294-5976, www.vedantaberkeley.org.

Fremont Hindu Temple & Cultural Center. This is the oldest Hindu Temple and Cultural Center in the San Francisco Bay Area. It offers a rendition of the Bhagavad Gita in English, and Hindi with Sanskrit verses. 3676 Delaware Dr., Fremont; 510/659-0655, www.fremonttemple.com.

Hindu Temple and Community Center South Bay. The Silicon Valley based HTCCSB offers ongoing daily activities from devotional worship to weekly Yoga Classes. Private *Pujas* and rituals are also available. 420-450 Persian Dr., Sunnyvale; 408/734-4554, www.sunnyvaletemple.org.

The International Society for Krishna Consciousness (ISKCON). The temple offers daily chanting and devotional practices based in the *Gaudiya Vaishnava* faith, a 5,000 year-old devotional tradition based on the teachings of the *Bhagavad-gita* and the *Bhagavat Purana* (*Srimad Bhagavatam*). 2990 Union Ave., San Jose; 408/559-3197, www.virtualtemple.org.

Livermore Shiva-Vishnu Temple/Hindu Community and Cultural Center. "Promoting Hindu religion and culture and providing a sanctum for human beings of all creeds." The Livermore Siva-Vishnu temple is an impressive structure, finished in 1986 and built with traditional Northern and Southern Indian architectural styles. Up to 10,000 people attend the temple on major holidays. Daily, monthly, weekly, *pujas*. Comprehensive services for ritualistic worship of Hindu deities (*Homas, Abhishekas, Archanas*). 1232 Arrowhead Ave., Livermore; 925/449-6255, www.livermoretemple.org.

M.A. Center. The M.A. (*Mata Amritanandamay*) Center hosts a special gathering followed by a vegetarian Indian dinner every Saturday evening. The daily schedule includes chanting, meditation, and *bhajans*. The Center is an ideal setting for those seeking a spiritual retreat, and modest overnight accommodations and vegetarian meals are available for a nominal fee. 10200 Crow Canyon Rd., Castro Valley; 510/537-9417, www.ammachi.org/bayareasatsang.

Buddhasinndara Temple. 14671 Story Rd., San Jose; 408/926-8000.

Sanathana Viswa Dharma Temple of Cosmic Religion. 174 Santa Clara Ave., Oakland; 510/654-4683.

San Francisco Brahma Kumaris Center. 401 Baker St., San Francisco; 415/563-4459.

Sathya Saibaba Center. 573 S. Clement St., San Francisco; 415/626-8921.

Shiva Murugan Temple. 1803 Second St., Concord; 925/827-0127, www.temple.org.

Sikhism

The Sikh Centre. A beautiful building overlooking the El Sobrante Valley, the center has been serving the Sikh community in the Bay Area for over 25 years. Previously local Sikhs held ceremonies in their homes, but with generous contributions of local and other California Sikhs, the new building was completed in 1993. 3350 Hillcrest Rd., El Sobrante; 510/223-9987, www.angelfire.com/ak/satguru.

Gurdwara Sahib. 300 Gurdwara Rd. (Hill Side Ave.), Fremont; 510/790-3755.

Guru Ram Das Ashram. 1390 Waller St., San Francisco; 415/864-9642.

Islam/ Mosques

Abu Bakr Sidique Mosque. Named for the first Khalif of Islam the mosque, built in 2001 with the support of local Muslims, is officially called the Afghan Islamic Refugee Community. 29414 Mission Blvd., Hayward; 510/393-5648.

Masjid-Ul-Jamia. The Masjid-Ul-Jamia offers daily *salat* and weekly lectures. This mosque strives to be a community center for Muslims in the South Bay and Fremont. A special "Young Companion Course" which draws inspiration from the young followers of the Prophet Mohammed is also offered on a weekly basis. 33330 Peace Terrace, Fremont; 510/429-4732, www.iseb.org.

Muslim Community Association of the San Francisco Bay Area. Offering a wide variety of services for the Muslim Community in the Silicon Valley, including weekly prayers and other religious services including funerals and wedding ceremonies, educational services, a job network, and programs for youth. Both MCASF locations are in Santa Clara. MCA Islamic Center/Granada Islamic School, 3003 Scott Blvd., Santa Clara; 408/970-0647, and Masjid An-Noor, 1755 Catherine St., Santa Clara; 408/246-9822, www.mca-sfba.org.

Shia Muslim Association of Bay Area. Based in San Jose, SMABA offers weekly evening classes on Tuesdays and Wednesdays focusing on understanding the Quran: Islamic practices, underlying philosophy, Quaranic recitation, and Arabic and Persian language classes are all part of the educational choices. 2725 White Rd., San Jose; 408/238-9496, www.saba-igc .org.

Al-Iman Masjid. 4606 Martin Luther King Jr. Way, Oakland; 510/654-7542.

Berkeley Masjid. 2366 San Pablo Ave., Berkeley; 510/549-9465.

Berkeley Mosque. 2434 Wais Way, Berkeley; 510/549-9465.

Islamic Center & Masjid of SF. 400 Crescent St., San Francisco; 415/282-9039.

Masjid Al-Jame (Fiji Jam'atul Islam of America). 373 Alta Vista Dr., South San Francisco; 415/876-9763.

Masjid Muhammed. 1652 47th Ave., Oakland; 510/436-8031.

San Francisco Masjid Dar El-Salam. 20 Jones St. 3rd floor, San Francisco; 415/863-7997.

Sufism

The Golden Sufi Center. The Golden Sufi Center is the vehicle for the work of the Naqshbandiyya-Mujaddidiyya Order of Sufism. Naqshbandi Sufis are known as the "silent Sufis" because they practice the silent meditation of the heart, and the central focus of the center is its meditation groups. Contact the center for ongoing meetings and retreats in both the Bay Area and internationally. 415/663-8773, www.goldensufi.org.

Sufi Sonoma. The best place to get information on both Sufism and numerous Sufi activities from a number of traditions in the Bay Area. Defining themselves as "a loosely-defined membership of people" Sufi Sonoma is the gateway into such activities as *ikrs* (the Remembrance of Allah) and The Dances of Universal Peace. There are also many links to online Sufi reading. For updated calendars go to www.sufisonoma.org.

SERVICES

WHETHER YOU ARE MOVING HERE, DOING BUSINESS HERE OR just visiting for fun, the San Francisco Bay Area has a wide range of Asian-focused resources, including community-based organizations, educational institutions, human services, and media. Not all of them are in San Francisco, and many of them have been covered elsewhere in the book. This section lists services in more detail, as well as providing phone numbers and other points of reference. Information about Asian American film festivals, dating services, summer camps, financial services, and museums can all be found on the following pages.

COMMUNITY ORGANIZATIONS

While the Bay Area is home to many organizations focused on the enrichment of Asian American lives, just as many have dedicated themselves to providing basic human services to lower income Asians. Huge population shifts were set in motion starting with the Korean War, ballooning upwards with the loosening of Chinese immigration laws in the 1960s, and then increasing again during and after the Vietnam War. Language barriers prevented existing groups from providing services to these populations, so new groups from immigrant populations began springing up to meet the surging demand for government, state, and local government health and welfare assistance.

Yet Asians are still the second most uninsured group in California. And a high percentage of parents has had little formal education, even less in English. The following human services organizations in San Francisco and the East Bay have been instrumental in overcoming the practical as well as political problems immigrants face in a new land. In addition, they have the ability to research and monitor workplace problems, anti-Asian violence, or police brutality.

Afghan American Association. Based in Fremont, the association says it represents the 65,000 Afghan Americans living in the East Bay. "Little Kabul" in Fremont provides residents and tourists alike the sounds of the Pashto language and the tasty reminders of Afghanistan's capital. 37485 Fremont Blvd., Fremont; 510/792-4444.

CAPA Community Education Fund. CAPA is a nonprofit organization and the largest community-based organization representing Asian Americans in Alameda and Contra Costa counties. A quarterly newsletter now reaches nearly 2,000 readers. P.O. Box 4314, Walnut Creek; 925/945-1901, www.capa-news.org.

Chinatown Community Development Center. The Center's goal is to build community and enhance the quality of life for San Francisco residents. Chinatown CDC also serves other San Francisco neighborhoods, including North Beach and the Tenderloin. It is a community development organization with many roles, serving as neighborhood advocate, organizer, planner, and developer and manager of affordable housing. 1525 Grant Ave., San Francisco; 415/984-1450, www.chinatowncdc.org.

East Bay Asian Local Development Corporation. In the last quarter century, EBALDC has developed over 600 units of affordable housing as well as 190,000 square feet of retail and office space in Oakland and Emeryville. From a modest beginning, the agency has made life better for many thousands of people and has grown to be one of the Bay Area's most capable and respected community developers. EBALDC client base is now

41 percent African American, 36 percent Asian and Pacific Islander and 11 percent Latino, and the geographic focus has also expanded to include Contra Costa and Alameda counties. Services have moved beyond afford-able housing to home ownership programs for low-income families and other neighborhood economic development programs. 310 8th St., Ste. 200, Oakland; 510/287-5353, http://ebaldc.com.

Korean Community Center of the East Bay. KCCEB was formed in 1979 to assist monolingual immigrants with English lessons and access to basic health and legal needs. It has since grown to serve everyone in the Korean American community, running summer camps, voter registration, and small business assistance, as well as the more traditional services, such as translation and assistance with access to affordable legal and health care. 4390 Telegraph Ave., Ste. A, Oakland; 510/547-2662, www.kcceb.org.

Southeast Asian Community Center. Since 1975, SEACC has run pro-grams focusing on self-sufficiency, economic viability, advocacy, and com-munity empowerment. SEACC currently has offices in San Francisco, Santa Clara, and Alameda counties. SEACC provides needed business, social, and health-related services to refugees, immigrants, and low-income Southeast Asian Americans. 875 O'Farrell St., San Francisco; 415/885-2743.

LEGAL SERVICES

Asian Law Caucus. Founded in 1972, the Asian Law Caucus is the nation's oldest legal and civil rights organization serving the low-income Asian Pacific American communities. ALC became famous when in 1983 it helped Japanese American Fred Korematsu win his lawsuit against the U.S. government, leading to a federal apology and reparations. Pro-bono lawyers and staff help strengthen the Asian Pacific American community by educating local communities, providing key legal advice, and launching lawsuits. 939 Market St., Ste. 201, San Francisco; 415/896-1701, http://asianlawcaucus.org.

ACADEMIC AND CONTINUING EDUCATION

The Bay Area is home to some of the best universities in the world, and the research and teaching available in the various fields of Asian Studies and Asian American Studies are no exception. The three Asian Studies programs profiled are only a few of the many university and college courses available. Others include excellent language courses at community colleges such as City College of San Francisco.

Institute of East Asian Studies. IEAS serves as the focal point for all University of California Berkeley's programs related to East Asia and the Pacific. East Asian Studies at Berkeley is an invaluable asset for the Bay Area and beyond, including the Center for Chinese Studies, the Center for Japanese Studies, the Center for Korean Studies, and the East Asia National Resource Center.

The Institue fosters the indisciplinary study of contemporary and historical East Asia, including the region's realtionship to the United States. It draw on a broad spectrum of eminent Berkeley faculty in a variety of areas, such as anthropology, architecture, art history, business, economics, East Asian languages and cultures, film studies, geography, history, journalism, law, public health, political science, psychology, social welfare, and sociology. 2223 Fulton St. #2318, Berkeley; 510/642-2809, http://ieas.berkeley.edu.

Center for the Pacific Rim. Led by Dr. Barbara Bundy, the Center was established on top of the Lone Mountain Campus of University of San Francisco in 1988 to promote understanding among the nations, peoples, and economies of the Pacific Rim. Engaged with the San Francisco Bay Area's Asia-oriented business and nonprofit communities, the Center is committed to the enduring value of the Jesuit tradition in public service and humanities education. Along with its Matteo Ricci Institute for Chinese-Western Cultural History, the Center presents timely seminars, lectures, and international conferences on a wide range of Asia-related subjects.

Room 202, Lone Mountain Campus, University of San Francisco, 2130 Fulton St., San Francisco; 415/422-6357, wwwificrim.usfca.edu.

Center for East Asian Studies. East Asian Studies is the largest and most diverse component of Stanford University's extensive programs in international studies. Besides providing a physical space for academic, administrative, and social functions, the Center is the principal mechanism for coordinating East Asian Studies at Stanford. The Center is involved in a number of programs that link the university's resources on China and Japan with civic groups, secondary schools, and local colleges in the San Francisco Bay Area. For instance, its China and Japan SPICE project trains elementary and secondary school teachers how to bring Asia into the classroom by developing innovative curriculum materials and organizing workshops. Room 51-L, Building 50, Stanford University, Stanford; 650/723-3362, www.stanford.edu/dept/CEAS.

The Institute for Teaching Chinese Language and Culture. The Institute is a division of the Chinese American International School, a Chinese-English immersion school primarily serving students from English speaking families. The Institute serves as a resource for pre-collegiate programs in Chinese language and culture in the Bay area and throughout the US. The Institute coordinates teacher workshops and intern programs, supports Chinese language curriculum development efforts, provides support for elementary school teachers and opportunities for elementary students to travel to China on exchanges and study tours, and participates in cultural events that promote greater understanding of China in the United States. Contact: Min Zhang, Associate Director, Chinese American International School, 150 Oak Street, San Francisco, CA 94102. Tel: 415-865-6096; m_zhang@cais.org

HEALTH AND MEDICAL SERVICES

Asian Health Services. Started in 1974, the clinic now serves 12,000 patients, 90 percent of them speaking limited English. Interpretation services are available 24 hours a day, and new languages are added according to surges in immigrant populations to the area. Along with defeating language barriers, other challenges still face Asian Americans in the healthcare realm, since Asians remain the second most uninsured group in California. 818 Webster St., Oakland; 510/986-6830, www.ahschc.org.

Chinese Community Health Care Association. This 20-year-old association has 160 doctors and physicians, all of them bilingual. They work in Chinese Hospital as well as other city hospitals, and accept a wide variety of health plans. 170 Columbus Ave., Ste. 210, San Francisco; 415/834-2118, www.cchca.com.

Chinese Hospital. First started in 1900 as a Chinese medicine dispensary, Chinese Hospital is one of the oldest and most successful models for a nonprofit corporation. Fifteen Chinatown benevolent associations revamped the dispensary in 1923, creating the Chinese Hospital Association and building a hospital in San Francisco's Chinatown. A larger, 54-bed facility opened next door in the mid-1970s, and the hospital is still flourishing today, with 235 doctors on staff. 845 Jackson St., San Francisco; 415/677-2480.

INTERNATIONAL ADOPTION SERVICES

When asked to lift his country's oppressive restrictions on emigration, the late Chinese senior leader Deng Xiaoping once famously remarked to President Jimmy Carter, "We have plenty of people, how many millions do you want?" Since then, emigration has become far easier. Now, spurred by a culture that prefers boys and a one-child policy that remains strict in many areas, the Chinese government has allowed a massive outflux of adopted girls to the United States and other countries. In 2000, the number topped 5,000. In the fall of 2001, the Chinese government adoption agency placed a quota on single parent adoptions, dipping the annual number slightly to 4,723.

Parents are also flocking to other Asian countries such as India, Vietnam, and Cambodia, each in the top 10 worldwide in terms of infant adoptions. Many adoption agencies and services have been established to handle the planeloads of parents and paperwork. The two organizations below are support groups with fantastic links to services and advice.

Families with Children from China, Northern California Chapter. FWCC is a successful nationwide community of parents who have adopted children from China, Taiwan, or Hong Kong. The network takes dues of $25 per year, which support orphanages in China, and helps underwrite this massive volunteer organization. Chinese language and culture classes are only a few of the many programs this chapter—one of the largest in the country—runs. FWCC Northern California also has excellent links to Bay Area Chinese American communities. www.fwcc.org/SanFrancisco.

Families with Children from Vietnam. The Bay Area chapters of FCVN cover San Francisco, the Peninsula, South Bay, East Bay, and North Bay. FCVN Bay Area members meet to celebrat traditional Vietnamese holidays such as Tet (new year) and the Mid-Autumn Festiveal. www.fcvn.org.

PUBLIC AFFAIRS AND BUSINESS DEVELOPMENT

Asian Business League of San Francisco. This business development organization was formed in 1980. 564 Market St., Ste. 404, San Francisco; 415/788-4664, http://ablsf.org.

Asian Pacific Islander and Information Services. This organization which goes by the acronym apiBIS, encourages small business development with a particular emphasis on Asian Pacific Islander entrepreneurs. The apiBIS is sponsored by the San Francisco Mayor's Office of

Community Development and managed by two community-based agencies. The apiBIS offers business development services, including capital access and loan packaging assistance; marketing and business plan consultation; and management consultations targeting low- to moderate-income entrepreneurs with a focus on Chinese, Pilipino, Korean, Japanese, and other Asian Pacific Islander communities. The apiBIS lead agencies are the Southeast Asian Community Center and the Northeast Community Federal Credit Union, supported by the Filipino American Development Foundation and the Korean Center. 875 O'Farrell St. and 51 Walter U. Lum Pl., San Francisco; 415/989-0672.

Chinese Chamber of Commerce. This association handles the business and promotional activities of Chinatown and aims for community improvement. It organizes the Chinese New Year Festival and the Miss Chinatown USA Pageant. 730 Sacramento St., San Francisco; 415/982-3000.

Chinese Consolidated Benevolent Association. This group, also known as the Chinese Six Companies, is the oldest advocacy group for Chinese Americans in the United States, having set up 150 years ago when some of the first workers were immigrating. The Chinese Six Companies is actually seven now. Even more confusing, the seven benevolent associations that make up the Chinese Six rotate the post every two months. This group advocates for commerce and business in the community, but is not allowed to back a candidate. It also manages the Chinese Hospital and other charitable organizations. 843 Stockton St., San Francisco; 415/982-6000.

Chinatown Merchants Association. This association is similar (and a rival) to the Chinese Chamber of Commerce. Like the CCC, it is a pro-business advocacy group with good access to the mayor and top officials. 667 Grant Ave., San Francisco; 415/982-6306.

POLITICAL CLUBS AND ORGANIZATIONS

Chinese for Affirmative Action. CAA was born out of the civil rights era, and since its inception in 1969 has enjoyed major success in winning educational and employment equality for immigrants and their families. Co-founded by former Superior Court Judge Lillian Sing and UC Berkeley professor Ling-chi Wang, CAA has now expanded its services from Chinatown to San Francisco's Visitacion Valley neighborhood, an area that has witnessed explosive Asian growth. The Kuo Building, 17 Walter U. Lum Pl., San Francisco; 415/274-6750.

Chinese American Voter Education Committee. Formed in 1976, CAVEC is a nonprofit citizen education organization that helps Chinese Americans understand and participate in the voting process. There is plenty of work to do: While Asian Americans made up 32 percent of San Francisco's population in the 2000 census, the voting population has been less than 10 percent Asian. CAVEC's Executive Director David Lee has led a strong grassroots organizing effort, and his punditry and vote tallying skills will become increasingly important as the Bay Area's Asian American community continues to grow in size and influence. 838 Grant Ave., Ste. 403, San Francisco; 415/397-8133.

Tibetan Association of Northern California. TANC is a nonprofit organization created to revive, preserve, and promote Tibet's unique culture, as well as to raise awareness of Tibet in the world in general and the United States in particular. P.O. Box 9128, Berkeley; 510/204-9792, http://tanc.org.

CULTURE AND ARTS ORGANIZATIONS

Asia Foundation. For 50 years, the Asia Foundation has been providing communities in Asia with grants and training on how to improve governance, as well as sending young scholars, seasoned ambassadors, and executives to study and work in Asia. Headquartered in San Francisco, the foundation has distributed $44 million in grants and more than 750,000 books and educational materials throughout Asia. 465 California St., 9th Floor, San Francisco; 415/982-4640, www.asiafoundation.org.

Asia Society. America's leading organization dedicated to fostering an understanding of Asia and communication among Americans and the peoples of Asia and the Pacific. The Society provides a forum for building multidisciplinary awareness of the more than 30 countries broadly defined as the Asia-Pacific region—from Japan to Iran, and from Central Asia to New Zealand. Founded in 1956, it is headquartered in New York. There are nine offices around the globe. Asia Society Northern California, 500 Washington St., Ste. 350, San Francisco; 415/421-8707, www.asiasociety.org.

Chinese Culture Center of San Francisco. The CCC is a community-based organization established in 1965 to foster the understanding and appreciation of Chinese and Chinese American art, history, and culture in the United States. The facilities of the Center, totaling 20,000 square feet, include an auditorium, a gallery, a bookshop, a classroom, and offices. The Center attracts a broad spectrum of audiences from the Chinese community, the greater Bay Area, as well as visitors from all over the country. 750 Kearny St., 3rd Floor, San Francisco; 415-986-1822, www.c-c-c.org.

Chinese Historical Society of America. Conceived in 1963, the Society is the first such Chinese American historical society in North America. Its first major publication, *A History of the Chinese in California: A Syllabus* has become a classic resource book used by students, historians, educators, and scholars in their research and writing about the Chinese in America. CHSA opened the Chinese Historical Society of America Museum and Learning Center in the historic Julia Morgan Chinese YWCA building in November 2001. 965 Clay St., San Francisco; 415/391-1188, www.chsa.org.

Japan Society. The Japan Society of Northern California is the West Coast's leading forum dedicated to building awareness, fostering understanding, strengthening cooperation, and facilitating cross-cultural communication between Americans and the peoples of Japan and the Pacific. For nearly 100 years, the Society has been a bridge to the Pacific by giving members and the community the opportunity to meet world leaders, distinguished scholars, government officials, community and industry leaders, and prominent authors, artists, and performers. 312 Sutter St., Ste. 410, San Francisco; 415/986-4383, www.usajapan.org.

LOTUS. Local Talent UnderScored is a platform for Northern California artists to showcase their performance skills in Indian Classical Music. The concerts are held on a specific date each month (usually the last Saturday or Sunday of every month in the afternoon). The program has two segments. The first hour is dedicated to budding artists and the next two hours is for skilled talents who have the capability of giving solo concerts. Ever since it's inception in February 2000, LOTUS has promoted and encouraged numerous talented local artists. Email bvmuralidhara@yahoo.com or subhapriya@narada.org.

Pacific Film Archive. Run by UC Berkeley, the PFA houses the largest collection of Japanese files outside Japan—especially those made in the 1960s and 1970s from the Shochiku, Daiei, Nikkatsu, and Toei studios. The PFA also presents film series from China, Taiwan, Thailand, Vietnam, and India, often with participation of native directors. 2575 Bancroft Way, Berkeley; 510/642-0808, www.bampfa.berkeley.edu.

MUSEUMS

Asian Art Museum. After growing out of its 30-year-old Golden Gate Park location, the Asian Art Museum reopened in March 2003 on the site of the former San Francisco Main Library. Designed by famed Italian architect Gae Aulenti, and ably led by Director Emily Sano, the new site houses more than 15,000 pieces of Asian art, making it the largest of its kind in the United States. Contact: Asian Art Museum, 200 Larkin Street, San Francisco; 415/581-3500.

Berkeley Art Museum. BAM houses one of the finest university Asian art collections in the United States, developed mainly through private gifts and bequests. It contains more than a thousand items, including hanging scrolls, screens, fans and ceramics from China, Japan, and India as well as a number of important individual works in Yangchow and Japanese Nanga paintings and woodblock prints. 2575 Bancroft Way, Berkeley; 510/642-0808, www.bampfa.berkeley.edu.

MEDIA

Whether the topic is Asia or Asians right here in the Bay Area, both English and non-English talk radio and television represents the fastest-growing segment of the news industry. Meanwhile, unlike the mainstream print media, non-English magazines and newspapers are still growing their subscriber bases, fueled by an insatiable appetite for reading, as well as reading about the home country. Niche audiences in English (such as international news from a non-mainstream-American perspective) are also enjoying a renaissance.

Asian American Journalists Association. AAJA was founded in 1981 by a few Asian American journalists who felt they were not well represented. By 1985, AAJA's expansion into a truly national organization had begun, and now the organization boasts over 1900 members in 19 chapters across the United States and Asia. AAJA's largest membership bases are generally concentrated in metropolitan areas on the West Coasts (Los Angeles, San Francisco, and Seattle) and East Coast (New York City and Washington, D.C.). And the organization is growing: AAJA has a growing number of members working throughout Asia—in Tokyo, Singapore, Hong Kong, and Bangladesh. AAJA has also relied on leadership in the community and Asian-language media to further its reach. 1182 Market St., Ste. 320, San Francisco; 415/346-2051, www.aaja.org.

Print

Asahi Shimbun International Satellite Edition. This paper was stablished in 1986 and popular with Japanese businessmen and their families. www.asahi.com.

Asianweek. Founded 25 years ago by journalist John Fang, this monthly English language magazine serves both a local audience and Asian Americans nationwide. Owned and managed by Fang's wife, former *San Francisco Examiner* publisher Florence Fang. 809 Sacramento St., San Francisco; 415/397-0220, www.asianweek.com.

Filipinas Magazine. Founded by Mona Lisa Yuchengco, this monthly is perhaps the best for the Filipino community in the United States. 1486 Huntington Avenue, Ste. 300, South San Francisco; 650/872-8650, www.filipinasmag.com.

Korea Times. First published in 1967, this daily is published every day except Sunday. Based in Los Angeles, the paper also puts out a San Francisco edition. 323/692-2000, www.koreatimes.com.

Pacific News Service/New California Media. These news outlets were the brainchild of UC Berkeley Journalism School Dean Orville Schell and history professor Franz Shurmann, who founded PNS in 1969 to provide diversity of views and stories on the Far East during the Vietnam War. Shurmann's wife, Sandy Close, a former China editor, has led the news service since 1974, winning a MacArthur genius grant award in 1995. In 1995, Close founded New California Media to broaden the scope of all ethnic California-based media. 275 9th St., San Francisco; 415/503-4170, www.pacificnews.org.

Siliconeer Magazine. *Siliconeer* is a monthly magazine distributed free of charge on the West and East Coasts. It bills itself as the first Asian Indian magazine to cover science and technology, even though the Bay Area Indian population is predominantly techie. But like many other magazines aiming for a wider audience, it also covers the film industry, especially Bollywood. 460 Persian Dr., Ste. 3, Sunnyvale; 408/745-9663, www.siliconeer.com.

Sing Tao Daily. Published daily, this paper is a rival to *World Journal* in U.S. circulation wars. Its parent company is in Hong Kong, and it has a higher readership in south Chinese and Taiwanese American communities. 215 Littlefields Ave., South San Francisco; 650/872-1188, www.singtaousa.com.

Viet Merc. A weekly newspaper published by *San Jose Mercury News* owner Knight Ridder, the *Viet Merc* reaches the largest audience of any Vietnamese language paper in the United States. 750 Ridder Park Dr., San Jose; 408/920-5000.

World Journal. This is the largest-circulation Chinese-language daily newspaper in the United States. The parent company is in Taiwan. 231 Adrian Rd., Millbrae; 650/692-9936.

TV/Radio

KTSF—Channel 26. KTSF is northern California's best-known multilingual television station having been around since 1976. KTSF offers programming in 14 languages, including Mandarin, Cantonese, Vietnamese, Tagalog, Japanese, Korean, and Hindi. KTSF is the only television station nationwide to air nightly, live Mandarin and Cantonese newscasts, and its signal covers more than 2.75 million households in the San Francisco market. www.ktsftv.com.

Sing Tao Radio. Sing Tao Radio claims a high listenership of 85 percent of all Chinese language on the airwaves, but the market is highly fragmented. Based in the East Bay, the two AM Cantonese stations (1400 and 1450) are high-powered, but Mandarin FM Channel 96.1 is low-power and unable to be heard well in San Francisco. www.chineseradio.com.

The Growth of Chinese Business and Commerce in 19th-Century San Francisco

by Dr. Andy Anderson

Though dreams of a vast commercial exchange with Asia had existed in America since the 1780s, when the first American-flag ship, Empress of China, sailed from New York to Canton (Guangzhou) with a cargo of ginseng, they became an economic reality only with the worldwide spread of "gold fever" in 1848, the year gold was discovered in California.

At the center of America's great Gold Rush and its attendant "China trade," was the City by the Golden Gate—San Francisco—home to anyone serious about creating mercantile wealth on the Pacific Coast of America in the 19th century. Much of the gold and silver discovered in the West flowed to or through San Francisco on its way to minting into U.S. gold dollars and to fulfilling obligations in the exchange, investment, and manufacturing centers of the world.

In the course of three decades, from the mid-1840s to the mid-1870s, San Francisco grew from being a sleepy, backwater port of about 1,000 people to being the major commercial center of the American West, with a remarkably diverse population of nearly a quarter-million people from every corner of the world. Of that number, somewhere between 10–15 percent were Chinese. Smaller percentages of immigrants and sailors from Japan, the Philippines, Southeast Asia, and the Hawaiian Islands contributed to the diversity.

By the end of the 1870s, most of the 100,000-plus Chinese living in America had passed through San Francisco, with about 75,000 staying in California and the remainder distributed throughout the West. By cultural choice and economic necessity and by political exclusion, most early Chinese immigrants lived in communities referred to as Chinatown, the largest being San Francisco.

Gold was the initial draw. It created the possibility of an exchange of the precious metals of the mining fields for the foods, finished goods, and labor supply of Asia. Most of all, it brought the promise of family wealth for a generation of Chinese "sojourners" wishing to escape political and economic turmoil at home by traveling to America, often in an indentured capacity, to mine, farm, build railroads, and run the hundreds of small businesses needed to service the town and country economy of the labor-scarce American West.

California was Gum Shan, the golden mountain, the place of imagined wealth for many immigrants who came from the Pearl River delta region of southern China. San Francisco was usually their first glimpse, and sometimes lasting impression, of this powerful economic dream.

The initial growth of the Chinese population and business community in California was greeted with enthusiasm, especially in newspaper editorials, witness the Daily Alta California, the state's largest newspaper, on May 12, 1852:

"Many letters pass to and from between China and California and at each departure of ships for the Celestial Empire, its children here send off to their friends, beyond the Pacific, great numbers of California papers. It may be seen from this how intercourse is increasing and knowledge extending. The day of fencing the world and information out of China has forever passed away."

This passing of letters, goods, gold, and financial information between China and California was, to a large extent, the handy work of shipping and trading companies, such as the Pacific Mail Steamship Company, and express and banking companies, such as Wells, Fargo & Co.

Wells Fargo, founded in 1852, was a vast transportation, communications, and financial services network connected by stagecoaches, railroads, riverboats, ocean steamers and telegraph. As such, it was one of the principal carriers, exchange companies, and commission agents for gold and silver shipments, monetary payments, debt settlements, investments, and business information in the U.S. and around the world.

Most importantly, for Chinese immigrants, merchants and small business owners, Wells Fargo was the principal carrier of money and information (via its mail system) among Chinese communities in the western United States and Canada. With agents on Pacific Mail Steamship Company ships, it carried gold, financial instruments, trade goods, and business information to and from Hong Kong and Shanghai.

This same network serviced smaller populations of immigrants from the Hawaiian Islands, the Philippines, and Japan.

The clearest indication of the mutual benefit Wells Fargo and Chinese communities afforded each other is seen in the series of publications entitled Wells Fargo & Co.'s Directory of Chinese Business Houses. Published in the late-1870s and 1880s, they are a bilingual series of directories listing hundreds of Chinese businesses in San Francisco, Sacramento, Stockton, Marysville, Oakland, San Jose, and Los Angeles, California; Portland, Oregon; Virginia City, Nevada; and Victoria, British Columbia. As might be expected, San Francisco had the most extensive street-by-street lists of businesses.

This commercial relationship between Wells Fargo and Chinese communities became very important when anti-Chinese sentiment and economic downturns resulted in political and social violence, and in legal moves to officially exclude the Chinese from America in the 1870s and 1880s. Wells Fargo Agents were among the very few who testified in court against the deportation of the Company's longstanding clients and customers from China.

Though the growth of Chinese businesses in San Francisco waned for a long period after the 1880s, one thing remained constant: the mutual respect and benefit of Wells Fargo and the Chinese—at 150-plus years, one of the longest continuous commercial relationships in the history of American business and in the history of San Francisco.

INDEX

G

About the Authors

The **Asia Society** is America's leading institution dedicated to fostering understanding of Asia and communication between Americans and the peoples of Asia and the Pacific. A nonprofit, nonpartisan educational organization, the Society provides a forum for building awareness of the more than 30 countries broadly defined as the Asia-Pacific region. Through art exhibitions and performances, films, lectures, seminars and conferences, publications, and initiatives to improve elementary and secondary education about Asia, the Asia Society presents the uniqueness and diversity of Asia to the American people.

Established in 1998, the Asia Society Northern California strives to offer fresh perspectives on the forces and issues that are shaping Asia's relations with California and the rest of the world. Founded in 1956 and headquartered in New York, the Asia Society has a network of regional centers around the globe.

Dr. Andy Anderson is Senior Vice President and Chief Historian of Wells Fargo & Company. Over the past 26 years, he has built the Wells Fargo archives, Wells Fargo history museums and a fleet of stagecoaches. He has managed Wells Fargo's corporate marketing, advertising, and brand management and the initial development of wellsfargo.com in 1994. He is the author of *Stagecoach: Wells Fargo and the Rise of the American Financial Services Industry* (Simon & Schuster, 2002).

Neelanjana Banerjee is the managing editor of *YO!* Youth Outlook magazine, where she helps young people produce their own media. The former editor-in-chief of *AsianWeek* newspaper, she has also been published in *Audrey, Hyphen,* and *Clamor* magazine among others.

Vera H-C Chan, a former newspaper reporter, is a freelancer writer specializing in popular culture, arts and entertainment, and travel. Born in Hong Kong, bred in Boston, and raised in Oakland, Chan serves as co-president of the Asian American Journalists Association's San Francisco Bay Area chapter.

Jeff Cranmer is a freelance writer and editor living in San Francisco. He is coauthor of the *Rough Guide to Laos* and has contributed to Rough Guides to the USA and Washington, D.C.

Sarah A. Drew studied religious studies at U.C. Berkeley with an emphasis on cross-cultural myth and semiotics. She has lived in Japan and traveled extensively throughout Asia visiting sacred sites and studying with various lineage teachers. She is a published writer and international lecturer on such topics as the "Cybernetic Sensorium," and "Media and Consciousness."

Nicholas Driver spent over 13 years in Beijing analyzing and writing about the business and political climate in China, and has covered similar topics locally as a *San Francisco Examiner* reporter. He earned his BA in Asian Studies from UC Berkeley and has studied in Nanjing, China and Tokyo, Japan. He reads, writes, and speaks fluent Mandarin Chinese.

Marlene Goldman is a freelance writer and photographer who contributes to the *San Francisco Chronicle, Christian Science Monitor, Healing Lifestyles and Spas,* and other publications. She was the winner of the 1999 Book Passage Travel Writing award and has won numerous awards for her photography. When she's not traveling and writing, she can also be found in San Francisco teaching yoga.

Joyce Nishioka received her BA in Journalism in 1998 from San Francisco State University. She is the Dance Critic/Arts & Entertainment Editor for *AsianWeek.* Her work has also appeared in *Nikkei Family, San Francisco Bride Magazine,* and *Pacific Time.*

Barbara Jane Reyes is the author of *Gravities of Center*. She is currently a MFA candidate in poetry at San Francisco State University; her writing is included in the literary journals *Interlope, Tinfish, Asia Pacific American Journal*, forthcoming in *North American Review*, and in the anthologies *Babaylan, Eros Pinoy, InvAsian, Going Home to a Landscape, Coloring Book*, and *Not Home But Here*.

Thy Tran is a San Francisco–based writer who specializes in the history and culture of food. She has coauthored *The Kitchen Companion*, an award-winning culinary reference guide; written articles for The Los Angeles Times and The Washington Post; and created wanderingspoon.com. Generous community leaders made the San Jose chapter possible: Helen Duong and Peggy Flynn at the San Jose Redevelopment Agency, Hien Duc Do at San Jose State University, Mai Bui at the Association for Viet Arts, and Beth Gates at Pacific Bridge, all offered invaluable advice and assistance.

Patricia Unterman has been San Francisco's most respected food critic for three decades, writing for the *San Francisco Chronicle* and the *San Francisco Examiner*. Her work appears in national food magazines such as *Gourmet* and *Food & Wine*. She also publishes a newsletter, *Unterman on Food*, six times a year and is the author of *Patricia Unterman's San Francisco Food Lover's Guide*. She lives, eats, and cooks in San Francisco, where she is also the chef/owner of the Hayes Street Grill and Vicolo Pizzeria.

Pamela Yatsko is a freelance journalist and author of *New Shanghai* (John Wiley & Sons, 2000). She covered China as the Shanghai Bureau Chief for the *Far Eastern Economic Review* in the 1990s. She received her Bachelor's degree from Smith College in 1984 and her Master's degree specializing in China Studies and International Economics from Johns Hopkins University's School of Advanced International Studies (SAIS) in 1988. She currently lives with her husband and son in Mill Valley, California.

Dr. Farid Younos is an Afghan American who fled his country shortly before the Soviet invasion in 1979. He studied cultural anthropology in Denmark and obtained his Doctorate degree in International and Multicultural Education from the University of San Francisco. He is a researcher and lecturer of Islamic studies, the founder of Afghan Domestic Violence Prevention in the United States, and the Director of Public Relations for the Afghan Coalition, a nonprofit organization serving the Afghan community in Northern California.

Acknowledgments

All guidebooks are collaborative efforts, and this one is no exception. Indeed, *Asia in the San Francisco Bay Area* is the West Coast spin-off of the extremely successful *Asia in New York City*, published in 2000. This successful first effort provided both model and motivation for a Bay Area companion piece. From the outset it was clear Northern California's demographic provided uniquely rich material for a cultural travel guide on all things Asian. Over the three-year development period, many members of the Asia Society in both San Francisco and New York contributed ideas, knowledge, contacts and time. Were it nor for the generous seed funding provided by Wells Fargo in support of the project, the book would never have gotten off the ground. Wells Fargo has been an invaluable partner in this effort from start to finish and the Society is indebted to them for their shared vision and commitment.

The editors, publisher, and writers are to be commended for their focused efforts to produce and deliver a high-quality, innovative product under consistently tight deadlines. Avalon Travel Publishing has been a committed and dedicated professional partner. Publisher Bill Newlin possessed the early belief that *Asia in the San Francisco Bay Area* would be a significant local resource. Editor Matt Orendorff worked tirelessly to ensure smooth production of the book with creative solutions to numerous roadblocks. The ATP production staff provided a wonderful design. Finally, significant gratitude goes to Pam Joyce and Karen Karp of the Asia Society for the perseverance and enthusiasm to bring this project to fruition. For all involved, it has been a dedicated and fulfilling journey.

About Our Sponsor

Wells Fargo (NYSE: WFC) is a diversified financial services company - providing banking, insurance, investments, mortgage and consumer finance from 5,900 plus stores, the Internet and other distribution channels across North America and elsewhere internationally.